Essays and Studies 2017

Series Editor: Elaine Treharne

The English Association

The objects of the English Association are to promote the knowledge and appreciation of the English language and its literatures, and to foster good practice in its teaching and learning at all levels.

The Association pursues these aims by creating opportunities of co-operation among all those interested in English; by furthering the recognition of English as essential in education; by discussing methods of English teaching; by holding lectures, conferences, and other meetings; by publishing journals, books, and leaflets; and by forming local branches.

Publications

The Year's Work in English Studies. An annual bibliography. Published by Blackwell.

The Year's Work in Critical and Cultural Theory. An annual bibliography. Published by Blackwell.

Essays and Studies. An annual volume of essays by various scholars assembled by the collector covering usually a wide range of subjects and authors from the medieval to the modern. Published by D. S. Brewer.

English. A journal of the Association, *English*, is published four times a year by the Association.

English 4–11. A journal supporting literacy in the primary classroom, published three times a year

The Use of English. A journal of the Association, *The Use of English*, is published three times a year by the Association.

Newsletter. Published three times a year giving information about forthcoming publications, conferences, and other matters of interest.

Benefits of Membership

Institutional Membership

Full members receive copies of *The Year's Work in English Studies, Essays and Studies, English* (4 issues) and three *Newsletters.*

Ordinary Membership covers *English* (4 issues) and three *Newsletters.*

Schools Membership includes copies of each issue of *English* and *The Use of English*, one copy of *Essays and Studies*, three *Newsletters*, and preferential booking and rates for various conferences held by the Association.

Individual Membership

Individuals take out Basic Membership, which entitles them to buy all regular publications of the English Association at a discounted price, and attend Association gatherings.

For further details write to the Membership Administrator, The English Association, The University of Leicester, University Road, Leicester LE1 7RH.

Essays and Studies 2017

Textual Distortion

Edited by
Elaine Treharne and Greg Walker

for the English Association

D. S. BREWER

ESSAYS AND STUDIES 2017
IS VOLUME SEVENTY IN THE NEW SERIES
OF ESSAYS AND STUDIES COLLECTED ON BEHALF OF
THE ENGLISH ASSOCIATION
ISSN 0071-1357

First published 2017
D. S. Brewer, Cambridge

D. S. Brewer is an imprint of Boydell & Brewer Ltd
PO Box 9, Woodbridge, Suffolk IP12 3DF, UK
and of Boydell & Brewer Inc.
668 Mt Hope Avenue, Rochester, NY 14620–2731, USA
website: www.boydellandbrewer.com

ISBN 978-1-84384-479-2

A CIP catalogue record for this book is available
from the British Library

This publication is printed on acid-free paper

Printed and bound in Great Britain by TJ International Ltd, Padstow, Cornwall

This book is dedicated to Helen Lucas, Chief Executive of the English Association, who has tirelessly worked for the organisation and its members, and unstintingly supported Essays and Studies, as well as all other initiatives of the Association.

Thank you, Helen.

Contents

Illustrations

Preface and Acknowledgements

The contributions in this volume of Essays and Studies were inspired by the Stanford Text Technologies Collegium on 'Distortion', held in May 2015 at Stanford University. Funded by the Denning Gift, this three-day intensive collegium examined one of the key themes in the history of textual communication: how texts are distorted even as they are disseminated, sometimes as a result of accidental manipulation, or careful mediation; sometimes through wilful perversion or falsification. At the Stanford Collegium, we were delighted to host Benjamin Albritton, Mark Algee-Hewitt, Emma Cayley, Paul Fyfe, Tom O'Donnell, Sarah Ogilvie, Timothy Powell, Colin Reeves-Fortney, Giovanni Scorcioni, Elizabeth Tyler and Greg Walker, and each gave powerful and intellectually stimulating papers on very different topics, centred on the concept and practice of distortion.

We are grateful to be able to include the work of some of these original participants in this book, and other essays we have specifically commissioned for inclusion here. We are pleased to thank the attentive and engaged audience at the Collegium, whose informed questions and focused responses allowed invigorated discussion. We also wish to thank the Dean of Humanities and Sciences at Stanford; the Denning Fund for Humanities and Technology, which supports Text Technologies; the Center for Spatial and Textual Analysis (CESTA), which hosted the Collegium; and Daeyeong Kim, who, as Text Technologies Graduate Administrator, organised the proceedings with great skill and professionalism.

Elaine Treharne and Greg Walker
Feast Day of St Baldus, 2016

Notes on Contributors

Matthew Aiello is a Ph.D student in English at the University of Pennsylvania, having completed his Master's degree in Medieval Literature at Worcester College, University of Oxford. His research interests are primarily focused on book history in early medieval England, addressing questions about the relationship of the literature to its physical context. He is particularly interested in smaller, non-elaborate, feasibly portable manuscripts from the two centuries following the Norman Conquest.

Emma Cayley is Associate Professor of Medieval French at the University of Exeter. She teaches and publishes in the area of late medieval French poetry and culture, and her research interests extend across the digital humanities; manuscript studies and the history of the book; text editing; and gender studies. Her publications include *Debate and Dialogue: Alain Chartier in his Cultural Context* (Oxford University Press, 2006); and *A Companion to Alain Chartier c.1385–1430: The Father of French Eloquence* (Brill, 2015) with Daisy Delogu and Joan E. McRae. She is currently working on two critical editions; *Debate Culture in Medieval Europe* for the University of Florida Press; and the Exeter Book app in partnership with Stanford and Glasgow Universities. She has been a Leverhulme Trust Fellow and a Text-Technologies Fellow at Stanford.

Aaron Kelly is Senior Lecturer in the Department of English Literature at the University of Edinburgh. His research interests include modern and contemporary Irish, Scottish and English literature; working-class writing; and the interfaces between literature, ideology and politics. Among his recent publications are *Irvine Welsh* (Manchester University Press, 2005), *The Thriller and Northern Ireland since 1969: Utterly Resigned Terror* (Ashgate, 2005) and *James Kelman: Politics and Aesthetics* (Peter Laing Publishing, 2012). He is currently working on a major project to recover and republish neglected working-class writing from the 1920s and 1930s.

Daeyong (Dan) Kim is a senior doctoral candidate in English at Stanford University. His dissertation, 'Migrant Identities: Converts, Immigrants and Cosmopolitans in Early Modern English Drama', investigates the ways in which culturally hybrid figures performed and renovated their identities in relation to their changing worlds, both as self-fashioners and world-makers. He is Graduate Associate Director of Stanford Text Technologies.

Sarah Ogilvie teaches Linguistics at Stanford University. Prior to coming to Stanford, she taught at Cambridge University and at Australian National University where she was Director of the National Dictionary Centre and Chief Editor of Oxford Dictionaries, Australia. A trained lexicographer, she has worked as an editor on the *Oxford English Dictionary* and *Macquarie Dictionary*. Her books include *Words of the World: A Global History of the Oxford English Dictionary* (Cambridge University Press, 2013) and *Keeping Languages Alive: Documentation, Pedagogy, and Revitalization* (Cambridge University Press, 2014).

Timothy Powell is a faculty member of the Religious Studies department at the University of Pennsylvania and Consulting Scholar at the Penn Museum. He is Director of Educational Partnerships with Indigenous Communities (EPIC) at Penn Language Center. He is the author, most recently, of 'Digital Knowledge Sharing: Forging Partnerships between Scholars, Archives, and Indigenous Communities' and '"The Songs are Alive": Bringing Frances Densmore's Recordings Back Home to Fond du Lac Tribal Community College'.

Giovanni Scorcioni, founder of FacsimileFinder.com, is a professional bookseller specialising in facsimile editions of medieval manuscripts. His comprehensive knowledge of facsimiles – from production, to distribution, to academic use – has earned his company the trust of libraries across the globe. Additionally, he is regularly invited by major universities to illustrate the making process of manuscript facsimiles to students involved in medieval studies courses.

Elaine Treharne is Roberta Bowman Denning Professor of Humanities, Professor of English, Director of the Centre for Spatial and Textual Analysis, and Director of Stanford Technologies at Stanford University. She is the author or editor of almost thirty books and sixty articles, nearly all focused on Old and Middle English literature, and manuscript technologies. Her most recent work is *A Very Short Introduction to Medieval Literature* (Oxford University Press, 2015) and *Text Technologies: A History*, with Claude Willan (Stanford University Press, 2017); and she is currently completing *The Phenomenal Book.*

Greg Walker is Regius Professor of Rhetoric and English Literature at the University of Edinburgh. He has published widely on the literature and politics of the later medieval period and the sixteenth century, on early drama, and the political and religious history of the reign of Henry

VIII. Among his recent publications are *Writing Under Tyranny: English Literature and the Henrician Reformation* (Oxford University Press, 2005); *The Oxford Anthology of Tudor Drama* (Oxford University Press, 2013); and *Imagining Spectatorship from the Mysteries to the Shakespearean Stage* (Oxford University Press, 2016), co-written with John J. McGavin. He is currently working on a study of the work of the playwright John Heywood.

Claude Willan received his Ph.D in English from Stanford University and is Postdoctoral Research Associate in the Center for the Digital Humanities at Princeton University. His research interests include historical poetics, digital humanities, disciplinarity, media theory, and verbal and visual satire. He is working on his first book, *The Seizure of Literary History in the Eighteenth Century*.

Introduction

ELAINE TREHARNE

'The most dangerous untruths are truths slightly distorted'[1]

'Distortion' is nearly always understood as negative: it can be defined as perversion, unnoticed alteration, impairment, caricature, twisting, corruption, misrepresentation, deviation. Unlike its close neighbour, 'disruption', currently enjoying a makeover in British government-speak as a newly positive term (in such collocations as 'disruptive technologies' and 'disruptive industries'), it remains resolutely associated with the undesirable, the lost or the deceptive. The process of distortion is generally seen to create a form of the original (factual, true, authentic, real) that is not transubstantive as such, but deformed: warped, misshapen, skewed, shrunken, amplified or simulated. Even in acoustics or music, the notion of distortion, however aesthetically pleasing in itself, most often connotes loss of purity or clarity of signal. And yet, it might equally be said that only through distortion can one find the presence of the original. Indeed, in literary and historical studies, one might argue that all textual transmission is inevitably distorted – either through mediation, translation, appropriation, colonisation, canonisation and authorisation of an elite corpus or authentic version, digitisation, remediation or, more obviously negatively, through misunderstanding, lack of contextualisation, deliberate falsification or pretence.

In the Collegium held at Stanford University in 2015, at which some earlier forms of these essays were presented (Cayley, Ogilvie, Powell, Scorcioni, Walker), the three-day discussion ranged from core issues of space, place, time and context in the production of literary and artefactual meaning, to the archive and its necessary interpretation – whether through sorting and cataloguing or editing, retrieval and display. In tussling with the term and its implications, we returned frequently to the concept of the undistorted and what it might imply, whether in theory or practice. An antonym of 'distortion' seems always to be the search for the authentic, the original, the true, as if that might exist textually. Yet, alongside this

[1] Georg Christoph Lichtenberg, *The Waste Books*, trans. R. J. Hollingdale, New York Review Books Classics (New York: NYRB Classics, 2000), p. 118.

inbuilt distrust of the text or artefact as a bearer of undistorted meaning, there is an equally evident suspicion of the oral, and of sound or speech – with their evanescence and ephemerality, even when recorded (as is shown brilliantly in Powell's essay). Distortion is part of the larger knowledge system, filling the gap between the authentic event and its experience; it has its own ethics and practice, as a number of writers here point out, and it is necessarily incorporated in all meaningful communication.

What results from distortion? Need it always be a negative phenomenon? How does distortion affect producers, transmitters and receivers of texts? Are we always obliged to acknowledge distortion? What effect does a distortive process have on the intentionality, materiality and functionality, not to say the cultural, intellectual and market value, of all textual objects? The essays in this volume seek to address these questions, focusing on a broad range of literature, language and textual objects.

The essays in this book are, then, all carefully themed around 'distortion'. Within the compass of this term, though, the contributors range from the medieval to early modern to contemporary periods and, throughout, deliberately challenge periodisation and the canonical. Subjects treated range from early English manuscripts to Native American animated matters; from lexicographical compilation to the performance of texts in new contexts. From the written to the spoken, the inhabited object to the remediated, distortion is demonstrated to demand a rich and provocative mode of analysis.

Matthew Aiello offers a compelling essay, arguing through the case studies of Oxford, Bodleian Library, Junius 85 and Junius 86, against the distortion that inevitably follows from the investigation of manuscripts via individual texts, or incoherent evaluations of script, scribal practices and codicology. He shows that a scrupulous holistic investigation of a pair of manuscripts previously dismissed as 'scruffy' provides new and important evidence for the ways in which scribes worked with inherited materials in the earlier medieval period. In this case, books that were thought to be ill-constructed and produced, but split up at a much later date, are proven to be the result, rather, of a careful pair of scribes working in the eleventh century. The distortion of models of manufacture in traditionally received scholarship is thus replaced with verifiable evidence in this fastidious study.

Emma Cayley's essay looks at distortion more positively, focusing on ways in which texts might be amplified, continued, debated and adapted through time and across media and cultures. She describes how some of the Old English riddles in the tenth-century Exeter Book have been strikingly reimagined as a sculpture illustrating a key tourist feature of Exeter;

a multi-purpose app aimed at a range of audiences; and as furnishings in a modern Exeter hotel. Then, demonstrating further the *afterlife* of texts, Cayley moves into the later medieval period, switching attention to the little-known French medieval debate poem of the mid to late fifteenth century, the *Songe de la Pucelle* (Dream of the Virgin). In this case study, Cayley shows how successive printed editions of this ambivalent text in French and English offer in their prefatory materials – and still more in their woodcut illustrations – often quite sharply distinct interpretations of the text and its implications, designed to refashion the text's functionality for new readers.

Aaron Kelly's contribution looks at notions of distortion in the work of Lionel Britton, a neglected working-class English writer of the 1920s and 1930s. He shows not only how contemporary understandings of time, history and causality are explored, contorted and reframed in Britton's work, most obviously in his visionary plays, *Spacetime Inn* (1932) and *Animal Ideas: A Dramatic Symphony of the Human in the Universe* (1935), but also how attending to Britton's eccentric genius and particular brand of 'proletarian aesthetics' allows, indeed forces, us to rethink conventional models of class consciousness and the relation of 'those who work' to ideology and the imperatives of history.

Dan Kim's essay is also both broadly and pointedly political. It focuses on the issue of nationhood in the global landscape of Shakespeare studies. Inspired by MacMorris in *Henry V*, who asks 'What ish my nation? Who talks of my nation?', Kim reflects upon this vexed question in relation to the many versions of Shakespeare around the world today – a world of permeable borders and transnational networks of media and movement. Kim attends to the remapping of Shakespeare in Korea, and Korea in Shakespeare, asking how that country is represented on the international stage, through its performances of *Hamlet* and *The Tempest*, plays that, as Kim sensitively shows, have particular resonance for Korea's past and present.

Sarah Ogilvie's engaging account of the distortion inherent in dictionary history examines the origins and twentieth-century evolution of *The Oxford English Dictionary* (*OED*). From her own experiences writing for and about the *OED*, Ogilvie provides a detailed account of the ways in which words and their meanings are distorted by lexicographers, by published narratives of words' histories, and by public desire either to maintain stasis or to bring about unrealistic change in language. Ogilvie's discoveries about the motivation for particular instantiations of lexicographical compilation and suppression surprise, and she exhorts researchers and the engaged public to pay particular attention to evidence not only within the *OED* and other dictionaries, but also evidence accrued over decades of that publication's history. She shows how all endeavours to describe and record are, in the end, subjective and potentially distortive efforts.

Timothy Powell's powerful narration of his experiences with Indigenous storytelling highlights the inadequate (and always already colonising) framework of western scholars' canonical accounts of early American literature, and of temporal considerations. 'Indigenous stories like this', he argues, 'possess the power to teach us to see anew the distorted origins of American literary history in ways that may yet prove to be transformative': storytelling as 'social activity' that deepens scholarly understanding of history, existence and its own literary explorations within the academic community. Ojibwe drums enact code-switching, as the drum becomes animated 'vibrant matter' at the hands of those medicine men who know how to engage with the inhabited object. Powell insists upon the need for scholars to work with Indigenous literature and matter on its own terms, with a more sensitive apprehension of space, time and the existential.

Giovanni Scorcioni's technical and agenda-setting essay reveals his experiences as the manufacturer of deluxe 'exact' replicas of medieval manuscripts. He takes the reader through the processes of facsimile production, highlighting the photographic and artisanal effort undertaken by the publishers to ensure the proximity of the replica to the original. While never diminishing the value and testimony of the original artefact, Scorcioni effectively highlights the complexity and professionalism of the facsimile maker, raising the issues of light, colour and materiality in the first essay of its kind. In this piece, distortion is seen to be both troublesome and essential; to be avoided and, simultaneously, a core component of the process of facture, or, to quote Scorcioni: 'distortion is itself an essential means to get rid of distortion'.

Greg Walker focuses on the period of the Reformation Parliament (1529–36) to assess the curious acts of haunting manifested by 'revenant' Lollard texts resuscitated in print as part of the English church's internal struggles over its own history, destiny and relationship to revealed 'truth'. Even as the Reformation appeared to be an historical and theological novelty, Walker suggests, it also clearly resonated with multiple moments of forestalled revolution from the past – especially during the later fourteenth and earlier fifteenth centuries, seeking evidence for its own eventual victory in the evidence of ongoing failure they provided. As Walker demonstrates with close analysis of key texts, including the pseudo-Chaucerian *Plowman's Tale*, at this critical juncture in Henry VIII's reign, 'history folded in upon itself and declared its own indecisiveness, even as those involved most actively in the folding process claimed both the familiarity and the absolute decisiveness of what was happening'.

In the final essay in the collection, Claude Willan's focus on 'the presence of the book' launches with an appreciation of the uniqueness of all textual artefacts, contra Harold Bloom. Willan sees distortion as emerging from moments when materiality intervenes in the transmission of a text's meaning. Using the Jacobite work, *An Answer to the Arguments in the Lord Bishop of Oxford's Speech, on the impeachment of Dr. Henry Sacheverell*, as a case study, Willan illustrates how the particularities of material production – in this case a gash in the book – physically reflect the instability of terms inherent in the text's discussion of government. Such interpretation of material objects is problematised further by the recognition of the distortion of the digital image, distortion that often seeks to render less visible or obtrusive the infelicities of surviving artefacts. Willan looks at multiple technologically rendered manifestations of early text, including online versions where the tools have struggled to represent the object, and, indeed, critical editions that wilfully mediate. He concludes that new models of investigation taking full account of the material are essential.

Through these essays, covering a thousand years of literature across continents and languages, the varied, dynamic and often positive role of distortion in the transmission and reception of texts has been productively examined. This discussion ties into core issues within text technologies and text technological transformation; it elucidates major characteristics in the studies of book history and digital humanities; and it exposes the benefits of the close reading and interpretation of texts, both at the level of the word and with respect to the animated essence of the textual object. We hope to inspire further reflection and scholarship with this work on distorted notions of visible and invisible things.[2]

[2] Percy Bysshe Shelley, 'A Defence of Poetry' (1821), in Percy Bysshe Shelley, *Essays, Letters from Abroad, Translations and Fragments* (London: Edward Moxon, 1840), p. 36: 'The distorted notions of invisible things which Dante and his rival Milton have idealized, are merely the mask and the mantle in which these great poets walk through eternity enveloped and disguised.'

The Curious Production and Reconstruction of Oxford, Bodleian Library, Junius 85 and 86[1]

MATTHEW AIELLO

Oxford, Bodleian Library, Junius 85 and 86 are two manuscripts that contain mostly anonymous, vernacular homilies that focus on the fate of the human body and soul. They also contain an Old English translation of the *Visio Sancti Pauli*, four bilingual charms, and a homily by Ælfric (c.955–1010). This may seem surprising, as Ælfric explicitly condemned the copying of apocryphal literature, like the *Visio Pauli*,[2] and, moreover, repeatedly denounced the vernacular textual traditions of his time, cautioning against charms, prognostications and heterodox writings.[3] It is interesting, then, that Ælfric's homily comes directly after a sequence of charms and vernacular homilies of questionable orthodoxy. Many studies have focused their critical efforts on making sense of these unusual groupings,[4] but hardly any explore the material text as the form in which these works survive. As such, this essay will argue that current

1 Many thanks to Elaine Treharne for bringing these two books to my attention and pointing out that they lacked a complete palaeographic study. I would also like to extend thanks to Seamus Dwyer and Thomas Kittel for reading drafts of this essay. Also, many thanks to Daniel Wakelin for his assistance with the quire collations.

2 See Homily 20 for Tuesday in Rogationtide in Malcom Godden's edition of *Ælfric's Catholic Homilies: The Second Series*, Early English Text Society, Supplementary Series 5 (London: Oxford University Press, 1979), where Ælfric states, 'Humeta rædað sume men. ða leasan gesetnysse. ðe hi hatað *paulus gesihðe*' ('How may some people read that false testament, which they call the *Vision of Paul*', lines 14–15; my emphasis).

3 See the Old English Preface in Peter Clemoes, ed., *Ælfric's Catholic Homilies: The First Series*, Early English Text Society, Supplementary Series 17 (Oxford: Oxford University Press, 1997), where Ælfric finds 'mycel gedwyld on manegum Engliscum bocum' ('much heresy in many English books', line 51).

4 Most notably Frederick M. Biggs, *Sources of Anglo-Saxon Literary Culture: A Trial Version* (Binghamton: State University of New York Press, 1990), pp. 66–8. Also see Rudolph Willard, 'The Address of the Soul to the Body', *PMLA*, 50.4 (1935), 957–83; Karen L. Jolly, 'Tapping the Power of the Cross: Who and for Whom?', in Catherine E. Karkov et al., eds, *The Place of the Cross in Anglo-Saxon England* (Woodbridge: Boydell, 2006), pp. 58–79.

scholarly understanding of Junius 85 and 86 is distorted by a focus only on specific texts, or on the general appearance of the codices, rather than on a more holistic approach to details of compilation and production.

One useful study of these books is that by Jonathan Wilcox in his examination of the Ælfric homily.[5] Wilcox, however, focuses solely on that text to make a case for its independent transmission amongst the laity in booklet form, and so only briefly mentions the manuscript as a whole. Indeed, when scholars have commented on the state of the material text, their brief remarks are almost wholly negative. Wilcox refers to them as 'a strikingly low status pair of manuscripts' that are 'incongruously scruffy, messy' and 'materially poor'.[6] Richard Gameson focuses on the collection's fragmentary nature and observes that the manuscripts are 'badly damaged'.[7] N. R. Ker's only assessment of the physical condition of the books is that the 'parchment varies in quality' and that a few of the *mise-en-page* features are 'unusual'.[8] Aside from their shared aesthetic judgements, scholars are also unanimous in their belief that Junius 85 and 86 once constituted a single manuscript that was split into separate volumes at a later date.

What a study of the material text reveals, however, is that these books are not soiled and materially poor, but well-used volumes that have been expertly constructed and cared for. Moreover, the lack of critical attention that has been paid to the materiality of these books has distorted their true significance and suggests a larger problem in English manuscript studies – the tacit belief that less ornate, visually modest manuscripts are somehow 'low status' and have little to offer the field. In reality, these two volumes are replete with rich insight into a number of the unique material obstacles that Anglo-Saxon scribes were forced to overcome when copying non-deluxe books. The folios in Junius 85 and 86 detail how a single scribe ingeniously navigated material challenges – a lack of sufficient materials and materials of inconsistent quality – to produce a beautiful, visually cohesive text. The methods he employs are extraordinary, and they deserve careful attention.

5 Jonathan Wilcox, 'The Use of Ælfric's Homilies: MSS Oxford, Bodleian Library, Junius 85 and 86 in the Field', in Hugh Magennis and Mary Swan, eds, *A Companion to Ælfric* (Leiden: Brill, 2009), pp. 345–68.

6 Wilcox, 'Use of Ælfric's Homilies', p. 355.

7 Richard Gameson, *The Manuscripts of Early Norman England (c.1066–1130)* (Oxford: Oxford University Press for the British Academy, 1999), p. 145.

8 N. R. Ker, *Catalogue of Manuscripts Containing Anglo-Saxon* (Oxford: Clarendon Press, 1957; reprinted with Supplement, 1991), p. 411.

This essay, then, aims to both clarify and explain the narrative of production that a close study of the material text is able to provide. Specifically, I suggest that the division of these miscellaneous homilies into separate volumes is not contemporary with its current binding, but is probably a medieval separation that was both intentional and concurrent with one of the two main scribes of the text as it stands today. Moreover, I aim to prove that the entirety of Junius 85 was written in the early to mid-eleventh century by a scribe who will henceforth be referred to as Scribe A, and that a relatively close contemporary of his, Scribe B, later sought to repair portions of this manuscript within fifty years of its original composition. As a result of these repairs, Scribe B recopied many of the quires in Junius 85, but left two quires (II and IV) unaltered from Scribe A's work. Scribe B was then the first to copy the texts currently in Junius 86, but chose to treat this grouping as a separate book, as he was no longer beholden to Scribe A's pre-existing quires. As such, Scribe B was able to wield autonomous control over Junius 86's physical layout, evidenced by specific features of the *mise-en-page* that are exclusive to the text. Not only did Scribe B treat Junius 86 separately from Junius 85, but he is the one responsible for the mid-homily separation of these volumes. The bridging homily, then, was only placed between these manuscripts to ensure that the texts travelled in tandem with one another. This is an intricate and complicated history, but an examination of the key features within these books adds significant weight to a narrative of intentional reconstruction.

Key Physical Descriptors

Both of these manuscripts were collated by Ker in his *Catalogue of Manuscripts Containing Anglo-Saxon*. However, Ker's single collation for both Junius 85 and 86 is inaccurate.[9] A careful and thorough reassessment of the quires and ruling patterns has resulted in the following collations:

Junius 85
i + 2 singletons + I^{8} + 1 singleton + II^{6} (5 cancelled) + 1 singleton + III^{8} (8 cancelled) + IV^{8} + V^{2} (2 cancelled) + 2 singletons + i

[9] Ker's collation (*Catalogue*, p. 411) reads as follows: '1 seven (ff. 2, 12–17: ff. 14–15 are a bifolium), 2^{10} wants 10 after f. 11, 3^{8} wants 8, probably blank, after f. 24, 4^{8}, 5 three (ff. 33–5), 6^{6}, 7^{10} + 1 leaf after 6 (f. 48), 8^{8} +1 leaf after 7 (f. 60), $9–10^{10}$'.

Junius 86
ii+ VI^6 +VII^{12} (5 cancelled) + VIII^{12} (2, 3 and 9 are cancelled) + IX^{10}+ X^{12} (1 and 5 cancelled) + i

In conjunction with these collations, I have provided the reader with supporting data in the appendix to this chapter. Appendix A depicts these collations with quire diagrams.[10] The next step in detailing the history of production is to identify the two scribes who copied the text as it is extant today.

Most surviving Anglo-Saxon manuscripts were written by more than one scribe.[11] It is often possible, then, to determine a great deal about how a book is made by tracking where one scribe finishes and another begins. But as Jonathan Wilcox notes, in these particular manuscripts it is remarkably difficult to differentiate between scribes.[12] Both scribes write in Anglo-Saxon or English vernacular rounded minuscule, the individual features of which place the original production of the manuscript in the mid to late eleventh century. Both scribes are also adept at switching to a form of Caroline minuscule when copying Latin. Scribe B's hand is slightly more careful and calligraphic, but Scribe A's letterforms are also calligraphically impressive. The two scribes frequently cut the nib of their quill pens, or even switch pens, and thus the overall aspect of their writing changes often; in one particular instance, Scribe B even intentionally assumes the characteristics of Scribe A. Also adding to the difficulty of determining scribal stints, much of the faded writing has been retouched by a later, seventeenth-century hand that has at times made it impossible to determine which scribe first copied a folio.[13]

Bearing in mind all of these limitations, if one carefully examines both hands side by side (Plates 1 & 2), the differences become appreciably discernible; more importantly, one can note a few particulars about the *ductus* of the pen. These pen movements stay true to each individual scribe and are useful tools when identifying a scribe that tries to hide

[10] While the above collation may look unusual, I have tabulated specific information about each folio that corroborates the stated construction: the folio's respective quire number, the identity of the scribe who copied the page, the number of lines ruled, the folio's connected leaf within its quire and the dimensions of its writing block. For images of the folios cited, see http:/bit.ly/2t8dkG5

[11] Alexander Rumble, 'The Construction and Writing of Anglo-Saxon Manuscripts', in Gale Owen-Crocker, ed., *Working with Anglo-Saxon Manuscripts* (Exeter: Exeter University Press, 2009), pp. 25–59 (p. 50).

[12] Wilcox, 'Use of Ælfric's Homilies', p. 356.

[13] For a fuller discussion of this late editor in the collection, see Hiroshi Ogawa, 'The Retoucher in MSS Junius 85 and 86', *Notes and Queries*, 41 (1994), 6–10.

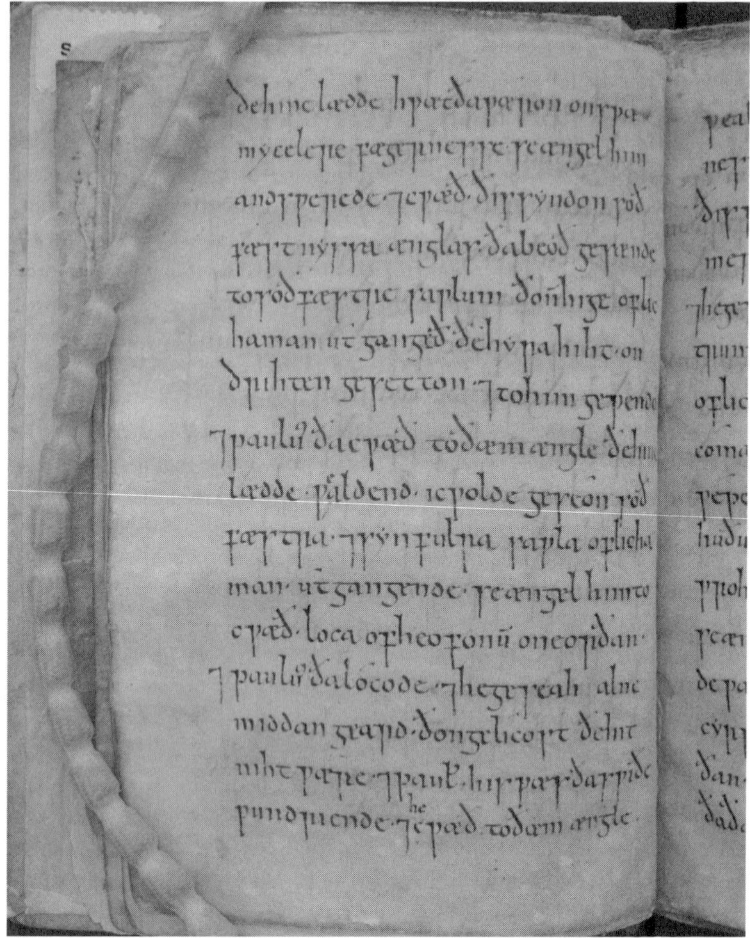

Plate 1: Oxford, Bodleian Library, Junius 85, folio 6v.

his own idiosyncrasies and engage in any attempted matched hand. At folio 6v (Plate 1), one can see that Scribe B bifurcates his ascenders, a feature that becomes common in the mid-eleventh century in the work of scribes trained at Worcester and Exeter, for example (see 'him', line 7; and 'wolde', line 9).[14] Also, other than in word initial position, the ascenders

[14] For other examples of Worcester bifurcations, see Christine Franzen, *Worcester Manuscripts*, in A. N. Doane and Phillip Pulsiano, eds, *Anglo-Saxon Manuscripts in Microfiche Facsimile*, 6 (Binghamton: SUNY Press, 1994-).

of **d** are typically very short. Scribe B always uses the long, insular **s** and the insular form of **r**; the tail of **g** is very fluid and is usually accomplished by one movement of the pen. Also, while the **t** is stoutly formed in the hands of both scribes, Scribe B tends to begin the downstroke in the centre of the cross-stroke, while Scribe A begins more to the left.

The feature that is most useful in scribal profiling, however, is the cross-stroke of **ð**. Scribe B's cross-stroke begins on the left-hand side of the ascender. The pen first moves in a slight, counter-clockwise motion before continuing at a 45-degree angle to cross the ascender until, finally, it reverses direction and drops down in a clockwise motion (see 'ðonne', line 5).[15] In contrast, Scribe A writes his cross-strokes quite differently. He writes them in two different ways, depending on the thickness of his pen. The first method, which is the most common on folio 12v (Plate 2), for example, is to do the reverse of what Scribe B writes. Scribe A begins his cross-stroke at the bottom, left-hand side of the ascender in a clockwise motion. He then moves in a straight line at a 60-degree angle as he crosses the ascender before reversing the motion and jerking the pen upwards in a counter-clockwise motion. The second form of **ð**, which becomes the most prominent form in quire IV, is the one represented in 'forðæm' in the first and fourth lines. Here, Scribe A starts the cross-stroke at the ascender and only moves in one direction (right) before dropping the pen down for added emphasis at the end.

Moreover, when it is in word final position, Scribe A uses the Caroline form of **r** (see Plate 2: 'for', lines 2 and 5) and the Caroline form of **s** (see 'godes', line 8). As he moves through the manuscript, the use of Caroline **r** and **s** become more prominent until Scribe A eventually uses these letterforms exclusively. It is also worth noting that while some of his ascenders show a slight bifurcation (see 'lichaman', line 16), the vast majority are flagged instead. The ascenders of **d** are generally taller than Scribe B's, and his **g** is often more rigid and 5-shaped, coinciding with two movements of the pen instead of one.

[15] All expanded abbreviations in this essay are underlined. Junius 85 and 86 are included in Peter Stokes and Stewart Brookes's *DigiPal* project, but, unfortunately, with no available images, available at: http://www.digipal.eu/digipal/manuscripts/1299/hands/ (accessed 25 February 2017). They state the hands are 'SE England', but provide no evidence. The manuscript's contents are fully described by Owen Roberson, in Orietta Da Rold, Takako Kato, Mary Swan and Elaine Treharne, *The Production and Use of English, 1060 to 1220* (Leicester: University of Leicester, 2010), https://www.le.ac.uk/english/em1060to1220/mss/EM.Ox.Juni.85.htm, with a link to Junius 86, but again, the scribal characteristics are not delineated and the place of origin is described as 'unknown'.

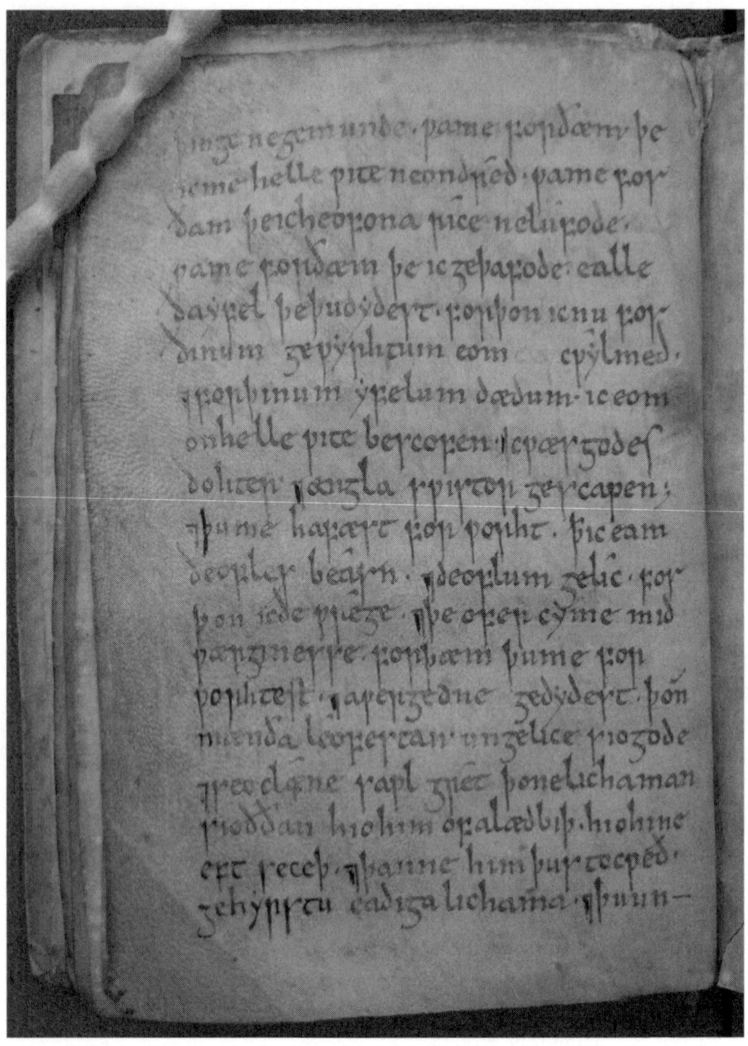

Plate 2: Oxford, Bodleian Library, Junius 85, folio 12v.

Junius 85

Now that the differences between these two scribes have been discussed, the next question is how these observations aid our understanding of the construction of Junius 85 and 86. Returning to the collations, one can see that Junius 85 has a number of singletons while Junius 86 has none at all. My study of the manuscripts has determined that every singleton in Junius 85 was added by Scribe B. Furthermore, these singletons come either directly before or directly after quires written by Scribe A (quires II and IV). This suggests that Scribe B, arriving at the texts in Junius 85, sought to replace a number of Scribe A's damaged quires by recopying them himself. He then found it necessary to add singletons when his new quires did not arrive at the correct place in the text where Scribe A's preserved quires began.

This is best illustrated through example. Folio 11 was copied by Scribe B and has been added between quires I and II. Quire I is written by Scribe B, and quire II is written by Scribe A. This folio is unquestionably a singleton, as it arrives after a perfect quire of eight and before a quire of six; more importantly, it is ruled for fifteen lines of text, while all of quire I's folios are ruled for sixteen lines and all of quire II's folios are ruled for nineteen lines. It is, in a sense, the odd one out both in location and design. But a glance at the opening of folio 11v and folio 12r in the *Anglo-Saxon Manuscripts in Microfiche Facsimile* edition, or at the online images (see fn. 10) shows that the writing grids appear to be even, despite the large difference in the number of lines ruled. Empirical data supports this observation as well. While folio 11r has a writing grid of roughly 125 x 86mm, its verso has a writing grid of 131 x 90mm (inclusive of run-over). This closely matches the writing grid of folio 12r, which is 130 x 86mm. These comparable figures are not simply happenstance, but a result of Scribe B's thoughtful process of production.

While it is difficult to show ruling photographically, due to the poor legibility of dry-point ruling, after line 7, Scribe B writes the text below the ruled line instead of on top of it. At line 13, which begins, 'þæt ðu sige on wyrolde', the text is actually written in the middle of a ruled line. Scribe B's process, then, is to move the written text slowly down the page in small, incremental jumps in order to expand the writing block. Also, while folio 11v has four fewer ruled lines than folio 12r, Scribe B cleverly matches his horizontal bounding lines (i.e. the top and bottom lines) with the bounding lines of the facing folio from Scribe A to give the illusion of conformity.

From a textual perspective, folio 11 also indicates that the singleton was necessary because Scribe B, when recopying quire I, was unable to arrive at the place in the text with which Scribe A begins folio 12r, as quire II begins mid-sentence. In Ker's collation, he states that there is a cancelled folio after folio 11.[16] This is erroneous, but an understandable mistake.

[16] Ker, *Catalogue*, p. 411.

Looking carefully at these folios, there are what appear to be remnants of a cancelled folio in the gutter of the page. When one actually reads the text, however, it follows across quires perfectly. Beginning with the run-over on folio 11v, the text reads, 'ðæs synfullan mannes . / [12r] sawl .' The remnants in the gutter are therefore just scraps of vellum that a later conservator has used to ensure that the singleton stays in place, and are in fact, not a cancelled folio.[17]

One must also consider the possibility that these scribes were not writing years apart (as I have suggested), but, rather, in tandem with one another. It was not unusual for two scribes to work on different quires within the same manuscript, as changes in hand are often separated by quire units. Occasionally, a change in hand can even come mid-text.[18] In this particular manuscript, however, the codicological features speak against this likelihood. A change in scribe mid-text is one thing, but a change in scribe mid-sentence is rarer. Moreover, the two quires (I and II) are radically different, both in the number of bifolia and in the number of ruled lines per page. If one were able to accept that a change in scribe can come mid-sentence, this would at least have to be corroborated with quires of similar make, as it would make sense that these features would be uniform within the same institution of production. Here, though, a more likely theory is that the first quire was originally copied by Scribe A and that Scribe B later recopied it (possibly because of damage). In so doing, Scribe B copied the text in a quire of his own construction that had fewer ruled lines than the original (assuming this older quire was also ruled for nineteen lines like quire II); because of this, Scribe B still had text left to be copied when he came to the end of his quire of eight. He therefore chose to add a singleton for the remainder of the text, but wanted the writing grid on the verso side (folio 11v) to match that of Scribe A's quire, so he adjusted the spacing accordingly. This is one of many examples where Scribe B must manipulate space in order to catch up with Scribe A. His methods, however, are always clean and consider the overall aesthetic of the page.

The need for a singleton also perhaps speaks to the manner in which this section of the text was copied, as it was possibly from a disbound exemplar where Scribe B's focus was solely on copying Scribe A's old

17 These remnants also appear in the opening gutter of the book, suggesting that a scrap of vellum was used to secure this folio to the previous quire.

18 Richard Gameson, 'Anglo-Saxon Scribes and Scriptoria', in Gameson, ed., *The Cambridge History of the Book in Britain c.400–1100* (Cambridge: Cambridge University Press, 2009), pp. 94–120 (p. 108).

quire, word for word. As such, it may be that Scribe B treated the recopying of this quire as a separate project that would later be inserted into the complete codex as it stands today. One must therefore consider the possibility of booklet production, as it is likely that all of the recopied quires in Junius 85 were copied as separate fascicles before being inserted into the current manuscript. P. R. Robinson famously defined the booklet as a textual unit, which 'could circulate independently and at the same time provide a complete copy of a text'.[19] This definition relies too much on the self-sufficiency of the literary text and not nearly enough on self-sufficient production. Robinson, based on her definition, would not categorise the quires completed by Scribe B in Junius 85 as booklets, because they do not always hold a self-contained text. Ralph Hanna has added a helpful addendum to Robinson's definition of booklets by stressing self-sufficiency in production:

> [R]ather than conceiving of the booklet as a basic unit, the producer begins to conceive of the unit of the whole codex. And when this step occurs, although production proceeds (or has proceeded) within booklet format, the 'self-sufficiency' of the booklet is frequently lost.[20]

As such, applying the title of 'booklet' to the miscellaneous quires in Junius 85 completed by Scribe B is an acceptable classification, though arguably slightly misleading, if the whole codex was conceived of. While most of the quires in Junius 85 do not contain a self-sufficient text, then, they were probably produced in a piecemeal fashion with consideration of the whole codex during production. Nowhere is this more obvious than in the Ælfric booklet (quire III). This quire actually does contain a self-sufficient text, but there are also clear indications that it was always intended to be inserted in the small codex. It is therefore only a 'booklet' insofar as it was self-sufficient in production, not because of any independent circulation.

The quire containing Ælfric's homily for the first Sunday in Lent begins on folio 18r. Wilcox argues for the independent transmission of this booklet by noting that it is 'self-contained and aesthetically distinct from the rest of the collection'.[21] While absolutely self-contained, it is

19 P. R. Robinson, 'The "Booklet": A Self-Contained Unit in Composite Manuscripts', *Codicologica*, 3 (1980), 46–69 (46–7).

20 Ralph Hanna, 'Booklets in Medieval Manuscripts: Further Considerations', *Studies in Bibliography*, 39 (1986), 100–11 (103).

21 Wilcox, 'Use of Ælfric's Homilies', p. 356.

by no means aesthetically different. Wilcox's evidence for this claim is based on the fact that the text begins with a 'hierarchy of scripts' that create a visual impact 'not echoed elsewhere in Junius 85 and 86'.[22] This, in fact, is not the case. There are multiple examples of decorated, large opening initials that occur throughout both manuscripts. A few of these decorated initials are actually even more elaborate than the one opening the Ælfric homily. There are also other examples of Scribe B writing in majuscules for the whole of the first line (folio 62r, for example), and thus this process is not unique to this quire. Furthermore, Wilcox also argues for the text's independent transmission because he believes that the pages show heavy signs of use, particularly on the outside folios. In reality, however, the pages of the Ælfric homily are some of the cleanest, least damaged and best preserved folios in the manuscript.

But there are a few visual inconsistencies within this quire that Wilcox correctly notes are not present elsewhere in the collection. The text block has been defined with margins at both sides of the leaves by double vertical bounding lines. The text initially began at the second bounding line, while the space between the first and second was probably left clear for enlarged capitals.[23] On close examinations of the margins on only the recto sides of the leaves, however, it is clear that in the left-hand margin, a small portion of text (roughly five to six characters) has been scribbled at the front of a few lines where these capitals were intended to go. This occurs uniquely throughout this quire. The process is also noted by points added at the end of each line to indicate when words must be added to the beginning of the following line. The revised text appears to have been added by the main hand (Scribe B), which dates this process to close to the original construction of the booklet. Wilcox observes that this whole procedure only makes sense if 'one assumes that the scribe expected the last characters on the right of each recto page to be lost due to cropping';[24] by this he means that the scribe must have been told that the right margin was going to be cut *before* he began writing. When it was actually placed in the codex, these considerations were ultimately unnecessary, and Scribe B then copied the left-out text in the space that had been previously reserved for enlarged or offset capitals. What this suggests, then, is that this particular booklet, from the very beginning of its construction, was copied bearing in mind the consideration that it would have its margins substantially cropped. For leaves that were already small to begin with,

22 Wilcox, 'Use of Ælfric's Homilies', p. 356.

23 Wilcox, 'Use of Ælfric's Homilies', p. 357.

24 Wilcox, 'Use of Ælfric's Homilies', p. 357.

these considerations only make sense if this booklet was always intended to be placed in an even smaller book, such as Junius 85. The booklet probably did not circulate independently as Wilcox suggests, but is only a 'booklet' insofar as it was produced in a self-sufficient manner.

Junius 86

Ignoring for a moment that Junius 86 begins in the middle of a homily, from a purely visual perspective, the manuscript looks like an entirely separate book from Junius 85. There are no erratic singletons, no last-minute marginal scribbles, and no indications that Scribe B had to develop creative solutions for joining his work with Scribe A's. Moreover, the first two quires of Junius 86 (quires VI and VII) are replete with elaborate run-over marks at the bottom of each page. Because they occur consistently at the bottom of every page, one might wonder if they are run-over marks at all. Michelle Brown defines 'run-on symbols' as the following:

> A decorative device (abstract, foliate, zoomorphic, or anthropomorphic) which indicates that the text of a line has been carried over to occupy the remainder of the line above or below a space that otherwise would have been left blank. Run-over symbols serve both decorative and space-saving functions, especially in verse forms such as Psalms, and were initially popularized in insular and pre-Carolingian art.[25]

The run-over symbols in Junius 86 are absolutely decorative, but they do not operate as 'space-saving functions', nor do they occur in a space that 'otherwise would have been left blank', as the lower margin would have been too large without them. To explain, without the run-over marks, the average writing block for the leaves in quire VI would be roughly 120 x 80mm. For quire VII, this average drops to 116 x 76mm. As the length and width of the pages stays fairly consistent throughout the collection, these two quires would then have the smallest average writing blocks anywhere in Junius 85 and 86. When one includes the run-over marks in the writing block, these figures jump to 127 x 80mm and 125 x 76, respectively. These new figures are closer to the standard writing blocks for the rest of the quires in the collection. These run-overs are therefore not operating in their prescribed role of space-saving functions – an additional line could have solved this problem – but are there to add drama to the page.

[25] Michelle Brown, *Understanding Illuminated Manuscripts: A Guide to Technical Terms* (London: British Library Publications, 1994), p. 112.

If a manuscript is decorated at all, it is normal for the first few pages to have the most elaborate decorations, as this helps give the illusion of high quality throughout the text.[26] The unnecessary use of ornate run-overs suggests that, at the very least, in the *production* of these last five quires Scribe B treated them as their own textual unit that deserved opening decoration. In texts as small as Junius 85 and 86, these run-overs make a significant impression on the manuscripts' users, whether they were intended to occur at the beginning of a new text (as I propose), or in the very centre of the text (as most scholars suggest).

An even closer look at these run-overs reveals more information about the order of their composition. The ink used for the boundary lines of these symbols appears to be the same ink in which the main text is written. It therefore points to the scribe himself as the artist behind these additions, rather than a third-party illustrator. It should be noted, though, that the run-overs in quire VI differ slightly from those in quire VII. The ones in quire VI have a thicker, more elaborate finish on their right-hand side. On the left-hand side, when the pen changes from a horizontal to a vertical stroke, tiny loops are present at the point of transition. By contrast, the run-overs in quire VII do not have these loops, and the right-hand side displays a simpler, less heavy flourish. These may be subtle differences, but they point to the scribal stints between quires VI and VII, suggesting that at least some time had passed between the addition of the run-overs in these consecutive quires. Moreover, when one examines folio 34v (a singleton in Junius 85 added by Scribe B), it is apparent that the tongue of the zoomorphic run-over matches the flourishes on the run-overs in quire VII. This gestures to the possibility that this singleton and quire VII were written close together, perhaps even on the same day, and further supports a history of an erratic reconstruction by Scribe B. It seems likely that Scribe B was recopying sections from Scribe A in Junius 85 at the same time that he was copying new material for Junius 86.

The facing folios of 47v and 48r also point to Scribe B's careful attention to aesthetics. Folio 47v is ruled in dry-point for thirteen lines, which run through the width of the page; folio 48r has been ruled for fourteen lines of text. Their writing blocks, however, are equal (123 x 72mm and 122 x 72mm, respectively). This is because Scribe B has chosen to ignore the final ruled line on folio 48r and has instead written the text from the run-over through the ruled line to maintain a cohesive spread.[27] These

[26] Gameson, 'Anglo-Saxon Scribes and Scriptoria', p. 111.

[27] This is difficult to see in any photographic replication, but it is there.

run-overs are absolutely more decorative than functional, as here it would have made more sense for Scribe B to simply write the final line *on* the final ruled line rather than through it. The desire for matching writing blocks, however, was too important to him. These are impressive considerations that are ubiquitous in Junius 86 and indicate that this book was made with great care and planning.

Based on this evidence alone, it would be fair to suggest that Scribe B treated the quires in Junius 86 as a separate text from Junius 85 – a text where he was able to control the layout of the page without the interference of Scribe A's quires. But there is further compelling evidence that suggests Scribe B not only treated Junius 86 as its own book, but made it a separate book as well. Scribe B, I suggest, then, is responsible for the mid-homily split.

The Eleventh-Century Separation of Manuscripts

Scholars are unanimous in their belief that Junius 85 and 86 once constituted a single manuscript that was split into two volumes by a later conservator. Exploring what this actually means in practice, however, indicates that this theory is unlikely. That is, if a later conservator split the manuscript into two volumes, then the only logical reason for the split's location is that the conservator believed the embellished run-overs, which begin at folio 36r, warranted their own codicological sequence of units. This would also mean that the conservator did not bother to read the text, as the split arrives mid-sentence. Even if such a person was unfamiliar with Old English, it is obvious where a new sentence begins in the text as it is signified by a distinctive majuscule letter. This would have been unpractised conservation work, but such is not altogether impossible. A more likely scenario, however, is that any conservation work completed on the collection was completed after the original manuscript was split into two volumes, and that the split was carried out in the late eleventh century by Scribe B. The clearest way to support this claim is to first examine the pages directly involved with the split (folios 35 and 36).

On the recto side of the last folio in Junius 85, one can see that a change in hand occurs at the end of line 4. The first four lines, I suggest, are written by Scribe A, and indicate a clear attempt to end the preceding homily. These are written by Scribe A because the scribe of those lines favours the Caroline form of **r** (see 'ðær' and 'brucan', line 3), which I noted as one of his identifying characteristics. His letterforms also gradually increase in size, and the spaces between words become larger (compare with folio 12r). It is almost as if Scribe A were intentionally trying to take up more space on the page and give a visual impression of finality to these words. Also, from a textual perspective, these final words come as a formulaic conclusion to a homily, which praises the soul for keeping the commandments and then rejoices in the soul's ability to enter heaven with God's beloved 'ænglum' (line 4). The written word, however, does not stop there. Although not signified by an enlarged capital, a new homily begins at the end of line 4. Its opening phrase, 'And nu, mæn ða leofestan' (lines 4–5), is a common invocation for the beginning of homilies, and the dramatic shift in subject matter from the soul's salvation to a discussion of eternal punishment further supports the separateness of these two homilies.[28] A quick and cursory glance might suggest that this new homily starting at line 4 appears to have been written by Scribe A with a smaller pen; it is, in fact, written by Scribe B.

Scribe B has now switched to Scribe A's characteristic cross-stroke of **ð** and is attempting to mask his own identity; but there are clear indicators that this is actually Scribe B. Most of the ascenders are still heavily bifurcated. Moreover, this scribe is not using Caroline letterforms. As stated above, at this point in the text, Scribe A was using Caroline forms of **r** and **s**, exclusively. One could argue that the return to insular letterforms after line 4 is simply indicative of a scribal stint, but Scribe A's previous stints (such as those between folios 32v and 33r) do not support this hypothesis. If this scribe was Scribe A, he would be using Caroline, not insular, letterforms. There is also the occasional slip into two-compartment **a** (see 'lera', line 10, and 'singallic', line 14). Scribe A never uses a two-compartment **a**, whereas Scribe B occasionally uses this form ('costnunga', line 13).

Scribe B as copyist of the second two-thirds of folio 35 becomes a more obvious proposition when his stint here is compared with the first folio of Junius 86. The same scribal stint that begins on the fourth line of folio 35r carries over to the recto side of folio 36 in Junius 86, the first folio in this manuscript. These hands are identical. They were therefore written by the same person, with a similar pen, possibly the same day. Further supporting this suggestion, the ink used to fill the run-over at the bottom of folio

28 In practice, it is impossible to know the definitive end to most of the homilies present in Junius 85/86, as many have no extant counterparts. However, a shift in subject of this size would suggest that these were two separate homilies, or, at the very least, different sections of the same homily. For a full transcription of the text with a facing Italian translation, see A. M. Luiselli Fadda, ed., *Nuove Omelie Anglosassoni Della Rinascenza Benedettina*, Filologia Germanica Testi e studi 1 (Firenze: Le Monnier, 1977), pp. 22–3.

36r is unique to that quire but was also used for the in-filled graphemes on folio 35r. The beginning of Scribe B's homily on folio 35r may not begin with an enlarged capital, but the majuscule 'A' in 'And' has been filled in for added emphasis. Also, the two shoulders and outer limbs of 'm' from the previous word (written by Scribe A) have small dashes of this ink that were added at a later date. It is almost as if Scribe B, highlighting the beginning of his own work, tried to smooth the visual transition between his own homily and Scribe A's preceeding one by also adding colour to the end of the previous homily.

It is also interesting to note that the run-over on folio 36r is slightly different than the rest of the run-overs in quire VI. It is the only symbol in that quire that does not have loops at the directional transition point, indicating that this symbol (and therefore this folio) was written on a different day than the rest of its quire. Collectively, this information points to a single stint between folio 35r and folio 36r. It is curious that this stint only covers two pages (the smallest in the collection) and, moreover, that these two pages happen to be the ones that both end and start the two manuscripts. This suggests that the scribe set aside more time for these two pages, as he knew that this split in the manuscript was going to occur at this exact location. It would be difficult to suggest that the smallest scribal stint in the collection occurs here by pure chance.

Moving slightly outside these pages, there is other corroborating evidence that Scribe B is the author of these pages and is responsible for the intentional split. The whole of quire VI (the first quire in Junius 86) is written in a hand that looks like Scribe A's, but is not. On the verso side of folio 36, Scribe B continues to mimic Scribe A but has clearly switched to a pen with a thicker nib, as this is a new stint. However, after the word 'breohtnes' in line 13, one will notice that the scribe completed what would have been blank intertextual space with a small flourished line filler. This flourish is identical to one found on line 5 of folio 17r, which is another singleton from Junius 85 that was added by Scribe B. Thus, a few of Scribe B's customs betray his attempt to cover his own hand. The question is why he would seek to emulate Scribe A's hand like this before returning to his normal hand in quire VII? And, if it is truly Scribe B's hand at the end of Junius 85, why did he not just start his continuation of the homily at the beginning of Junius 86 instead of beginning mid-sentence, and leave the remainder of Junius 85 blank? These decisions cannot be explained away by a desire to save material, for as suggested earlier, Scribe B favours aesthetics over more practical, space-saving methods. This whole process only begins to make sense if one suggests that all of these oddities are intentional and serve a larger purpose.

I propose the following justification: Scribe A's final contribution to the text was on folio 35r. Scribe B then continued Scribe A's previously closed homily and did so by imitating Scribe A's hand to smooth his continuation, as visual cohesion was important to him. Once the last singleton had been fully filled out, Scribe B then had the opportunity to continue the text in a separate book of his own construction, a text where he decided to add elaborate run-overs for opening drama. The split, then, was purposefully carried out in order to link Scribe A's ending homily in Junius 85 with Scribe B's own continuation, as one could not read the opening homily to Junius 86 without the closing homily from Junius 85. This had the added benefit of ensuring that the two volumes would travel in tandem with one another in the future. This is the narrative that the constructive features suggest. I wonder, also, if Scribe B made this decision to split the texts because he was simply proud of his work in Junius 86 and wanted it to stand on its own. Such satisfaction in one's own work is something not typically associated with medieval scribes, but perhaps that should be reconsidered. Bookmaking is a craft like any other, and a scribe's pride in his work and subsequent desire to preserve the longevity of his creation are understandable motives.

Conclusions: A Later History

During this study, I have imagined a scene where Scribe B, arriving at the original text made by Scribe A, sought to improve, wherever he could, damaged portions of the manuscript that he inherited. Then, as a continuation of Scribe A's last homily, Scribe B had the opportunity to add to the text in a separate book and took on this job with alacrity and aesthetic inspiration.

My point is not simply to offer a possibility for the previously unknown provenance, process and construction of these books. I also mean to stress the need for close study of non-deluxe medieval manuscripts. Studies of manuscript materiality are crucial, and not just as a means to an end. A manuscript's context is always tied to the literature it contains. As Karen Jolly notes in her essay on the power of the cross in Anglo-Saxon England, the construction of the charms and homilies present in early medieval books can assist in determining audience.[29] The texts may be bilingual, but prayers, for example, prescribe fairly simple Latin that the

29 Karen Jolly, 'Tapping the Power of the Cross: Who and for Whom?', in Catherine E. Karkov, Sarah Larratt Keefer and Karen Jolly, eds, *The Place of the Cross in Anglo-Saxon England* (Woodbridge: Boydell, 2006), pp. 58–79 (p. 73).

laity would or could know, such as excerpts from the *Pater Noster* and the invocation of Longinus. Her larger point, however, is that whether the scribe intended it or not (which I think he did), the texts he copied made it easy for the clerical user of this collection 'to teach [a] lay congregation biblical concepts'.[30] If Jolly had room for a material analysis in her study, she would have also noted how Scribe B worked tirelessly to improve the sustainability of these two books to allow, I think, the clerical user to do just that: teach.

After the eleventh-century renovation of these books, however, their provenance is unknown until the seventeenth century when Isaac Vossius acquired the manuscripts. Even this later history presents students of the material text with wonderful mysteries, though, particularly concerning the manuscript's paratext. Junius 85 contains a palimpsest that has been added to the front of the text as a protective flyleaf. While Ker did not note the substrate's palimpsested qualities, he did attribute this added single leaf to Isaac Vossius, as it is his hand that details the contexts of the manuscript (in Latin) as an opening to the collection.[31] Examining this leaf carefully, it is possible to see that there are horizontal ruled lines that expand the length of the page. The verso of the same folio confirms its nature, as it is filled with faded Latin in an early hand. My own research into the folio's origin has turned up no results. However, Vossius's complete library was catalogued after his death by Paul Colomiez, and it is likely that this folio came from a loose leaf in one of Vossius's other manuscripts.[32] Anyone desiring to know the palimpsest's origin could cross-reference the details on the page with early Latin manuscripts in Colomiez's extensive catalogue to see if he has noted a missing page.[33]

While little may be definitively stated about the provenance between these two volumes' eleventh-century renovation and Vossius's seventeenth-century acquisition of them, this examination has shone some light on the collection's early history. My study stresses the importance of

[30] Jolly, 'Tapping the Power of the Cross', p. 74.

[31] Ker, *Catalogue*, p. 411.

[32] The entire catalogue can be found in F. F. Blok's translated edition, *Contributions to the History of Isaac Vossius's Library*, Verhandelingen der Koninlijke Nederlandse Akademie van Wetenschappen, Afd, Letterkunde 83 (Amsterdam: North Holland, 1974).

[33] Due to technological limitations, I was not able to uncover the full text of this palimpsest. Few words and phrases are visible to the naked eye; the ones that are legible are extremely common in Latin ecclesiastical texts, such as *sancte* and *perpetua domine*, and were therefore unhelpful in determining the identity of the work.

fully investigating books that are humble in design, and plain in production. For even in small, materially poor books, a deep consideration for sustainability and professional manufacture, and a concern for aesthetic and visual cohesion can be found.

Appendix A

Quire Diagrams

Junius 85:

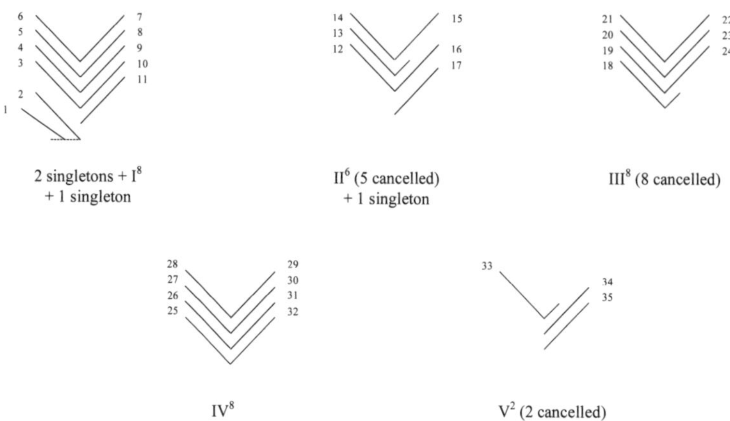

2 singletons + I^{8} + 1 singleton

II^{6} (5 cancelled) + 1 singleton

III^{8} (8 cancelled)

IV^{8}

V^{2} (2 cancelled) + 2 singletons

Junius 86:

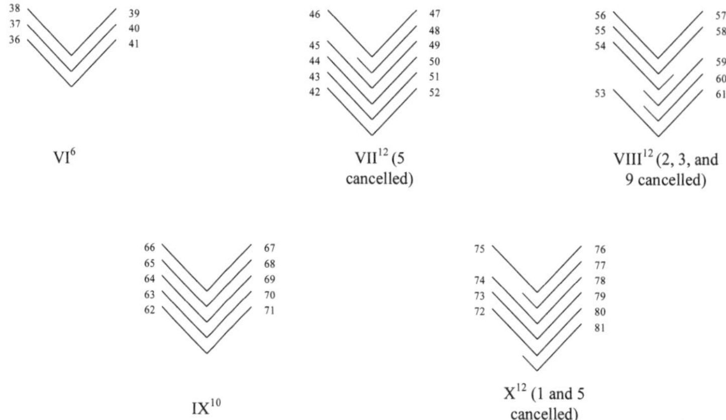

VI^{6}

VII^{12} (5 cancelled)

VIII^{12} (2, 3, and 9 cancelled)

IX^{10}

X^{12} (1 and 5 cancelled)

'Through a glass darkly', or, Rethinking Medieval Materiality: A Tale of Carpets, Screens and Parchment

EMMA CAYLEY

This essay approaches the topic of distortion from an unashamedly recuperative angle. The epigraph here is that most famously reprised biblical quotation: 'For now we see through a glass, darkly; but then face to face: now I know in part; but then shall I know even as also I am known', from 1 Corinthians 13:12.[1] It is cited out of context in a hundred different songs, television shows, films and poems, including as the title of a 1961 Ingmar Bergman film, which exploits the notion of human misapprehension and the distorted or partial nature of human knowledge, of human works and endeavours in the face of the divine.[2] The perhaps questionable reception of this quotation forms a jumping-off point for our investigation of the reception and/or distortion of medieval texts, from the moment they emerge in written form, to their modern manifestations under foot or digitally translated and transformed.

Within the field of medieval French literature and manuscript studies, the textual and material phenomena of incompleteness, instability and fragmentation – or perhaps what we might rather more positively call continuations, variance and multiplication – have been the subject of a number of studies in recent decades.[3] The discrete text is often left incomplete or unfinished through the common medieval trope of the refusal or deferral of ending or judgement (especially in the dialogued or debate poem), which is projected beyond the diegetic frame of the text through a number of textual devices: an unreliable narrator; an absent

[1] See https://www.kingjamesbibleonline.org/ (accessed 10 February 2017).

[2] *Through a Glass Darkly*, directed by Ingmar Bergman (Janus Films, 1961). See also Gene D. Phillips, 'Ingmar Bergman and God', in Stuart M. Kaminsky and Joseph F. Hill, eds, *Ingmar Bergman: Essays in Criticism* (New York: Oxford University Press, 1975), pp. 45–54.

[3] For the bright side of manuscript variance, see Bernard Cerquiglini's *In Praise of the Variant: A Critical History of Philology*, trans. Betsy Wing (Baltimore: Johns Hopkins University Press, 1999), originally published in French as *Éloge de la variante* (Paris: Seuil, 1989).

judge; a delay to find legal representation; ambiguity, and so on.[4] This might seem unsatisfactory until one realises that a continuation is usually offered, often in the shape of a further text or texts; and indeed that the 'original' text gains from its contextual – or as Jean-Claude Mühlethaler puts it, 'co-textual' – reading across the linguistic surfaces of a manuscript or printed compilation, or cycle.[5]

In this context, the 'original' itself is held up as imperfect, unfinished, *continuable*; and therefore any 'distortion' in the sense of continuation or adaptation may be seen as a positive gain. Indeed, 'distortion' itself is a not unproblematic word, since while more often than not used to indicate deviation from a norm or original form in a pejorative sense, it can signify positively in certain contexts.[6] In music, for example, 'Distortion is what results when the electronic output signal of an amplifier becomes "clipped" or interrupted in a way that produces an overflow of harmonious resonances.'[7] Such distortion is sometimes thought to enhance the music.

This notion of a proliferation of 'harmonious resonances', of amplification or augmentation, can be read across the chequered reception and

[4] On the deferral of ending in medieval French literature see Adrian Armstrong, 'The Deferred Verdict: A Topos in Late-Medieval Poetic Debates?', *French Studies Bulletin*, 64 (Autumn 1997), 12–14; Michèle Perret, 'Typologies des fins dans les oeuvres de fiction (XIe–XVe siècles), *PRIS-MA*, 14.2 (1998), 155–74; Emma Cayley, *Debate and Dialogue: Alain Chartier in his Cultural Context* (Oxford: Clarendon Press, 2006); Emma Cayley, 'Drawing Conclusions: The Poetics of Closure in Alain Chartier's Verse', *Fifteenth-Century Studies*, 28 (2003), 51–64.

[5] See Jean-Claude Mühlethaler, 'Inversions, Omissions and the Co-textual Reorientation of Reading: The *Ballades* of Charles d'Orléans in Vérard's *La Chasse et le Départ d'Amours* (1509)', in Adrian Armstrong and Malcolm Quainton, eds, *Book and Text in France 1400–1600: Poetry on the Page* (Aldershot: Ashgate, 2007), pp. 31–47. On medieval French literary cycles, see Bert Besamusca, W. P. Gerritsen, C. Hogetoorn and O. S. H. Lie, eds, *Cyclification: The Development of Narrative Cycles in the Chansons De Geste and the Arthurian Romances* (Amsterdam: Royal Netherlands Academy of Arts & Sciences, 1994); Sara Sturm-Maddox and Donald Maddox, eds, *Transtextualities: Of Cycles and Cyclicity in Medieval French Literature* (Arizona: MRTS, 1996); and Thomas Hinton, *The Conte du Graal Cycle: Chrétien de Troyes's 'Perceval', the Continuations, and French Arthurian Romance* (Cambridge: D. S. Brewer, 2012).

[6] See the Oxford English Dictionary definition at http://www.oed.com/ (accessed 28 February 2017).

[7] John Shepherd, David Horn, Dave Laing, Paul Oliver and Peter Wicke, eds, *Continuum Encyclopedia of Popular Music of the World: Volume II: Performance and Production* (London: Continuum, 2003), p. 286, 'Guitars'.

multifarious adaptations of the Exeter Book of Old English poetry,[8] as across the manuscript and printed tradition (reception, adaptation, translation) of late fifteenth-century French amatory debate poems, as we will see further on in this essay through a closer analysis of their varied textual afterlives.[9] The manuscript anthology itself can be experienced as a space of play in which discrete texts are understood as moves in a wider game, and co-textual reading then becomes a necessary part of this game-play.[10] This is a game that is played out in material contexts too, within and across manuscript compilations.[11] Medieval poets operate in collaborative, yet competitive networks that I have termed 'collaborative communities', after Brian Stock's notion of textual communities.[12] These communities or networks are located through the medieval cyclical composition or continuation mentioned above, and through what Jane Taylor has termed the 'collective phenomenon' of a participatory poetics in late medieval France. That is to say, this is a collaborative poetic endeavour producing a body of texts, which are incomplete as individual pieces, but signify relationally through their co-textual links:

[8] See Bernard Muir's two-volume edition, *The Exeter Anthology of Old English Poetry* (Exeter: University of Exeter Press, 2000), and 2006 Liverpool University Press reprint with DVD-ROM.

[9] I borrow this term from the 'Textual Afterlives' project, co-organised by Jeremy Smith (University of Glasgow), Ian Johnson (University of St Andrews), Crawford Gribben (Trinity College Dublin) and John Thompson (Queen's University Belfast).

[10] For the manuscript as a space of play see Emma Cayley, 'Debating Communities: Revealing Meaning in Late-Medieval French Manuscript Collections', *Neuphilologische Mitteilungen*, 105. 2 (2004), 191–201; Emma Cayley, 'Players and Spaces of Play in Late-Medieval French Manuscript Collections', in Emma Gilby and Katja Haustein, eds, *Space: New Dimensions in French Studies* (Bern: Peter Lang, 2005), pp. 23–39; Cayley, *Debate and Dialogue*; Emma Cayley, 'Polyphonie et dialogisme: Espaces ludiques dans le recueil manuscrit à la fin du Moyen Âge. Le cas de trois recueils poétiques du quinzième siècle', in Tania Van Hemelryck and Claude Thiry, eds, *Le recueil à la fin du moyen âge. La fin du Moyen Âge* (Turnhout: Brepols: Texte, Codex & Contexte, 2010), pp. 47–60.

[11] For poetic games and competitions see Jane H. M. Taylor, *The Making of Poetry: Late-Medieval French Poetic Anthologies* (Turnhout: Brepols, 2007); Adrian Armstrong, *The Virtuoso Circle: Competition, Collaboration, and Complexity in Late Medieval French Poetry* (Arizona: MRTS, 2012); and Cayley, *Debate and Dialogue*, esp. chs 1 and 4.

[12] See Brian Stock, *Listening for the Text: On the Uses of the Past* (Baltimore: Johns Hopkins University Press, 1990); and Emma Cayley, 'Collaborative Communities: The Manuscript Context of Alain Chartier's *Belle Dame sans mercy*', *Medium Ævum*, 71.2 (2002), 226–40.

> A collective phenomenon, where the poets who participate in the social field of poetry construct themselves, as Bourdieu would have it, relationally, and where the dynamism of their relationship underpins the word on the page.[13]

In the later Middle Ages, we have ample evidence of networks of texts that respond to, debate and question – even undermine – an 'original' or prior text. We could think in the French context, for example, of the fifteenth-century epistolary quarrel that sought to debate the infamous thirteenth-century *Romance of the Rose*,[14] or the later fifteenth-century poetic quarrel, which erupted over Alain Chartier's *La Belle Dame sans mercy* (1424).[15] In either case, the debates took issue with the supposed 'authority' of a unitary 'original', and in the latter instance, sequels and imitation poems reshaped and recast Chartier's poem for more than half a century. Indeed the reuse by John Keats in his 1819 poem of Chartier's title,[16] if not the substance, of Chartier's poem, has led to a proliferation of nineteenth-, twentieth- and twenty-first-century adaptations in a variety of media, including a series of Pre-Raphaelite paintings,[17] and, more recently, a stop-motion children's film, *Coraline* (Henry Selick, 2009), based on a 2002 novella by Neil Gaiman.[18] The witch-like character Beldam of

[13] Taylor, *The Making of Poetry*, p. 81.

[14] For the letters and other documents in this quarrel, see *Le Débat sur le Roman de la Rose*, ed. Eric Hicks (Paris: Champion, 1977); *Querelle de la Rose: Letters and Documents*, ed. Joseph L. Baird and John R. Kane (Chapel Hill: University of North Carolina Press, 1978); *Le Débat sur le 'Roman de la Rose'*, ed. and trans. Virginie Greene (Paris: Champion, 2006); Christine McWebb, ed., *Debating the Roman de la Rose: A Critical Anthology* (New York: Routledge, 2007); and *Debate of the Romance of the Rose*, ed. and trans. David F. Hult (Chicago: University of Chicago Press, 2010).

[15] For the poems in this network, see Arthur Piaget, ed., 'La Belle Dame sans merci et ses imitations', *Romania*, 30 (1901), 22–48, 317–51; 31 (1902), 315–49; 33 (1904),179–208; 34 (1905), 375–428, 559–602; Alain Chartier, *Le Cycle de La Belle Dame sans Mercy*, eds David Hult and Joan E. McRae (Paris: Champion, 2003); *Alain Chartier: The Quarrel of the Belle Dame sans mercy*, ed. and trans. Joan McRae (New York and London: Routledge, 2004); Cayley, 'Collaborative Communities'.

[16] John Keats, 'La Belle Dame sans merci', in *John Keats: The Complete Poems* (London: Penguin, 2003), pp. 334–6.

[17] For a comprehensive overview of the paintings and illustrations produced in response to Keats's poem, see Grant F. Scott, 'Language Strange: A Visual History of Keats's "La Belle Dame sans Merci"', *Studies in Romanticism*, 38.4 (Winter, 1999), 503–35.

[18] Neil Gaiman, *Coraline* (Bloomsbury/Harper Collins, 2002).

Gaiman's *Coraline* is a terrifying amalgam of Middle English other wordly hag ('beldam'), and Keatsian 'faery's child' (Belle Dame).[19] On a different note, in 1996, Sting released a song entitled, 'La Belle Dame sans regrets':[20] 'harmonious resonances', indeed.

The very existence of a unitary, authoritative and 'authentic' text on which a secondary distortion is practised is destabilised – if not thoroughly undermined – by its textual and textural afterlives. We can extend Mühlethaler's notion of co-textual reading to the whole textured body of materials that proliferate from a central (rather than originary) point, looking at textual reception and traditions not in a linear or vertical, but in a horizontal way, much like the links between nodes in social network theory.[21] So authority is not achieved through 'originality' or coming before. Indeed, philologically and linguistically speaking, the notion of an '*ur*-text' is of course highly problematic when applied to medieval literature.[22] And if there is no 'original', authentic, unitary or perfected text we can value as such, how are we to speak of distortion or its adaptation as imperfection, let alone condemn or devalue variation, linguistic variety, translation and adaptation? In similar vein, the very notion of a prestige vernacular or vernaculars and the devaluing of linguistic currencies that vary from the prestige is something currently being called into question by a number of scholars, especially in the areas of medieval English and French studies.[23] Digitisation work

19 I am grateful to my incredibly sharp final-year undergraduate students at Exeter who brought this fascinating reuse of the Belle Dame motif to my attention.

20 Sting, 'La Belle Dame sans regrets', on *Mercury Falling* (Magnetic Publishing Ltd, 1996).

21 See for example Peter J. Carrington and John Scott, eds, *The SAGE Handbook of Social Network Analysis* (London: Sage, 2011). Nick Crossley, Siobhan McAndrew and Paul Widdop, eds, *Social Networks and Music Worlds* (Abingdon: Routledge, 2014); and recent work by Peter Knowles, 'A Continuum from Medieval Literary Networks to Modern Counterparts: The Attractions and Operations of Social Networks', unpub. Ph.D dissertation (University of Exeter, 2016).

22 Cerquiglini, *In Praise of the Variant*.

23 There has been considerable attention paid to this issue across a series of high-profile funded projects on multi-lingualism; for example, Jocelyn Wogan-Browne and the French(es) of England at Fordham University (https://frenchofengland.ace.fordham.edu/); Bill Burgwinkle, Jane Gilbert and Simon Gaunt's AHRC-funded Medieval Francophone cultures outside France (MFLCOF, http://www.medievalfrancophone.ac.uk/); and Simon Gaunt's more recent ERC-funded project (2015–20), with Hannah Morcos, Maria Teresa Rachetta and Simone Ventura, The Values of French Literature and Language in the European Middle Ages (TVOF, https://blogs.kcl.ac.uk/tvof/).

is going on at an unprecedented rate, opening up collections to scholars and the general public through new visualisations and platforms.[24] The demise of the physical book has been much anticipated, and its modern avatars often criticised, but it is clear that not only is the book not really threatened, but also that modern forms of the book can and will multiply and enhance reading experiences in ways that medieval authors in particular would surely have approved of, and in ways that take us closer to what a medieval reading experience might have looked like.[25] People are reading more, not less, and significantly, they are not reading alone but as part of networks or communities of readers, be that of 140-character-long tweets that can link to articles and signal richer content; posts on Facebook; or blogs, recalling Jane Taylor's 'communal phenomenon' mentioned above. The future of reading is more reading, and more diverse content, whether the platform is a physical book or a smartphone, or something else.[26] This particular reading of 'distortion' reflects the musical model of amplification, then, and is of course an overwhelmingly positive phenomenon. Increased attention by scholars to medieval materiality has drawn welcome attention back to the embodied lives and afterlives of texts in their manuscript, printed, or other manifestations.[27] In the French context, Sarah Kay has drawn attention to the manuscript as flayed skin, stripping back the layers of materiality as textile/textual covering to reveal a potentially troubling encounter between the human and the animal, and introducing the notion of an

[24] See for example Elaine Treharne's Text Technologies project based at CESTA, Stanford, and especially the collaborative MOOC, 'Digging Deeper' (https://lagunita.stanford.edu/courses/English/DiggingDeeper1/Winter2015/about).

[25] On medieval reading experiences, see for example Joyce Coleman, *Public Reading and the Reading Public in Late Medieval England and France* (Cambridge: Cambridge University Press, 1996).

[26] On the future of the book, digital literacy and the new technologies, see Geoffrey Nunberg, ed., and Umberto Eco (afterword), *The Future of the Book* (Berkeley: University of California Press, 1996); G. Kress, 'Visual and Verbal Modes of Representation in Electronically Mediated Communication: The Potentials of New Forms of Texts', in I. Snyder, ed., *Page to Screen: Taking Literacy into the Electronic Age* (London: Routledge, 1997), pp. 53–79; Gunther Kress, *Literacy in the New Media Age* (London: Routledge, 2003); Guy Merchant, 'Writing the Future in the Digital Age', *Literacy*, 41.3 (2007), 118–28.

[27] On medieval materiality in the Old English context, see Elaine Treharne's current and forthcoming work, especially *Living Through Conquest: The Politics of Early English, 1020–1220* (Oxford: Oxford University Press, 2012), and *Text Technologies: A History*, with Claude Willan (Palo Alto: Stanford University Press, 2017).

ethics of reading whereby readers become hyper-aware of the animality of the page, leading to a series of uncanny effects.[28]

Stephen Milner's recent collaborative work at the juncture of the humanities and the sciences, using a technique referred to as 'non-invasive peptide fingerprinting', has enabled us to go beyond the parchment surface to extract proteins that can reveal species, and even the locations where animals whose skins were stripped for books are likely to have lived.[29] So we can now look into the former lives of the book, as well as its afterlives. The focus here, though, is very much on textual and textural afterlives. Through an Old English and a Middle French example, we see how variance, reproduction, translation and flexibility of textual form are not always distorting, but rather have an amplifying effect, and can present a celebratory and harmonious continuation and development of textual and textile threads, even when spun in non-conventional ways.

Carpets, Screens and Parchment

If you walk along the High Street in Exeter city centre from the Sidwell Street end down towards the Guildhall, you will come across two curious man-made features: one rather more obvious, and one easy to miss.

First is the 6.5m high stainless steel Exeter Riddle Sculpture by Michael Fairfax (see Plate 1),[30] commissioned as part of a multi-million pound renovation of Exeter High Street and Princesshay in 2005. Its eight sets of mirrored panels reflect and refract modern English translations of the famous Exeter Book riddles, which were laser-cut backwards into the steel faces;[31] putative solutions are reflected in spheres at the base of

[28] See Sarah Kay, *Animal Skins and the Reading Self in Medieval Latin and French Bestiaries* (Chicago: University of Chicago Press, 2017); 'Legible Skins: Animals and the Ethics Of Medieval Reading', *Postmedieval*, 2.13 (2011), 13–32; and her earlier work on flayed skin – 'Flayed Skin as Objet A: Representation and Materiality in Guillaume de Deguileville's *Pèlerinage de vie humaine*', in E. Jane Burns, ed., *Medieval Fabrication: Dress, Textiles, Cloth Work, and Other Cultural Imaginings* (New York: Palgrave Macmillan, 2004), pp. 193–205 and 249–51; and 'Original Skin: Flaying, Reading and Thinking in the Legend of Saint Bartholomew and Other Works', *Journal of Medieval and Early Modern Studies*, 36.1 (2006), 35–74.

[29] See https://manutiusinmanchester.wordpress.com/ for details, and Milner's co-authored article: Sarah Fiddyment et al., 'Animal Origin of 13th-Century Uterine Vellum Revealed Using Noninvasive Peptide Fingerprinting', *Proceedings of the National Academy of Sciences*, 112.49 (2015), 15066–71.

[30] See http://www.michaelfairfax.co.uk/exeterriddle.html.

[31] The English translations are by Kevin Crossley-Holland, *The Exeter Book Riddles* (London: Enitharmon Press [2008], 2010). The Exeter Book in Exeter

Plate 1: The Exeter Riddle Sculpture, Michael Fairfax, 2005.
Exeter High Street.

the sculpture. Further on, modestly inset in the pavement is a so-called 'new' Exeter Book riddle by Richard Skinner.[32] However, Exeter residents remain, by and large, unaware of the priceless manuscript that inspired these two features. In addition to these two public artworks, the Exeter Book enjoys a more unusual afterlife in the Mercure Exeter Southgate Hotel in Southernhay, in the centre of Exeter. In 2014, the hotel underwent a £2 million refurbishment, which included the installation of a specially commissioned carpet, themed around the Exeter Book.[33] A recurring motif in the carpet is an extract from the opening of the Exeter Book's famous elegiac poem, *The Wanderer* (see Plate 2).

Ironically, this is a most appropriate choice for a hotel floor that travellers are perennially passing over. Not all parts of the carpet feature the Exeter Book: some squares are woven with passages of Latin and modern French. It is a carpet, therefore, that speaks in tongues, and of distant shores. More intriguing perhaps than even the Exeter Book light feature in the lobby are the shower panels, installed in approximately half of the hotel's bathrooms, which display Exeter Book Riddle 26 (the Book Riddle) on an 'antiqued' image of a battered scroll in a blackletter or Gothic font, sliced vertically in half so as to obscure the sense of the riddle yet further. Indeed, anyone who was able to decipher the Old English would still need some advanced code-breaking skills to piece the riddle back together from the available text on the wall (or a neighbour with the other half in her/his bathroom) (see Plate 3).[34]

The hotel explained that the panels had been too large to install two halves in each bathroom, and so they are split into left and right halves

Cathedral Library, MS 3501, dated to c.960, and localised to the south-west of England. On the Exeter Book, its background and its significance, see the classic study by Patrick Conner, *Anglo-Saxon Exeter: A Tenth-Century Cultural History* (Woodbridge: Boydell, 1993).

[32] 'Conjure with me three letters of the alphabet, or two and one, or one,/ Run me backwards and I would seem to be unchanged,/ But that would be an uphill task of course,/ My name speaks of former times, / While I am still current,/ Though what current can be still', Kevin Crossley-Holland and Lawrence Sail, eds, *The New Exeter Book of Riddles* (London: Enitharmon Press, 1999).

[33] For a series of images of the inside of the hotel, see http://www.devonlive.com/pictures/Gallery-look-inside-refurb-d-Mercure-Southgate/pictures-26487839-detail/pictures.html#1.

[34] I was called in by the hotel as a consultant in January 2015 after the refurbishment was done, and was able to connect the hotel with Exeter Cathedral Library, inform their staff about the narrative behind the new furnishings, and to provide a leaflet of information about the Exeter Book to use in the bedroom folders and enable guests to interpret their material surroundings.

Plate 2: A section from the opening of *The Wanderer* in The Exeter Book Carpet at the Mercure Exeter Southgate Hotel.

of the riddle: left halves in some bathrooms, right halves in others. So far, so surreal, but can these extreme instances of textual deviation or appropriation be seen in a positive light? My suggestion would be that we can read these instances of textile and sculptural reinterpretation as part of the rich textured body of materials that proliferate from the distortion or adaptation of an 'original': as a series of more or less 'harmonious resonances'. In how many hotels in the world can you step on a material rendering of a thousand-year-old book, or take a shower with half a riddle? In terms of functionality, certainly, a carpet is doubtless a more useful material underfoot than a manuscript, and more absorbent. For any of the approximately four hundred guests who stay at the hotel every week, in the 156 rooms that have been refurbished with the theme, the Exeter Book becomes, quite literally, part of the fabric of their visit.

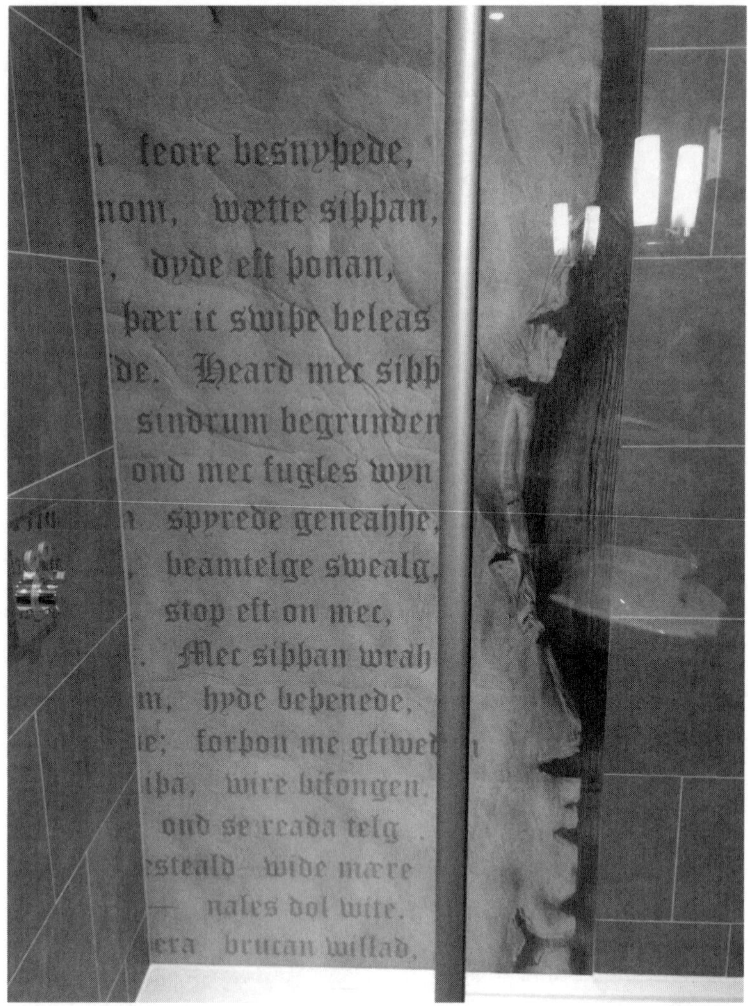

Plate 3: Right Half of Exeter Book Riddle 26, a bathroom, Mercure Exeter Southgate Hotel

Riddle 26 is, of course, an intriguing choice for the shower panel, since the supposed answer to the riddle is a manuscript, and specifically perhaps a copy of the Gospels.[35] The riddle describes the process of making a

[35] Muir, *Exeter Anthology*; Crossley-Holland, *The Exeter Book Riddles*, pp. 29, 93–4.

medieval manuscript by scraping and drying animal skin, cutting and folding it, then writing on it with ink and a quill pen, made from a slain bird, decorating and binding it in a cover. In terms of distortion that is pretty much as good as it gets: the repurposing of animal into paper and pen.[36] That a hotel guest stepping into their bathtub might become aware of all this through the information in their room seems a quite wonderful example of how distortion and reception or adaptation can have positive effects, while the form of the distortion of the 'original' textual object itself may not be to all tastes.

The Exeter Book App or Visualising the Manuscript in Digital Space

From 2012–15, I received funding through the Arts and Humanities Research Council (AHRC)'s Research and Enterprise in Arts and Creative Technology (REACT) hub,[37] as well as the Higher Education Funding Council of England (HEFCE) Higher Education Innovation Funding (HEIF) to work with creative industry partner Antenna International.[38] I led a team across the University of Exeter, Exeter Cathedral Library and Antenna International to develop a prototype iPad app based around the Exeter Book. Currently, the Exeter Book – though of global cultural significance, and inscribed on the UNESCO UK Memory of the World Register in 2016[39] – is available to consult only in Exeter Cathedral Library and Archives, or virtually via the two-volume critical edition and DVD/CD-ROM created in 2006 by Bernard Muir; this is now very difficult to use due to its outdated software.[40] Our app aimed to explore the materiality of the manuscript in digital space and, crucially, to enable

36 I am grateful to Andrew Prescott whose comments about the afterlives of the Lewis chessmen at the Medieval Materialities conference at St Andrew's, 19–20 January 2017, proved most helpful in my thinking about the afterlives of objects as well as texts.

37 See details of the REACT hubs at http://www.react-hub.org.uk/, and my project at http://humanities.exeter.ac.uk/research/react/projects/exetermanuscripts/.

38 See http://antennalab.org/about-us/. I was awarded a collaborative doctoral studentship (2012–16), to supervise a student at the University of Exeter, in partnership with Antenna International where he undertook three work placements during the course of his studies. Peter Knowles, who worked with us on the prototype, successfully defended his Ph.D at Exeter in 2016, and now works as a content designer at Antenna.

39 See https://www.theguardian.com/books/2016/jun/22/unesco-lists-exeter-book-among-worlds-principal-cultural-artefacts.

40 Muir, *Exeter Anthology* (revd. edn with DVD-ROM, 2006).

public access to what had previously been inaccessible to all but scholars. In addition, the funding enabled us to undertake a range of public engagement initiatives, including an exhibition at Exeter Cathedral,[41] and schools' workshops in collaboration with artists, content designers and storytellers. The main features of the prototype are accessed via a screen, which displays Riddle 47, known as the 'Bookmoth Riddle', as it appears in the Exeter Book.[42] The prototype build took place in just one day, using a rapid prototyping model (see Plate 4).[43]

My conception of the app has developed since the prototype build, thanks to a series of fascinating research conversations with Elaine Treharne and Benjamin Albritton at Stanford, and Johanna Green at Glasgow,[44] as well as other individuals whose feedback on the prototype has been invaluable over a period of years. The University of Exeter launched its new £1.2 million Digital Humanities facility in 2017. As its flagship project, the University and Exeter Cathedral Library have an agreement to undertake a new digitisation of the Exeter Book, returning copyright of the images to the Cathedral Library, and to produce an aca-

41 Our exhibition, 'From Medieval Manuscripts to "Calligraffiti": Discovering Exeter's Written Heritage', took place at the Chapel of St James and St Thomas in Exeter Cathedral from 23 October to 4 November 2012. This exhibition explored Devon's written heritage from the earliest medieval manuscripts kept in the Cathedral Library and Special Collections at the University of Exeter, through the dawn of printing and early printed books, to modern calligraphy in the shape of Gospels handwritten and painted in the 1950s, and the arrival of the e-book and kindle. Our tagline was 'From Codex to Kindle in twenty centuries'. In addition, the exhibition featured artwork created by local Devon schoolchildren (from ISCA College and St Sidwell's CE Primary School), inspired by manuscript calligraphy and by the art of 'calligraffiti'.

42 Muir, *Exeter Anthology*; Crossley-Holland, *The Exeter Book Riddles*, pp. 50, 100–1.

43 See the Antenna blog at http://antennalab.org/exeterbookrapidprototyping/.

44 I am grateful to Elaine Treharne, Benjamin Albritton and Johanna Green for their enthusiasm and the intellectual generosity with which they have shared ideas, and pointed me in the right direction. Their work has been hugely influential for me. See, for example, Elaine Treharne and Orietta Da Rold, eds, *Textual Cultures: Cultural Texts* (Cambridge: D. S. Brewer, 2010); Johanna M. E. Green, 'Textuality in Transition: Digital Manuscripts as Cultural Artefacts', in G. Hulsman and C. Whelan, eds, *Occupying Space in Medieval and Early Modern Britain and Ireland* (Oxford: Peter Lang, 2016), part II. Dr Green is also preparing an edited book of essays on the Exeter Book with F. McCormack, eds, *The Texts and Contexts of Exeter Cathedral Library MS 3501: The Exeter Book* (Leiden: Brill, forthcoming). I was Text-Technologies Fellow at Stanford in May 2016, and worked on the development of the Exeter Book app with Stanford Text Technologies and the Center for Spatial and Textual Analysis.

demic public interface based on an existing open source framework with modifications released back to the developers and wider community. Our team plans to use this new digitisation as the basis for an Exeter Book WebApp, developing techniques and content from the app prototype for use in a different platform. This platform will enable the use of embedded audio, video and 3D models. The Exeter Book app aims to incorporate a variety of manuscript views, visualising the manuscript as a 3D object that occupies physical space, rather than a series of flat-screen images.[45] This app aims to go beyond mere replication of analogue layout (often criticised in digital editing projects),[46] to reimagine digital interaction with manuscripts through the use of existing and emerging technologies. The model could be made available for any Special Collections department, and the tools could be adapted for use by other researchers and editors beyond the scope of the current project. While this app forms one of the outcomes of collaborative research into materiality of the codex, and is designed to reach a scholarly audience, a second research-led public-facing educational app, this time designed to be used from an iOS or android tablet platform, is also in development. In this second version, which incorporates a range of manuscripts including but not restricted to the Exeter Book, younger users would be able to engage fully with a range of game functionalities within the app environment, enabling them to discover manuscripts and medieval narrative through play (avatars, levels

[45] On the potential of the digital to enhance manuscript studies, see the work of Bill Endres (University of Kentucky) and his multi-spectral visualisations of the St Chad Gospels using reflectance transformation imaging. The Augmented Palimpsest project run by Tamara O'Callaghan (Northern Kentucky) and Andrea Harbin (State University of NY, Cortland) is another novel augmented reality (AR) experiment, based on a digital version of Chaucer's *General Prologue* with a mocked-up manuscript frame from which QR codes enable the reader to launch images, information and video clips. See Bill Endres, 'The St Chad Gospels: Ligatures and the Division of Hands', *Manuscripta: A Journal for Manuscript Research*, 59.2 (2015), 159–86; Bill Endres, 'Imaging Sacred Artifacts: Ethics and the Digitizing of Lichfield Cathedral's St Chad Gospels', *Journal of Religion, Media and Digital Culture*, 3.3 (2014), 39–73; and https://lichfield.ou.edu/; https://augmentedpalimpsest.wordpress.com/.

[46] See Emma Cayley, 'Response on Modern Languages and Digital Archives', in C. Taylor and N. Thornton, eds, 'Modern Languages and the Digital: The Shape of the Discipline', *Modern Languages Open* (2017). DOI: http://doi.org/10.3828/mlo.v0i0.156. See also Elaine Treharne, 'Fleshing out the TEXT: The Transcendent Manuscript in the Digital Age', in Holly Crocker and Kathryn Schwarz, eds, *Flesh*, special issue of *PostMedieval: A Journal of Medieval Cultural Studies* (2013), 1–14.

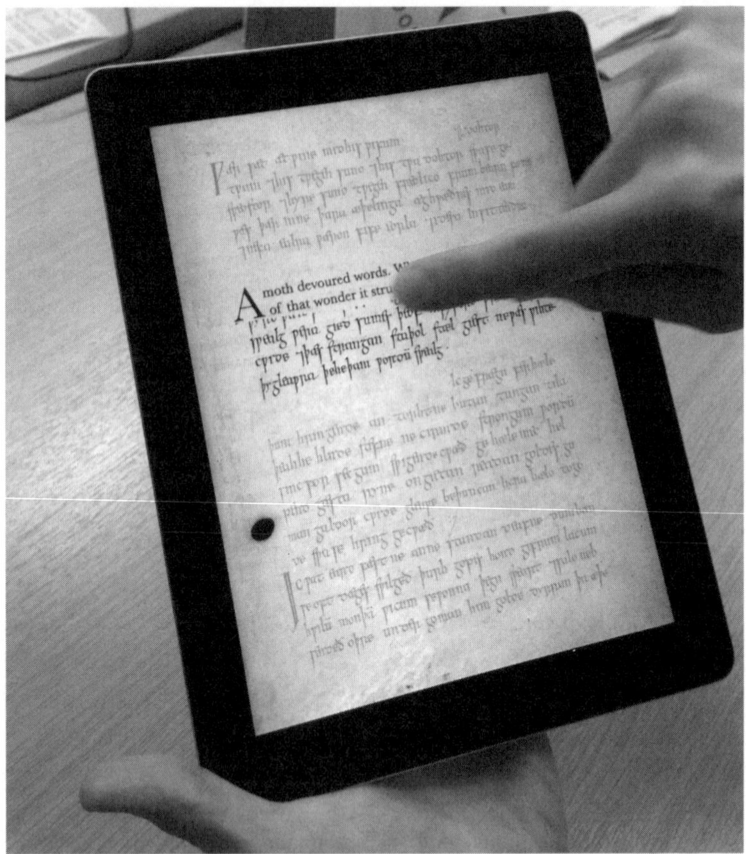

Plate 4: The 'Bookmoth' Riddle 47 on the Exeter Book app prototype, November 2013, Antenna International Offices, London.

and decision making). Among other functionalities, the app will develop the innovative finger-swipe translation functionality available in our prototype (see Plate 4).

It will provide a mapping functionality, and possible geo-location tool to track the journeys of some manuscripts; enable users to share illuminations they have created or quizzes they have completed within the app to social media; and introduce users to the sounds of the original texts through audio and video clips, which can be launched from hotspots on the screen. A pinch and zoom functionality will enable users both to examine and luxuriate in the manuscripts.

Parchment and Print: 'Harmonious resonances' in the Tradition of the *Songe de la Pucelle* (Dream of the Virgin)

From this discussion of the manuscript as mediated by the digital, and the medieval text in its modern material contexts, we move to a final case study, which examines a little-known French medieval debate poem of the mid to late fifteenth century, the *Songe de la Pucelle* (Dream of the Virgin), which has a fascinating narrative of distortion via manuscript and early printed copies, both French and English, and via a fifteenth-century English translation.[47] The *Songe* was a popular fifteenth-century poem, and enjoyed a wide contemporary circulation as well as a series of visual and textual reinterpretations. I have identified a total of ten manuscripts that contain or contained the *Songe*: seven fifteenth-century manuscripts; two later copies; and one fifteenth-century manuscript that contained the *Songe* but is now lost.[48] This popularity continued well beyond the fifteenth century, with the poem recorded as appearing in seven separate French early printed editions and a number of later collected editions.[49] Julia Boffey notes that the *Songe* was also translated into English by Christopher Goodwyn in 1513, as *The Maiden's Dream*, and possibly printed in an early edition by Wynkyn de Worde, as well as the edition that survives from 1542 by Robert Wyer.[50] Crucially, Boffey notes that Goodwyn has added a prologue to his version of the debate and an envoy in which he makes clear the audience at which the debate, and the edition,

[47] I am grateful for permission to draw on material from published work on the *Songe de la Pucelle*. For a full account of this poem and context, see my article, 'Between Manuscript and Print: Literary Reception in Late Medieval France: The Case of the Dream of the Virgin', *Fudan Journal of the Humanities and Social Sciences* (FJHSS), 8.2 (March 2015), 137–65, and chapter 'Entre deux sommes: Imag[in]ing desire in the *Songe de la Pucelle*', in Rosalind Brown-Grant and Rebecca Dixon, eds, *Text-Image Relations in Late Medieval France* (Turnhout: Brepols, 2015), pp. 47–64. See my forthcoming edition of the *Songe de la Pucelle, Sleepless Knights and Wanton Women*, 1: The Debate Poems (Arizona: MRTS).

[48] For all details of manuscripts and printed copies, see Cayley, 'Between Manuscript and Print'.

[49] See 'Le Songe doré de la Pucelle', in Anatole de Montaiglon, ed., *Recueil de poésies françoises des XVe et XVIe siècles*, III (Paris: P. Jannet, 1856), pp. 204–31; 'Le Songe de la Pucelle: poème moral du XVe siècle d'après le texte du manuscrit Supersaxo 97bis', in P. Aebischer ed., *Vallesia* 16 (1961), pp. 225–41; and my forthcoming edition of the *Songe de la Pucelle, Sleepless Knights and Wanton Women.*

[50] Julia Boffey, 'Banking on Translation: English Printers and Continental Texts', in Alessandra Petrina, ed., *The Medieval Translator: Traduire au Moyen Age* 15, *In principio fuit interpres* (Turnhout: Brepols, 2013), pp. 317-29, esp. pp. 323–4.

is targeted: 'yonge ladyes and maydens of eche astate'.[51] The manuscript tradition invariably collects the poem with other fifteenth-century debates and moral texts while the early printed copies tend to be monotextual, and enjoy a separate circulation as individual pamphlets (although these may have been later collected into *Sammelbände* at some point).[52]

The *Songe de la Pucelle* unfolds as the Pucelle, the first-person narrator of the debate, falls asleep at dawn only to be approached in a dream by two apparitions, whom the Pucelle discovers to be Love and Shame – discovered from looking at their clothing and from piecing together the visual clues from their mottos. There is an emphasis here, as in many debate poems of the period between debating women, on appearance and the visual, in direct conflict with the written or textual.[53] The scene is familiar: it is the first of May, the Pucelle is ripe and ready for love, and requires guidance. Love and Shame present themselves as willing moral guides through the fraught negotiations of love service and reputation that the Pucelle must embark upon. As the debate develops, Love predictably encourages the Pucelle to take a lover and enter into the courtly sphere, whereas Shame cautions chastity and silence. The poetic exchange totals sixty-eight octosyllabic *septains* (476 lines), and the debate is framed by the Pucelle, who upon waking, goes to find a male scribe to copy out the debate for her (lines 456–62). The Pucelle is thus substituted or usurped in her authorial/narratorial role by an anonymous male *clerc* in the narrative frame of the debate, and she is effectively recast as impotent participant in her own narrative. Similarly, in the paratext of one of the nine extant manuscripts of the *Songe*, Paris, BnF, MS fr. 25553, a further gender substitution or disruption is observed.[54] This is the only miniature that survives for the *Songe* in the manuscript tradition. We observe the Pucelle foregrounded in the centre of the image with her hand on her cheek and eyes closed, framed by the two figures of Love and Shame.

The figure of Love, though often male in medieval literature, is decidedly female in the written versions of the *Songe*, as we discover early on (lines

51 Boffey, 'Banking on Translation'.

52 Alexandra Gillespie, *Print Culture and the Medieval Author: Chaucer, Lydgate, and Their Books, 1473–1557* (Oxford: Oxford University Press, 2006); and Olivia Robinson, 'Alain Chartier: The Manuscript and Print Tradition', in Daisy Delogu, Joan E. McRae and Emma Cayley, eds, *A Companion to Alain Chartier* (Leiden: Brill, 2015), pp. 223–52.

53 See Cayley, 'Polyphonie et dialogisme'.

54 See Figure 1 in Emma Cayley, 'Entre deux sommes: Imag[in]ing Desire in the Songe de la Pucelle', p. 52. Love and Shame appear to the Pucelle in her sleep. *Songe de la Pucelle*, Paris, BnF, MS fr. 25553, fol. 50r.

64–7). Here, however, the illustrator has chosen (or been instructed) to depict Love as resolutely male, dominating the scene with his sparrowhawk, the tool of his trade and symbol of the courtly hunt, wherein women are the prey and not the hunters. This depiction of the female Love in men's clothing, masquerading as a man, might be read as a simple error on the part of the illustrator, but it provides us with an example of what Judith Butler might term 'gender trouble', and what we might read as a distortion or amplification effect.[55] The choice made by the illustrator of the *Songe* in Paris, BnF, MS fr. 25553, to foreground the debate framework by depicting the narrator physically within the dream sequence landscape, flanked by the two interlocutors of the debate, seems a deliberately distorting one. The choice of Love as a male rather than female figure serves (whether intentionally or otherwise) to emphasise the conflictual nature of the debate.

In the early printed editions of the *Songe*, we find a series of intriguing woodcuts, including a woodcut that introduces the English translation of the poem by Christopher Goodwyn. From the larger stage of the manuscript, and the multiple – often anonymous – texts and voices that crowd its folios, the focus here is on a single text, often printed in a small book (the Chantilly, Seville and Aix editions are small octavos), with fewer leaves, and a more limited number of interlocutors. One booklet printed in Lyon between 1488 and 1492 by the printer known as the Imprimeur du *Champion des dames* (ICD),[56] uses a woodcut that depicts the two figures of Shame and the Pucelle. Both are named in the margins, as with the manuscript image.[57] Olivia Robinson has shown how the ICD 'borrows' the woodcut used for the *Songe* from Jean du Pré's *Pierre et la belle Maguélonne* (1489). The ICD reuses Jean du Pré's *Pierre et la belle Maguélonne* woodcuts in a series of three texts (*Songe*; *La Belle Dame sans mercy*; *La Belle Dame qui eut mercy*), which form part of a wider programme of vernacular debates that this printer issued between 1489 and 1492 in Lyon.[58]

In the Lyon *imprimé*, the visual focus is solely on the two figures of Shame and the Pucelle, as Love is deliberately excluded. This choice of

[55] See Judith Butler, *Gender Trouble: Feminism and the Subversion of Identity* (New York and London: Routledge, 1990), *inter alia*.

[56] Robinson, 'Alain Chartier', cites Denise Hillard, 'Histoires d'L.', *Revue française d'histoire du livre*, 118.21 (2003), 79–104 (p. 89), on the identity of the Lyon printer referred to as ICD. According to Hillard, Jean du Pré and the ICD are not the same printer, though they are often confused.

[57] See Figure 3 in Cayley, 'Entre deux sommes', p. 55. Shame appears to the Pucelle in her sleep. *Songe [doré] de la Pucelle*, Paris, BnF, Rés., Ye 837, fol. 1r.

[58] Robinson, 'Alain Chartier'.

Shame as the solitary figure accompanying the Pucelle in these liminal images tends to point us towards a more moral interpretation and framework being imposed on the readership of the printed editions. Although the Pucelle never makes a final choice between her two advisers in the poem, she promises that she will 'be careful not to misbehave' (v. 445). It seems that the audience of these early printed editions is being given more of a framework with which to interpret the debate than that of the manuscript copies. They are subconsciously driven by this framework towards the silent election of Shame as the victor of the debate, and therefore to chastity as the route that the Pucelle should take.

A third French woodcut fronts a later edition of the *Songe* now kept in Chantilly, Bibliothèque du château.[59] This title-page woodcut depicts a wholly different scene from the more typical *Songe* woodcuts.[60] Here a standing figure we assume to be the Pucelle is framed in the upper part of the image with two kneeling men. She extends her left hand gingerly to one of the two bareheaded men whose lances are raised in a clearly phallic gesture.[61] The design may be intended as an interpretation of the Pucelle's naïve reception of courtship. A frieze of heads runs along the bottom part of the image; all are turned to watch the scene above. Like the manuscript miniature, here the scene is bucolic: a clump of grass is printed in the foreground. It is to be noted that this printed edition contains neither of the two 'moralising' ballades often found with the *Songe*. One might assume then that here, unlike the Lyon *imprimé*, the Pucelle has chosen Love over Shame, and is being courted by not one but two lovers. However, the remarkable frieze of onlooking male and female heads tends to suggest that the moral framework of the other editions is not far away here either.[62] If you take a lover, or indeed several, the woodcut seems to suggest, you must be careful of the gossips and *mesdisants* who will spread rumours abroad of your affairs.

A woodcut taken from the English tradition of the *Songe* presents a particularly intriguing trio of figures and through them a narrative of

[59] See Figure 5 in Cayley, 'Entre deux sommes', p. 57. The Pucelle is courted while onlookers observe. *Songe de la Pucelle*, Chantilly, Bibliothèque du château, XI. D. 54, fol. 3r.

[60] I have not been able to establish a direct borrowing here, though the image looks like a generic courtly scene, and is probably reused.

[61] Additionally, the two hanging ties of the lady's belt present a visual echo of the lances and may gesture to a future deflowering.

[62] It is difficult to make out the expressions on the faces depicted in the frieze, but they appear older than those of the characters they observe above, which may suggest a reflection on the folly of youth.

reuse and distortion.[63] The poet, an authoritative older man carrying a scroll, which we assume to be his poem, is flanked by two figures. These are either Love and Shame, or perhaps rather Love and the Pucelle. The identities of the figures remain ambiguous; *banderoles* flutter emptily above each. The central author-figure points towards the male figure to his right (our left), as if suggesting that the Pucelle should pay heed to his words. This woodcut uses a technique employed by Antoine Vérard in his *Therence en francoys* (1500–03) and *Jardin de plaisance* (1501).[64] Vérard, in common with fellow-printers Pierre Le Rouge and Michel Le Noir, was at this time using interchangeable printing blocks, which offered the printer a wide variety of permutations based on a series of assorted characters, architectural scenes and greenery. Therefore these figures are almost certainly reused from the *Therence* tradition.[65] The print of the far-left figure is noticeably less clear-cut than the other two, lending weight to the theory of reuse. The English woodcut, therefore, would represent the most complex of the framing narratives we have seen across the *Songe* tradition. *The Maiden's Dream* in its English translation would then foreground more evidently the creative process, rather than the dream landscape – whether it is bucolic or domestic – which is the focus of the manuscript miniature as well as the woodcuts from the French tradition. The reader is in no doubt from the 'Prohemye of the Authour' (Author's Prologue), which begins under the liminal image,

[63] See Figure 6 in Cayley, 'Entre deux sommes', p. 58. The poet is flanked by two figures. 'The maydens dreme compyled and made by Chrystofer Goodwyn, in the yere of our Lorde. M.CCCCC.xlij', San Marino, CA, Henry E. Huntington Library, Rare Books 81679, fol. 1r. I am grateful to Julia Boffey who generously shared her work on the English version of the *Songe* with me prior to its publication (see Boffey 'Banking on Translation'). She also kindly directed me to this woodcut she had located.

[64] A technique invented by Jean Gruninger of Strasbourg for his *Terence* in 1496, and used by Vérard for *Therence* and the *Jardin de plaisance*. See Martha Driver, *The Image in Print: Book Illustration in Late Medieval England and its Sources* (London: The British Library, 2004); Adrian Armstrong, 'Love on the Page: Materiality and Literariness in Jean Bouchet's *Amoureux transi* and its Avatars', in Adrian Armstrong and Malcolm Quainton, eds, *Book and Text in France, 1400–1600: Poetry on the Page* (Aldershot: Ashgate, 2007), pp. 95–115, esp. pp. 98–101; and Taylor, *The Making of Poetry*, pp. 239–40.

[65] Of course, Robert Wyer may be reprinting an earlier Wynkyn de Worde edition (see earlier, and Boffey, 'Banking on Translation'). Many English printers bought or rented continental woodcuts: see Valerie Hotchkiss and Fred C. Robinson, *English in Print from Caxton to Shakespeare to Milton* (Champaign: University of Illinois Press, 2008).

that this version of the *Songe* is designed as a moral framework or mirror to guide young women:

Beholde you yonge ladyes of hyghe parentage
And you yonge virgyns, of eche degre
Here is a pamphlet, even mete for your age
Where as in a myrrour, you maye lerne and se
How vycious love, you shulde eschewe and fle
Havynge alway shamfastnes, in your maydenly face
Then can you never mysse, of vertue and grace.[66]

So in this case study we have seen how the separate circulation of the *Songe* in its French and English early printed editions would seem to target a different audience from the manuscript copies. Distortion in the transmission of this text may then be read in the marked shift of reception between manuscript and print, orientating the text towards a different audience. Distortion in this case creates what we might term an amplification effect, ensuring the continued popularity of the *Songe* in a different medium and for new readers. The framing – visual, verbal and conceptual – of this surprisingly complex text in its various material contexts of reception foregrounds the creative process. While the poetic 'I' continues to protest the authenticity of her or his tale, the ways in which it is distorted or mediated in material context expose the complex artifice at its creative centre. This is an artifice echoed in the reuse of woodcuts in the printed copies of the *Songe*, just as it can be observed in the richly textured afterlives of the Exeter Book. As I suggested in my initial comments, distortion operates as an amplification or augmentation of the original via its multiple new contexts, textures and surfaces. Indeed, the very notion of an original on which a distortion can be practised is thoroughly undermined. It is, after all, only in the traces and echoes of a prior presence, essentially in distortion itself, that we can begin to locate any sense of an 'authentic' or original.

Across the reused blocks, as across the soon to be well-trodden hotel carpet, and through the darkened glass of our imperfect human understanding, then, echoes of other material contexts and other textures and texts surface to disturb, distort and yet simultaneously enrich the narrative. The variants, the continuations, material traces and adaptations, and the digital transformations, carpets and facsimiles are where the presence of the 'original' can be experienced, and not in the past. Memory and reception can be more powerful and more democratic than liveness.

66 Transcribed from California, Huntington Library, Rare Books 81679.

Distortion, Ideology, Time: Proletarian Aesthetics in the Work of Lionel Britton

AARON KELLY

Lionel Britton (1887–1971) was the son of Richard Britton, an eventually bankrupted and not fully qualified solicitor who died of tuberculosis in 1894 when Britton was seven, and Ira Britton, who supplemented the family income as a boarding-house keeper and briefly remarried. Despite the professional promise that might have bestowed a safely bourgeois existence from his father's side, Lionel Britton largely grew up with his maternal grandparents in Redditch and left home for Birmingham, where he lived on a loaf of bread for a week before heading to London. His family did not have the means to pay for his interest in learning and education – he attended a national school – and Britton was an errand boy for a greengrocer's and then a bookshop. He was imprisoned for over a year as a conscientious objector during the First World War and gained employment working for the Incorporated Society of British Advertisers in the 1920s. He unsuccessfully applied for Soviet citizenship in the late 1910s but is also notable for the fact that, unlike some leading intellectual figures in Britain during the 1920s and 1930s, he recognised that the Soviet Union was a dictatorship and not a worker's paradise.

His relatively brief but brilliant literary flourishing at the end of the 1920s and early 1930s resulted in a novel – *Hunger and Love* (1931) – and the plays *Brain: A Play of the Whole Earth* (1930), *Spacetime Inn* (1932) and *Animal Ideas: A Dramatic Symphony of the Human in the Universe* (1935).[1] *Hunger and Love* was a *Bildungsroman* of a kind, but supplants the normative alignment of individual becoming and socialisation with a shift towards a collective, communal temporality at odds with bourgeois modernity. *Spacetime Inn* and *Brain* might be deemed science-fiction plays, though such a designation does not do justice to how each again disorders time and history. The former is set in the eponymous hostelry where two working-class Cockneys, Bill and Jim, win the sweepstake

[1] Lionel Britton, *Brain: A Play of the Whole Earth* (London: G. P. Putnam, 1930); *Hunger and Love* (London: G. P. Putnam, 1931); *Spacetime Inn* (London: G. P Putnam, 1932); *Animal Ideas: A Dramatic Symphony of the Human in the Universe* (London: G. P. Putnam, 1935).

and traverse the dimensions of spacetime to join the company of fellow guests such as Shakespeare, George Bernard Shaw, Dr Johnson, Karl Marx, Napoleon, Queen Victoria, The Queen of Sheba and Eve. In the latter, the titular brain resides in the Sahara Desert and its supercomputer-type consciousness opens up phases of possible, conditional and future worlds, all of which harbour utopian and dystopian renderings of the logic of the present. *Animal Ideas* was begun before the other plays but published last in Britton's oeuvre. It emerged at the time he visited the Soviet Union in the mid-1930s, and its collision of cosmic longing for human potential with dystopian censure of state repression and power signals Britton's antipathy to the Soviet dictatorship and to the capitalism of his own society. Britton's publisher, Putnam, could barely bring themselves to promote his last work and, despite the fact that he had been a founder of Left Theatre and a teacher at Unity Theatre in London, Britton always struggled to find sustained backing for his work and ideas.

In their own way, Britton's works were a distortion, a twisting apart that flouted the common association of distortion with misrepresentation. For the orthodox Left in the 1920s and 1930s, especially the intellectual proponents of Soviet and socialist realism, misrepresentation was the skewed sway of bourgeois ideology and its thwarting of literature's capacity for truth-giving and objective representations of an alienated world. Literature's relation to history, as the objective gauge of our predicament, was crucial to such truth. Although, for example, Georg Lukács's reflections on the period acknowledged the 'qualitative, variable, flowing nature of time', he also despised modernism as pathological 'interiority', as a decadent bourgeois turn to a compensatory and false subjectivism that not only failed to resist the reified mechanisation of the world but also furthered our alienation from history and objectivity.[2] Britton's work departs markedly from the Lukács model of history and class consciousness as the means by which to redress the 'distorted' realm of reification, whereby self-alienated existence is reintegrated into meaning through 'the plane of historical reality and concrete praxis'.[3] Britton had other planes in mind. His main touchstone in his composite, self-educated worldview – he was a bookseller's errand boy who found time to read books he was only

[2] Georg Lukács, *History and Class Consciousness: Studies in Marxist Dialectics* [1968], trans. Rodney Livingstone (London: Merlin P, 1971), p. 90; Georg Lukács, 'The Ideology of Modernism', in *The Meaning of Contemporary Realism* [1957], trans. John and Necke Mander (London: Merlin Press, 1963), pp. 17–46.

[3] Lukács, *History and Class Consciousness*, pp. 93, 127.

destined to distribute for sale – during his writing was J. W. Dunne's *An Experiment with Time* (1927). Dunne was himself an idiosyncratic figure. An Anglo-Irish aeronautical engineer who pioneered the development of British military aircraft, Dunne also proposed a serial model of time in which we are travelling across moments between past, present and future. Aligning debates emerging from his scientific background, concerning quantum mechanics and the theory of general relativity with his faith in precognition and the capacity of dreams to predict and revise time, Dunne's version of temporality argued for the importance of the subjectivity of the observer in spacetime. Ultimately, for Dunne, beyond our individual consciousness there is a higher level outwith the quotidian and our physical selves in which we are all encompassed by 'human immortality' in communion with a greater duration of time that is eternity.[4] Future events may be experienced in serial and different ways by consciousness. Dunne's model is not quite that of Henri Bergson's concept of duration, long considered a key influence of the subjective rendering of temporality in opposition to clock time in modernism.[5] Instead it registers a relativity of time that proposes cosmic or eternal layers of a higher consciousness beyond the quotidian and linear.

In terms of literary influence, Dunne's work is often taken more seriously when deemed to influence the 'time plays' of J. B. Priestley, which split time and show what might have happened alongside what did.[6] Dunne, however, was satirised by H. G. Wells, an old friend of sorts, for taking too seriously Wells's fictional work such as *The Time Machine* (1895), particularly in Wells's *The Shape of Things to Come* (1933) and its Dunne-inspired character Dr Philip Raven, who declares that he has been reading a 'dream book' between sleeping and waking, which restores lost gaps in the past and envisages future worlds.[7] Another somewhat satirical take on Dunne is offered by Jorge Luis Borges, who nonetheless finds Dunne's effort to unfold an infinite number of temporalities to be 'less

[4] T. W. Dunne, *An Experiment with Time* [1927] (Charlottesville, VA: Hampton Roads Publishing, 2001), p. xiii.

[5] For a perceptive account of Bergson and time in modernism, see Randall Stevenson, *Modernist Fiction* (London: Routledge, 1997). For Bergson on duration, see *Time and Free Will: An Essay on the Immediate Data of Consciousness* [1889], trans. F. L. Pogson (New York: Dover Publications, 2001).

[6] For Priestley's own take on these issues, see his *Man and Time* (New York: W. H. Allen, 1964).

[7] H. G. Wells, *The Shape of Things to Come: The Ultimate Revolution* [1933] (London: Penguin Classics, 1993), p. 16.

convincing and more ingenious'.[8] In other words, if the Dunne model is not taken as science or gospel, it is better understood as enabling in a creative sense as a template by which we might reconfigure our present. Although mocking Dunne's style, which seeks to affirm the rectitude of his concept of serial time with a combination of diaristic accounts of premonitory dreams and mathematical diagrams, Borges commends the imagination of his work and the astral communion for which it yearns:

> Theologians define eternity as the lucid and simultaneous possession of all instants of time, and declare it a divine attribute. Dunne, surprisingly, presumes that eternity already belongs to us, as corroborated by the dreams we have each night. In them, according to him, the immediate past and the immediate future intermingle. Awake, we pass through [each …] successive time at a uniform speed; in dreams we may span a vast zone. To dream is to orchestrate the objects we viewed while awake and to weave from them a story, or a series of stories. We see the image of a sphinx and the image of a drugstore, and then we invent a drugstore that turns into a sphinx. We put the mouth of a face that looked at us the night before last on the man we shall meet tomorrow […] Dunne assures us that in death we shall finally learn how to handle eternity. We shall recover all the moments of our lives and combine them as we please. God and our friends and Shakespeare will collaborate with us […] So splendid a thesis, makes any fallacy committed by the author insignificant.[9]

In terms of Britton's work, given that he engineers a stage in which two 'proles' encounter Shakespeare in *Spacetime Inn*, it is evident that he took from Dunne a handbook by which to distort orthodox versions of history both in terms of their prior inequalities and their promise of future reconciliation. If, in Lukács, history is on our side and will repair the inequities of the past in stadial progress through which class consciousness transforms the world, Britton had already rejected that promise of the linear development of inevitable redress (most closely associated in the time in which he wrote with the Soviet state), and sought alternative methods through which to recast the flow of time and the promise of culture that we are all equal and free. It is clear in *Spacetime Inn* that history in its present version does not facilitate or presage such a dispensation, and that

[8] Jorge Luis Borges, 'Time and J. W. Dunne' [1940], in *The Total Library: Non-Fiction 1922–1986*, ed. Eliot Weinberger, trans. Esther Allen, Suzanne Jill Levine and Eliot Weinberger (London: Penguin, 1999), p. 218.

[9] Borges, 'Time and J. W. Dunne', p. 219.

a miraculous interruption of history's logic is necessary. Rather than being vague speculation, Britton's adaption of Dunne's serial time is a searing effort to challenge the reformist delusion that the way of the world is already its own reconciliation.

Britton's recourse to a cosmic temporality that might envision our future freedom partly explains his work's neglect, in that he refuses the adherence to realism and to history as an already established objective process that underpins most critical models on the Left. As such, his work is often conveniently labelled an ideological or compensatory retreat from the realities of the present, a distortion of sensibility and temporality from their proper, corrective home in objective social history. The very aspect of his work that does not fit such protocols, however, is also the key and distinctive facet by which it poses profound questions about the normative stipulations for an aesthetics of class. The interweavings and complications between aesthetics and social class tend, in the Marxist traditions of criticism (especially in its formalist or (post-)structuralist strands), to encounter distortion as an ideological process, in which an imaginary misrecognition displaces the real system of social relations by proffering a representational relation to the latter. Louis Althusser finds that such imaginative relations to social reality are not some 'great ideological mystification'. Rather, ideology has a material existence and grounding in social reality, in specific relations of production, stages in history, state formations and state apparatuses. The task is, thus, not to demystify ideology as pure falsity, but instead to ascertain how and why particular historical conditions generate specific ideological positions that are both always imaginative and necessary in our relation to the world. Althusser argues:

> [A]ll ideology represents in its necessarily imaginary distortion not the existing relations of production (and the other relations that derive from them), but above all the (imaginary) relationship of individuals to the relations of production and the relations that derive from them. What is represented in ideology is therefore not the system of the real relations which govern the existence of individuals, but the imaginary relation of those individuals to the real relations in which they live.[10]

As such, history – the real relations between human beings – is always an 'absent cause' in ideological critique; it is never experienced directly. Instead the interpretative mission is to decode how and why particular

[10] Louis Althusser, *Lenin and Philosophy and Other Essays* [1968], trans. Ben Brewster (New York: Monthly Review Press, 1971), pp. 164–5.

forms and ideas shape people's necessarily imaginative representation of the world. For this model, our relations are always and inexorably played out through these representations. Marxism should evaluate why a particular set of forms and ideas is dominant in a particular time, so that these specific representational forms disclose indirectly the power relations that are their absent cause – history itself – and which can only be experienced imaginatively through forms of representation. Althusser writes:

> [T]he question of the 'cause' of the imaginary distortion of the real relations in ideology disappears and must be replaced by a different question: why is the representation given to individuals of their (individual) relation to the social relations which govern their conditions of existence and their collective and individual life necessarily an imaginary relation? And what is the nature of this imaginariness? Posed in this way, the question explodes the solution by a 'clique', by a group of individuals (Priests or Despots) who are the authors of the great ideological mystification, just as it explodes the solution by the alienated character of the real world.[11]

In the Althusserian traditions of Marxism, ideology is therefore not pure false consciousness or a bogus myth propagated by a powerful elite that deludes the benighted many. It is a necessary relation to the world, allowing people to map themselves onto the conditions of their existence, but whose forms themselves yield to the political scientist the limitations and possibilities of a given society or historical moment. Althusser as critic stands in relation to the 'distortion' of necessarily imaginative forms and comprehends underlying forces.

This kind of method lends itself to formalist or (post-)structuralist Marxisms in literary criticism precisely because of the particular relationships they proposed between literature, ideology, reality, and science or truth. For Marxism, literature is an especially interesting terrain because it is not one and the same thing as reality (it is a literary and imaginative construction born out of real conditions but not one and the same as its context). So too, literature is not identical to ideology as such, precisely because of literature's form-giving capacity (it makes its materials into a sonnet or lyric poem, a piece of expressionist or epic theatre, a mystery story or a realist novel). Hence, even in a hypothetical scenario in which a work of literature is intentionally conceived as endorsing a given dominant ideology, the text itself is always heterogeneous to an ideological

11 Althusser, *Lenin*, p. 165.

formation because it has already given a new or different shape to its materials, creating a supplementary or imaginative excess, another form that is something-else-besides. Literature therefore retains restively and creatively a formal semi-autonomy between both reality and ideology. It is not completely commensurate with one or the other. It is, then, the critic as the bearer of truth or science who is able to adduce the total horizon of formal meanings generated by literature's migratory dynamics between and across ideology and reality.

Unlike Althusser, Pierre Macherey's model couches ideology as a broken mirror rather than a distorted one, in which literature is not a distortion but a space of absences of the things ideology cannot say or resolve, things that persist as formal tension and contradictions whose full ideological import is filled in by the critic:

> [T]he mirror is only superficially a mirror, or at least it reflects in its own special way. We are not concerned with just any reflecting surface which would give a direct reproduction of any object. And rather than the facile notion of a distorting mirror, Lenin suggests a fragmented image. Could it be a broken mirror? In effect, the relationship between the mirror and what it reflects (the historical reality) is *partial:* the mirror selects, it does not reflect everything. The selection itself is not fortuitous, it is symptomatic; it can tell us about the nature of the mirror.[12]

Hence, Macherey understands representation as both 'a reflection and the absence of a reflection: this is why it is itself contradictory'.[13] Such a model evaluates both the imaginary resolution (the literary form) and the social contradictions (the history) that the former is embedded in resolving or interrogating. It therefore resists allowing the imaginary resolution to make its historical conditions in its own narcissistic self-identity. Consequently, the ideology of form becomes part of the analytical process rather than a neutral lens through which we debate history and society. As Macherey puts it: 'The secret of the mirror is to be sought in the form of its reflections; how does it show historical reality, by what paradox does it make visible its own blindness without actually seeing itself?'[14] Thus, critical science lays bare the gaps and silences that betray the longing of form for resolution and in so doing unmasks a world that is unreconciled.

[12] Pierre Macherey, *A Theory of Literary Production* [1966], trans. Geoffrey Wall (London: Routledge and Kegan Paul, 1978), p. 210.

[13] Macherey, *A Theory of Literary Production*, p. 128.

[14] Macherey, *A Theory of Literary Production*, p. 122.

What Macherey shares with Althusser's model of necessary distortion is his commitment to interrogating the forms and shapes of ideology as they divulge the possibilities and limitations of society imaginatively, resources that recover for the critic an understanding of history's logic.

Fredric Jameson's *The Political Unconscious* most directly redeploys Althusser's version of history as an 'absent cause' as it grasps narrative as a socially symbolic act. Following Althusser, Jameson regards texts as 'inventing imaginary or formal "solutions" to unresolvable social contradictions'.[15] Jameson's model again contests the mimetic faith that representation is a unifying mirror and instead proposes that such is the force of history and its antagonisms that it cannot be encountered directly – as mere content reflecting the world around it – but rather embeds itself in form, in determinate structures negotiating what can be said and by whom, what cannot be consciously acknowledged and remains unreconciled and antinomic. Jameson argues:

> The type of interpretation here proposed is [...] grasped as the rewriting of the literary text in such a way that the latter may itself be seen as the rewriting or restructuration of a prior historical or ideological *subtext*, it being always understood that the 'subtext' is not immediately present as such, not some common-sense external reality, nor even the conventional narratives of history manuals, but rather must itself be always (re)constructed after the fact.[16]

Part of the process of that reconstruction of form is exactly to return to the literary text its submerged conflicts, the necessary and suppressed lack of synthesis in its encounter with history as conflict rather than stability.

More recently, the work of Slavoj Žižek has accented the Lacanian aspects latent in Althusser as a redevelopment of the thesis that ideology is not pure false consciousness but rather an exigent imaginative encounter with a submerged Real.[17] For Žižek, we have been dreaming the wrong dreams and indeed need to find new ways to dream.[18] Given his psycho-

15 Fredric Jameson, *The Political Unconscious: Narrative as a Socially Symbolic Act* (London: Routledge, 1996), p. 79.

16 Jameson, *The Political Unconscious*, p. 83.

17 For a critique arguing that Althusser's version of ideology and individual or collective subjects fails to push the psychoanalytical, Lacanian logic – touched upon in his work – to its full, disruptive potential, see Rosalind Coward and John Ellis, *Language and Materialism: Developments in Semiology and the Theory of the Subject* (London: Routledge, 2016).

18 See Slavoj Žižek, *The Pervert's Guide to Cinema* (dir. Sophie Fiennes, 2006); *The Pervert's Guide to Ideology* (dir. Sophie Fiennes, 2013).

analytical pathway into Marxism via Lacan, for Žižek the very status of the unconscious stands as a reminder that there are places that ideology and its formal hold on what can be imagined cannot reach. This notion of some remainder of fantasy, and our capacity to imagine through the unconscious in ways not already enlisted by dominant ideology, is obviously antithetical to the more structuralist and post-structuralist materialisms in which the subject is always a product of discourse. Instead, in Žižek's Lacanian Marxism, the subject is never quite one with itself and thus never monolithically compelled to dream in sanctioned ways only. To Žižek, the unconscious is the point at which the subject's agency exceeds the subject and dislodges its self-identity.[19]

In the case of all these versions of ideological analysis, even if via Žižek we might propose the analyst in Lacanian terms as 'the subject who is supposed to know' rather than the omniscient master, there is still the question of the primacy of the master-critic who is able to unravel as science and truth the lessons gleaned from the imaginative forms in which others are creatively but necessarily entrapped in their relations to social reality. Jacques Rancière's work is directly informed by his turning against the lessons of his one-time mentor, Althusser. In particular, an irony emerges in Althusser's assertion that ideology is not merely a great mystification by an elite but a lived and material relation, in view of Rancière's claim that Althusser sets up himself and other truth-bearers in a position of knowledge that eludes those who can only imagine the world ideologically. Rancière's work is distinguished by what he has termed *le partage du sensible*, the partition or distribution of the sensible: that is, how a society allocates who has the right to think, to sense, to perceive, to know, to act, to make.[20] The distribution of the sensible is the means by which a society partitions and distributes who has the rights to thought and expression, and simultaneously demarcates those who are excluded from those codes of citizenship, those whose very exclusion establishes the grounds of the enthronement of particular subjects, particular ways of seeing, particular regimes of what can or cannot be acknowledged. Crucial to the partition of the sensible is the division between thinkers who think and workers who work. That demarcation is found not only politically on the Right but also on the Left, in the model whereby it is the task of

[19] For a defence of the Žižek position against the more post-structuralist version of the subject, see Hilary Neroni, *The Subject of Torture: Psychoanalysis and Biopolitics in Television and Film* (New York: Columbia University Press, 2015).
[20] Jacques Rancière, *The Politics of Aesthetics: The Distribution of the Sensible*, trans. Gabriel Rockhill (London: Continuum, 2004), p. 21.

the learned to understand history fully and objectively and to impart or impute that knowledge to the workers.[21] Rancière's work is itself informed by the fractures in the French Left post-1968 and, most pertinently, by his disagreement with the thought of Althusser, who, in line with the French Communist Party, had judged the protests of the late 1960s to be untimely and misguided in the terms of their own avowed mastery of history's stages and development that licence and determine class struggle.[22]

To Rancière, Althusser's status, as the harbinger of truth outside of the ideologies in which everyone else is trapped, is itself blind to the socially mediated relations that produce the philosopher's judicious sovereignty over history in the first place: 'Dominant ideology is not the shady Other to Science's pure light; it is, rather, the space where scientific knowledges come to be inscribed, the space where they are articulated to the elements of knowledge constitutive of a social formation.'[23] Refusing the dichotomy of the knowledge of the few and the ideological consciousness of the masses, Rancière insists upon 'the capacity of the dominated',[24] upon people's ability to reinscribe their place in the world, to rearticulate and translate themselves in ways that contest not only their place in society and the processes of history but also the ownership of intelligence and philosophical agency.

Rancière's moment of departure from Althusser emanates from his research into the habits of nineteenth-century proletarians in France. In that work, his previously Althusserian quest is transformed by the finding that such workers were not the already agreed objects of his scrutiny and were not what he had been schooled to expect:

> These workers, who should have supplied me with information on working conditions and forms of class consciousness, provided me with something altogether different: a sense of similarity, a demonstration of equality. They too were spectators and visitors within their own class. Their activity as propagandists could not be separated from their idleness as strollers and contemplators. The simple chronicle of

[21] On the task of the philosopher or intellectual within orthodox Marxism to install *imputed* or *zugerechnete* consciousness in the proletariat, see Georg Lukács, *History and Class Consciousness*, *passim*.

[22] See, for example, Louis Althusser, 'The Althusser Case Part I, Marxist Humanism', *Marxism Today*, 16.1 (1972), 23–8; 'The Althusser Case [Part II]', *Marxism Today*, 16.2 (1972), 43–8.

[23] Jacques Rancière, *Althusser's Lesson*, trans. Emiliano Battista (London: Continuum, 2011), p. 142.

[24] Rancière, *Althusser's Lesson*, p. xvi.

> their leisure dictated reformulation of the established relations between *seeing*, *doing* and *speaking*. By making themselves spectators and visitors, they disrupted the distribution of the sensible which would have it that those who work do not have time to let their steps and gazes roam at random; and that the members of a collective body do not have time to spend on the forms and insignia of individuality. That is what the word 'emancipation' means: the blurring of the boundary between those who act and those who look; between individuals and members of a collective body. What these days brought the two correspondents and their fellows was not knowledge of their condition and energy for the following day's work and the coming struggle. It was a reconfiguration in the here and now of the distribution of space and time, work and leisure [...] Understanding this break made at the very heart of time was to develop the implications of a similarity and an equality, as opposed to ensuring its mastery in the endless task of reducing the irreducible distance. These two workers were themselves intellectuals, as is anyone and everyone. They were visitors and spectators, like the researcher who a century and a half later read their letters in a library, like the visitors of Marxist theory or the distributors of leaflets at factory gates. There was no gap to be filled between intellectuals and workers, any more than there was between actors and spectators.[25]

Most notably in the above passage, Rancière proposes something other than ideological distortion that might be remedied by the truth of the philosopher; instead he finds a radical rupture and distortion of time, particularly the historical narratives of stadial continuity underpinning the knowledge of the Marxist scientist that would ascribe places, roles and functions to workers.

Aesthetics, the distribution of the sensible for Rancière, distorts standard versions of historical temporality that would allocate time for philosophers to think, and an absence of time to those who merely work and become the objects of someone else's philosophical reflections. The awareness of workers as intellectuals confounds time as the regulator of the capacity to think in Althusser and, for Rancière, all the way back to Plato's *Phaedrus*, wherein the myth of the cicadas is deployed to contrast two categories of being: the workers who come to take a nap in the shade at the hot hour when the cicadas sing; and the congregated philosophers, separated from the former by their leisure for speech and exchange of

[25] Jacques Rancière, *Proletarian Nights: The Workers' Dream in Nineteenth-Century France* (London: Verso, 2012), pp. 19–20.

words. As Rancière puts it: 'philosophy defined itself in defining its other. The order of discourse delimited itself by tracing a circle that excluded from the right to think those who earned their living by the labor of their hands.'[26] In all this, the key factor is time. As with the myth of the cicadas, the capacity to think is regulated by leisure (*scholē*) or its absence (*ascholia*), the difference between the philosophers who can think and the mute workers who can only sleep before they resume their work.

Hence, for Rancière, ideological distortion is more a facet of the supposed knowledge that would deny workers the capacity and time to think and act in ways that disorder the consensus by which they are excluded from art and knowledge by such hierarchies of thinkers and labourers. Literature's promise is an equality of human intelligences rather than a set of ideological distortions of form whose historical secrets are disclosed to the master-critic. As a result, Rancière has a very particular aesthetic definition of emancipation:

> It means escaping from a minority. But nobody escapes from the social minority save by their own efforts. The emancipation of the workers is not a matter of making labour the founding principle of the new society, but rather of the workers emerging from their minority status and proving that they truly belong in society, that they truly communicate with all in a common space; that they are not merely creatures of need, of complaint and protest, but creatures of discourse and reason, that they are capable of opposing reason with reason and of giving their action a demonstrative form [...] Whence the proliferation in the literature of workers' emancipation – as also in that of women's emancipation – of arguments aiming to prove that those demanding equality have a perfect right to it, that they participate in a common world where they can prove their case and prove the necessity for the other to recognize it.[27]

However, for all that Rancière prioritises the capacity of the excluded to intrude upon and transform consensus through dissensual interventions that recalibrate what a society can acknowledge and express, his advocacy of 'discourse and reason' as the means by which such emancipation takes place tends to accept each as already agreed realms in which the excluded can partake in the demonstration of their equality of intelligence. My own point here, as we approach what might be meant by proletarian aesthetics and the work of Britton, is that discourse and reason might already be

[26] Jacques Rancière, *The Philosopher and His Poor*, trans. John Drury, Corinne Oster and Andrew Parker (Durham, NC: Duke University Press, 2004), p. 203.

[27] Rancière, *Proletarian Nights*, pp. 48–9.

socially mediated and bound by exactly the class hierarchies that Rancière's model of aesthetics designedly undermines. This is not, however, to fall back into the intellectual hierarchy that Rancière so rightly criticises in Althusser and others. It is not to propose that, if forms of literature and reason are historically contingent, then only the master-critic may unfold the total meanings of their imaginative, ideological distortion. Rather I wish to propose, in the spirit of Rancière's assertion of the equality of human intelligence, that working-class writers and readers can engage literary and discursive forms by themselves rather than simply joining the ongoing conversation of others. In other words, while taking on board Rancière's antipathy to the division between thinkers and workers, it is also possible to gauge and contest how form is impacted by social inequality and contradiction through the cultural work of workers themselves.

The main tenet to be drawn from the Marxist tradition is that culture exists precisely because what it promises does not. That is, the freedom, creativity and autonomy promised by art are not freely available to all but bought at the price of unfreedom and the inequality of the world in which we live. Relatedly, culture is therefore not some pure realm that already awaits the vanquished to find their voices in its eloquence; it is instead a fractious terrain that seeks to normalise particular, dominant modes of subjectivity, expression, discourse or reason, but in which these things may also be challenged, overturned and given new forms that express different, heterogeneous things. Such a radical process would entail a grasp of distortion in both its temporal and spatial senses, a reallocation of who has the time to think and produce culture, and a reorientation of the forms and shapes that such expression takes. So my purpose here is to engage aesthetics in terms of an ideology of forms, but to do so by both agreeing and disagreeing with elements of the Rancière model, in that such a venture is not and was not the preserve of Althusser or any other master-philosopher. Just as much as it is vital to divest the critic of her or his dominion over knowledge, so too eloquence is not to be vaunted as the already established expression of a culture by which the proles learn and insist upon their democratic place in the world. Instead, democracy might require a thorough critique of the available forms and modes by which it is to be expressed.

Lionel Britton is an interesting writer to consider in these terms. From the outset, he avowedly sought to experiment: 'I am trying to do new things with form, content and style.'[28] His experimentalism clearly

[28] Lionel Britton, letter to Winifred Holtby, 29 January 1933, Winifred Holtby Collection, Hull Local Studies Library.

contributes to his neglect in literary history, even in genealogies of proletarian writing.[29] He does not fit the realist template allocated to working-class writing in the 1920s and 1930s, nor does his experimentalism fit neatly with canonical modernism. Nonetheless, although Britton found it difficult to have his plays staged, it is worth recording that *Spacetime Inn* was the first work ever to be given a reading in an anteroom at the House of Commons, thanks to the assistance of his friend, J. S. Clarke, the then MP for Glasgow Maryhill. His sole novel, *Hunger and Love*, was published despite an ongoing battle with Britton's publisher over its form, style and scope. Again, although this work is largely invisible in literary histories, it too, like *Spacetime Inn*, spiked the interest of notable figures at the time. George Orwell read and reviewed the novel and discussed it during a BBC Home Service radio discussion with Desmond Hawkins on 6 December 1940 on the subject of proletarian writing. In Orwell's review, the novel was described as digressive, but nonetheless worthy as a 'social document'.[30] Implicit in these comments is a sense that Britton's formal and aesthetic radicalism is something of a tiresome diversion, and that the purpose of such writing is at best to authenticate some already agreed state of affairs. This condescension masquerading as faint praise permeates Orwell's radio discussion with Hawkins (despite its subsequent publication as 'The Proletarian Writer'), illustrating his sense that there is no meaningful tradition of working-class writing or aesthetics, and that the merits of such writing reside solely in its earthy documentation.

Orwell argued that, in a bourgeois society, the whole idea of a fully proletarian literature was impossible: 'I don't believe the proletariat can create an independent literature while they are not the dominant class. I believe their literature is and must be bourgeois literature with a slightly different slant.'[31] Certainly for the term 'working-class culture' to even approach the justification of its own designation, it would have to presume a sense of propriety: that is, as a culture not only produced by

[29] One shining exception to such neglect is Tony Shaw's Ph.D thesis, 'The Work of Lionel Britton', Open University, unpublished Ph.D thesis (2007).

[30] George Orwell, *The Complete Works of George Orwell*, ed. Peter Davison, 20 vols (London: Secker & Warburg, 1986–98; rev. and updated 2000); George Orwell, *A Patriot After All: 1940–1941*, ed. Peter Davison, *The Complete Works of George Orwell*, 20 vols (London: Secker & Warburg, 1986–98; rev. and updated 2000), p. 203.

[31] George Orwell, 'The Proletarian Writer: Discussion between George Orwell and Desmond Hawkins', in Sonia Orwell and Ian Angus, eds, *The Collected Essays, Journalism and Essays of George Orwell Vol.2: My Country Right or Left, 1940–1943* (London: Secker & Warburg, 1968), p. 38.

but also owned by the proletariat. Given that the working class has the least autonomy of all classes under capitalism, proposing the ownership of some self-authorising and self-identical proletarian culture is, at best, tokenism that fails to acknowledge the full effects of domination.

A kindred sentiment to Orwell's is found in his ostensible adversary on the Left, Raymond Williams's *Culture and Society*, where 'working-class culture' is made broadly synonymous with the mass or popular culture of technological modernity's entertainment apparatuses (which are most definitely not owned by the proletariat). Williams does credit a small amount of proletarian writing in England with some degree of literary merit, but surrounds his affirmation with circumspection:

> We need to be aware of this work, but it is to be seen as a valuable dissident element rather than as a culture. The traditional popular culture of England was, if not annihilated, at least fragmented and weakened by the dislocations of the Industrial Revolution. What is left, with what in the new conditions has been newly made, is small in quantity and narrow in range. It exacts respect, but it is in no sense an alternative culture.[32]

While Williams clearly and honourably seeks to valorise the dissidence of such writing as a residual register of human expression not totally or instrumentally standardised into conformity with bourgeois modernity, his own sense of working-class writing's attenuated scope ultimately and inversely makes it an unwilling index of precisely the hegemony of industrial capitalism. Here the perceived paucity of range in proletarian literature – in its form, technique, style – collapses out of its own seemingly limited self-containment into that which it already was: a consonance with the pervasive atomisation, fragmentation and regimentation of capitalist modernity's onward march. Although Williams acknowledges enclaves of dissent, they become commensurate with what they would nominally resist and thus cannot attain the requisite cohesion of a proper alternative.

Comparably, Orwell's BBC discussion finds proletarian writing more aggregated by its limitations than its possibilities. In response to Hawkins's suggestion that working-class literature is more a revolt in terms 'of content – not form or technique', Orwell concurs: 'As for technique, one of the things that strikes one about the proletarian writers, or the people who

[32] Raymond Williams, *Culture and Society 1879–1950* (Harmondsworth: Penguin, 1963), p. 320.

are called proletarian writers, is how conservative they are.'[33] Orwell could discern only two rather circumscribed benefits in the work of proletarian writers: 'new subject-matter' and 'crudeness and vitality. They have been a sort of voice in the gallery, preventing people from becoming too toney and too civilised.'[34] In other words, such literature provides bourgeois society with new subject matter (working-class life) and its edginess helps galvanise the mainstream, in some exotically barbarian way, so that it does not become too moribund. Despite his good intentions, Orwell can only ever regard working-class writing as a degraded or earthier version of bourgeois literature. To him, there is nothing to recommend it by way of formal or stylistic innovation and antagonism. It merely repeats – with a more vulgar content – the prevailing and already agreed modes of literary expression, which are robust and eager enough to withstand their sullying by this crude vitality, since the extension of such modes into the arena of this new working-class subject matter in fact burnishes the final triumph of bourgeois culture's dominance.

My purpose here is not to contest Williams's or Orwell's account of the hegemony of bourgeois culture as such. Or, at least, I would concur wholeheartedly with their caution in regard to the notion of some autonomous, ready-made working-class culture that could be shored against bourgeois modernity. Indeed, given Roland Barthes's understanding of bourgeois ideology as *ex-nominating*, as striving to 'un-name' itself – to shape everything yet remain invisible or appear natural – a vigilance is always required when encountering apparently grittily brash and authentic representations of working-class life which purport to articulate a self-ratified identity that scorns all that is bourgeois.[35] There is no greater example of bourgeois ideology in practice than when it disguises itself as the advocacy of someone else's class and interests. Barthes's interpretation of the *ex-nominating operation* of bourgeois ideology chimes with the model of dominant cultural super-saturation and pervasiveness advanced by both Orwell and Williams, whereby the signature of bourgeois identity authorises all cultural expression and forms (including those that ostensibly oppose it):

> [I]n a bourgeois culture, there is neither proletarian culture nor proletarian morality, there is no proletarian art; ideologically, all that is

33 Orwell, 'The Proletarian Writer', p. 40.

34 Orwell, 'The Proletarian Writer', p. 43.

35 Roland Barthes, *Mythologies*, trans. Annette Lavers (London: Vintage, 1993), p. 139.

> not bourgeois is obliged to *borrow* from the bourgeoisie. Bourgeois ideology can therefore be spread over everything and in doing so lose its name without risk.[36]

Clearly, the working class (as with all classes) is produced by capitalist society but, where bourgeois culture emerges in a society dominated by the bourgeoisie, working-class culture does not have the same unproblematic autonomy. Its 'working-class' status is the product of economic and social conditions that it does not control and that disempower it. In that sense, it is a class *In-Itself*, not through self-formation but on account of peremptory, underlying structural determinations. Any identity expressed in the name of an agreed working-class subjectivity under such conditions is really the passive, already-positioned endorsement of that system of relations. However, this essay is dedicated to the re-evaluation of proletarian writing via Lionel Britton's work in terms of how it opens up moments of the working class as a class *For-Itself*, with a commitment that dominant hegemonies are not fully exhaustive ones. In other words, it has been possible for working-class writers to produce work that is not homogenous with the system that dominates them. In doing so, they have not sought, on the one hand, compensatory solace in the tokenistic badge of a working-class identity already sanctioned as their lot by capitalism, in which they might wallow in the fantasy of their own autonomous authenticity; but nor, on the other hand, have they made themselves identical with prevailing bourgeois forms and modes (through the embrace of someone else's perceived culture or individual redemption). The task for any truly emancipatory literary project is to find a space of expression for the working class that is not made politically identical with the capitalism that would subordinate it.

Britton was initially considered by Orwell to be the one writer who might be an exception to his sense of working-class writing as formally conservative and inert, but he subsequently backtracked and judged Britton's *Hunger and Love* as a predictably typical 'representative of proletarian literature':

> It is about a young proletarian who wishes he wasn't a proletarian. It simply goes on and on about the intolerable conditions of working-class life, the fact that the roof leaks and the sink smells and all the rest of it. Now, you couldn't found a literature on the fact that the sink smells. As a convention it isn't likely to last so long as the siege

36 Barthes, *Mythologies*, p. 139.

> of Troy. And behind this book, and lots of others like it, you can see what is really the history of a proletarian writer nowadays. Through some accident – very often it is simply due to having a long period on the dole – a young man of the working class gets a chance to educate himself. Then he starts writing books, and naturally he makes use of his early experiences, his sufferings under poverty, his revolt against the existing system, and so forth. But he isn't really creating an independent literature. He writes in the bourgeois manner, in the middle-class dialect. He is simply the black sheep of the bourgeois family, using the old methods for slightly different purposes. Don't mistake me. I'm not saying that he can't be as good a writer as anyone else; but if he is, it won't be because he is a working man but because he is a talented person who has learnt to write well. So as long as the bourgeoisie are the dominant class, literature must be bourgeois.[37]

So, according to Orwell's argument, *Hunger and Love* is a typical representative of proletarian literature that is itself the passively expressive relay of bourgeois culture and hegemony. It is not simply that it lacks independence (as already acknowledged, that kind of total possession of a culture is a structural impossibility under capitalism), but that bourgeois hegemony is so thorough, and proletarian writing so supine, that the only representational possibility is a dark mirror in which the oppressed recognise themselves only in the reflection of their master's own image and form. If anything, it is Orwell's thinking that is saturated in prevailing bourgeois forms – he can only see this as the story of an individual, and therefore fails to recognise the formal radicalism of Britton's work, which distinctively shifts out of individual perspectives into collective enunciation. Throughout *Hunger and Love*, the individual remains non-identical to itself and becomes the impediment to, rather than the facilitator of, the educing move from *Bildung* to a common humanity or Hegelian *Allgemeniheit*. The Orwell reading of this novel reverts to the standard wisdom where the *Bildungsroman* encounters working-class life only to return it to itself as philistinism, while the protagonist – solely as a displaced *individual* – is alienated from both his background and the bourgeois order in which he seeks sanctuary.

Hunger and Love is a shape-shifter that seems to begin as a *Bildungsroman* but then completely negates and excavates the category of the individual when its main protagonist, Arthur Phelps, disappears with millions of others in the trenches of the First World War. At this juncture, the narrative dynamic tracing the development of the individual and its socialisa-

37 Orwell, 'The Proletarian Writer', pp. 41-2.

tion is occluded and divested of the complete aggregation of its plot with reality. Instead, a space of collective enunciation intervenes as a parallax view that negates the wholeness of the initial narrative thread: 'Gun-flashes and stench of rotting bodies, the bodies of men. Where is mankind? I do not know. The bourgeoisie are everywhere. Where is Arthur Phelps? I do not know.'[38] The circumscribed individual lens therefore becomes the broken mirror, unable to aggregate the world in its own self-identity, and resides in negating antagonism to a collective subjectivity unmediated by that individualism:

> Every man alive will say to himself, I am I, and you will be the man. You take no notice of position on the earth, of series or simultaneity in time, rank, station, condition, sublimation or degradation of intellect, hope or happiness, joy or despair or pain, squalor or comfort or grandeur or dignity or servile humiliation and abject and contemptible submission in filth and ignorance and disease. What can we know in a palace, university, workshop, slum – but that we are conscious of being alive, that life is grand and spacious and noble, that life is mean and vile and foul, that this is the quality of our lives or the quality of other lives, and that in oneself the self is a sublimity or a degradation? To They we are They, to Us we are Ourselves. We are the consciousness of the world, collectively among us, what we do to degrade, degrades it all.[39]

Here the primary narcissism by which the individual transfers its agreed becoming into a stable social reality, which in turn seamlessly and mutually deposits its universality back in such individuals, founders in the collision of perspectives in which the individual loses the import of its own name: literally, that which cannot be divided, that which is indivisible. It is divided from, to and by itself – less in the sense that it turns out that some individuals are rich and some are poor, more in that the very foundational category of the individual is divested of its universal suture. It therefore also becomes divided from, to and by the social reality over which it asserts sovereignty. It is unable to harmonise its own self-identity with an agreed and unifying representational frame. Instead an entirely different register of the real – the collective – short-circuits the correspondence between the individual's self-image and society. And the collective is not simply an aggregation of individuals. It stands as a clarity that radically negates the ideological distortion of the social and universal

38 Britton, *Hunger and Love*, p. 702.

39 Britton, *Hunger and Love*, p. 697.

placement of the individual. The very partiality of that self-identical individual makes the reality it names unfathomable; its antagonistic Other is not other individuals but a non-identical pathway to the real itself: the collective.

As such, *Hunger and Love* utterly negates the standard *Bildungsroman* and radically rewrites Orwell's assertion that the only thing to distinguish proletarian writing is its supplication to prevailing norms. Given that Mikhail Bakhtin, Franco Moretti and others have appraised this form as one of the most formative and expressive cultural orientations of bourgeois modernity, my choice might seem a perversely Sisyphus-like exercise in futility in light of Orwell's views. But the *Bildungsroman* proffers exactly the kind of illustratively hegemonic inheritance through which to demonstrate the unsoundness of Orwell's denial of any kind of aesthetic radicalism and contestation to proletarian writing. Moreover, this radicalism is heterogeneous to any generic play and fluidity that might be ascribed to the *Bildungsroman* as a form since its inception: in other words, it stands for something more than the assimilative, amorphous capacity of bourgeois ideology to frame all things. In terms of the historically adaptive aesthetic and political core of the *Bildungsroman*, Bakhtin – in keeping with his long-standing dedication both to formal and structural particularity and to an anti-totalitarian *nezavershennost* (unfinishedness or openness) – regards the genre as one of 'dynamic unity' rather than 'static unity'. [40] He places it as 'the novel of human *emergence*' in which the new fluidity of biography and the history of modernity intertwine in a modality that itself contains, conveys and keeps in creative tension the epochal transitions and processes of the late eighteenth century and beyond.[41] To Bakhtin, Goethe's *Wilhelm Meister* stands as the paradigmatic model that distils and reconciles the self as process with a newly sedimenting modern existence: 'the image of the emerging man begins to surmount its private nature (within certain limits, of course) and enters into a completely new, *spatial* sphere of historical existence'.[42] The culmination, for Bakhtin, of this consonance of the aesthetic and the social maturates the realistic novel of emergence, which itself facilitates the synthetic representational wholeness that he ascribes to nineteenth-century realism (Stendhal, Balzac, Flaubert, Dickens, Thackeray). Hence,

40 Mikhail Bakhtin, *Speech Genres and Other Late Essays*, ed. Caryl Emerson and Michael Holquist, trans. Vern W. McGee (Austin: University of Texas Press, 1986), p. 21.

41 Bakhtin, *Speech Genres*, p. 21.

42 Bakhtin, *Speech Genres*, p. 24.

Becoming – what Bakhtin terms *stanovlenie* and German Romanticism and idealism called *das Werden* – offers a reconciliation that is historically grounded and aesthetically realised.

Comparably, Moretti renders the *Bildungsroman* a partial 'synthesis' that agrees a shared and integral balance between the bourgeois individual subject and its social placement.[43] For Moretti, the novel more widely as a cultural form seeks 'to heal the rupture that had generated (or so it seemed) the French revolution, and to imagine a continuity between the old and the new regime'. In the 'marriage' of these two classes in historical compromise, Moretti proposes in the novel a kind of bourgeois ennoblement. In this logic there is a newly hegemonic and composite aggregation of the now dominant with the residually authoritative that arrives at synthesis.[44] Moretti feels that this is why the *Bildungsroman* is so deeply entwined with one social class and that it vanishes in the presence of the working class, so that the likes of Thomas Hardy's *Jude the Obscure* skew the synthetic promise by presenting a 'youth *without the right to dream*: this is what makes the working-class *Bildungsroman* incomparable to *Wilhelm Meister* or *Père Goriot* [...] no longer at home among his old fellow workers, but never accepted by the new bourgeois milieu, the hero suddenly sees the impossibility of his position'.[45] Moretti is most certainly attuned to the contradictions of the *Bildungsroman*, which makes modernity representable in the figure of youth and Becoming, but whose synthesis betrays the bourgeois hegemony laying claim to modernity:

> When we remember that the *Bildungsroman* – the symbolic form that more than any other has portrayed and promoted modern socialization – is also the *most contradictory* of modern symbolic forms, we realize that in our world socialization itself consists first of all in the *interiorization of contradiction*. The next step being not to 'solve' the contradiction but rather to learn to live with it, and even transform it into a tool for survival.[46]

However, rather than accepting the Althusserian model of form and proposing that the *Bildungsroman* is already an ideological distortion

[43] Franco Moretti, *The Way of the World: The Bildungsroman in European Culture* [1987], new edition (London: Verso, 2000), p. 214.

[44] Moretti, *The Way of the World*, p. viii.

[45] Moretti, *The Way of the World*, p. x.

[46] Moretti, *The Way of the World*, p. 10.

requiring the master-critic to excavate its distortive contradictions, or completely aligning with Rancière's sense that anyone can use it as he or she wishes in an aesthetic redistribution of already agreed eloquence, Britton's *Hunger and Love* robustly tears apart the hegemonic sedimentation by which bourgeois modernity lays claim to culture, progress and Becoming. Britton's cosmic register is less alienation and more a lens through which to coruscate the promise of a reforming history whose logic might allow us all to be free: 'The bourgeoisie sell you their sham fake substitute externals. Individualist like the Protozoa, their evolutionary minds are hundreds of millions of years behind the evolutionary level of one of their own liver cells.'[47]

Unlike so many takes on the *Bildungsroman* in working-class contexts, it is not that *Hunger and Love* places culture as an already agreed possession of someone else to which the proletarian youth aspires, and for which he or she must leave a milieu, *Hunger and Love* returns to bourgeois modernity its framing philistinism: 'So far as you can see, if the bourgeoisie were allowed to operate unrestrainedly, the work of civilisation would stop altogether. The whole principle of their existence is only get in the way [sic], prevent people doing anything at all. Just to exact tribute for permission'.[48] The bourgeois sanction of the telos to which Becoming yearns is unmasked in terms of a collective culture, unshackled from the logic of history's apparently progressive truth. Rather than a self-alienated bourgeois decadence that would distort our objective place in the world via Lukács, Britton's experiments with time disclose the false universal that is capital and its hold over reality at one and the same time, in that he divests aesthetics of an unmediated claim to all that is good. The universal mediator – capital – that would intercede in all things, and whose dominance is denied by the aesthetic promise of the standard *Bildungsroman*, is finally uncovered.

Given the fugitive reading of its author while working as an errand-boy for a bookseller, there is a strong autobiographical dimension to *Hunger and Love*'s defence of learning, but instead of straightforwardly endorsing the Rancière position in which proles can parade as bourgeois in a scrambling of entitlement that will disorder a hierarchy of souls, there is

47 Britton, *Hunger and Love*, p. 600.

48 Britton, *Hunger and Love*, p. 591. For a highly typical and illustrative example of the use of the *Bildungsroman* as the form by which the aspiring working-class youth seeks culture elsewhere in opposition to his supposedly moribund proletarian background, see Archie Hind, *The Dear Green Place* [1966] (Edinburgh: Birlinn, 2001).

a clear rebuttal of the already agreed status of culture and the formal eloquence ascribed by an unequal world: 'If man is to pass from the bubble of the individual life to the possibly immortal external existence in the race, we should all of us, units, individuals as we are, have this free access to the book. And you have been given a job, to sell books: for between mind and mind the bourgeois intercepts.'[49] Different messages are possible and can be imagined beyond the eloquence already laid down and given form in ways that return to such expressions their limits rather than their freedom. Another freedom exists that would extend eloquence beyond its status as something the vanquished might emulate. In Britton's distortion of culture from bourgeois hegemony, so that the former might be redefined as something other than the possession of the latter, which proles might mimic, *Hunger and Love* achieves something incomprehensible to the critical models in which workers simply repeat the forms of their masters, or for which master-critics are required to correct the ideological distortions of the falsely conscripted. And it also moves beyond Rancière's aesthetics in which the excluded intrude upon the eloquence of the vaunted, without this disruption requiring attention to the social mediation of such thought in the first place. Walter Benjamin had always dissected bourgeois ideology as materialism and capitalism rather than simply culture and *Bildung*, and his reading of Alexander Döblin's *Berlin Alexanderplatz* finds affinity rather than disparity between the bourgeois and the criminal:

> What we find here once again, in a beguiling form and with undiminished force, is the re-emergence of the magic of Charles Dickens, in whose works bourgeois and criminals fit each other like a glove because their interests (however opposed to each other they may be) inhabit one and the same world. The world of these crooks is homologous with the world of the bourgeoisie. Franz Biberkopf's road to pimp and petty bourgeois is no more than a heroic metamorphosis of bourgeois consciousness.[50]

From Britton all the way through to Irvine Welsh's *Trainspotting* – in which Renton's development and movement as an individual are enabled by the theft of money – class and aesthetics combine to rupture the synthesis of the *Bildungsroman* in proletarian terms that make capitalism

[49] Britton, *Hunger and Love*, p. 584.

[50] Walter Benjamin, *Selected Writings, Vol. II, Part I, 1927–1930*, ed. Michael W. Jennings, Howard Eiland and Gary Smith, trans. Rodney Livingstone and others (Cambridge, MA: Harvard University Press, 2005), p. 303.

the main character and the formal mediator by which individuals make something of themselves.[51] *Hunger and Love* also arrives at this insight – class consciousness but by radically different means than those outlined by Lukács's faith in history – and the effort to prophesy an alternative to the way of the world is much more than compensatory alienation.

Hunger and Love indicts commodification and reification, but also resists the hold of bourgeois hegemony upon culture as its untainted remedy by instead renaming the latter's complicity with an unequal world. The redress is not to be found in in workers acquiring a culture for which capitalism is already the guiding character and mediator, and nor is it to be unearthed through the truth of the master-critic. Much as Borges slyly winked at Dunne's vision of a world in which we all join up with Shakespeare and commune in our knowing eternity, in Britton's *Spacetime Inn* there is a clear understanding that the meeting of minds staged by the play is impossible in the logic of history. This is less a practical case of characters from the twentieth century encountering Eve, the Queen of Sheba, or Dr Johnson, and more a realisation that the collision of intelligences, the public acknowledgement of the equality of our minds, is unachievable in the prevailing way of the world. Although the vagaries of Britton's stage directions would frustrate those wishing for working-class realism or naturalism and a deep grounding in history – 'The following is an impression of the dialogue going on between them: spoken, or unspoken, who knows?' – *Spacetime Inn* is deeply historical in its comprehension of the social mediation of what can be spoken and by whom and in what form. Bill and Jim are continually the object of the musings of others:

> Marx to Jim: You, I perceive, belong to the proletariat?
> Marx: And have you any politics?
> Shaw: Now, my dear Marx, do be reasonable! People like this don't have politics, politics has them. Just look at them.[52]

Here it is the silence of the proles that equips the eloquent aphorisms of their masters, and when the following exchange takes place Shaw is told to be quiet, but then seeks to frame the speech of the proles in the terms of his own knowledge:

> Jim: Ow the ell can a man say wot e finks if you keeps on talking.
> Shaw: How will you know what he thinks if I don't? […]

51 Irvine Welsh, *Trainspotting* (London: Secker and Warburg, 1993).

52 Britton, *Spacetime Inn*, p. 23.

Jim: We've ad enough o livin wivout avin no life.
Shaw: Well, I'll be damned! Pure Shavianism!
Bill: You shut up![53]

Already wisdom and culture would have their masters. This stage and history's stages are not neutral spaces in which we might all talk on equal terms. Just as Rancière would rail against his Althusserian master, seeking to correct the ideological distortions of the workers in which they become one with their domination, there is still the distortion by which our humanity is mediated by an unequal world whose forms simultaneously enthrone and dispossess modes of thinking rather than already providing an equitable aesthetics that we all might eventually share. Britton's *Hunger and Love* and *Spacetime Inn* radically undermine the notions both that working-class writers require others to unpick the contradictions of their forms and, alternatively via Rancière, that forms immediately exist in which to express our democracy equality. One of the reasons that M. P. J. S. Clarke sought to have Britton's work performed at the House of Commons was a sense that it was a set of prophetic cautionary tales that would warn history's victors to treat its victims more fairly so as to avoid apocalypse and rupture. Underscoring such a narrative is the faith of history's reformist reconciliation and an interpretation of Britton that makes him an ameliorator. But Britton realises that history is a catastrophe. His Dunne-influenced scrambling of time is neither an ideological alienation from the objectivity of historical progress nor an effort to frighten us back into its logic. His formal experimentalism seeks new paths of living and thinking that might connect us with our collectivity in ways that trace possibilities from a forlorn past and anticipate the promise of what might have been rather than what is. His own distortions of form are themselves a response to the tearing apart of human equality, and they are a testament to a proletarian aesthetics that is non-identical to the governing logic of the world and hence requires no further correction by truth-giving critics on the Left. But, incommensurate with Rancière's aesthetics, they also acknowledge fully the iniquitous forms by which our redemptive capacity to imagine, feel and think are sullied by the mediations of capitalism.

[53] Britton, *Spacetime Inn*, p. 42.

Shakespeare and Korea: Mutual Remappings

DAEYONG (DAN) KIM

Since the seventeenth century, Shakespeare's drama has travelled to virtually every corner of the world – first to continental Europe, then Africa, Asia and the Americas. These routes have been remarkably well documented. Indeed, scholarship on Shakespeare in Germany, China, Japan, India and beyond has been instrumental in broadening our understanding of Shakespeare's global reach.[1] Studies of Shakespeare in Japan, for instance, have meticulously documented the fertile cross-pollination between his drama and Japan's long-standing theatre traditions: *Bunraku, Kabuki* and *Noh*.[2] In India, scholars have investigated the ways in which Shakespeare was co-opted as a colonial agent by Britain in the nineteenth century, and later renovated as an 'inciter of nationalism – as if the people of India had said, "We will learn your game of cricket and beat you at it"'.[3] By mapping his transmission nation by nation, however, the critical project of global Shakespeares has more recently threatened to become an obstacle to its own inquiry. What do we mean in the twenty-first century by Japanese, Indian or, in this study's case, Korean Shakespeares? That is to say, what are we constructing – intentionally or unintentionally – and what are we occluding when we examine Shakespeare's dissemination in units of the nation? How has nationhood inflected the study of Shakespeare, and what does Shakespeare bring to our sense of the nation as an empowering yet also inhibitive idea?

The problem of imagining the nation is, of course, a dilemma Shakespeare himself explored in *Henry V*, a play that registers the political tensions within and surrounding early modern England as it sought to establish its geopolitical relevance in a global context. Among the first

[1] Dennis Kennedy, ed., *Foreign Shakespeare: Contemporary Performance* (Cambridge: Cambridge University Press, 2004); Dennis Kennedy and Yong Li Lan, eds, *Shakespeare in Asia: Contemporary Performance* (Cambridge: Cambridge University Press, 2010).

[2] Ryuta Minami et al., eds, *Performing Shakespeare in Japan* (Cambridge: Cambridge University Press, 2001); Tetsuo Anzai, *Shakespeare in Japan* (Lewiston, NY: Edwin Mellen, 1999).

[3] Kennedy, *Foreign Shakespeare*, p. 258; Ania Loomba, *Gender, Race, Renaissance Drama* (Oxford: Oxford University Press, 1992).

plays to be staged at the newly constructed Globe Theatre in London, Shakespeare's last history play is a literary enterprise that reaches back into England's past as a way to reconstruct, celebrate and project its national and imperial ambitions. King Henry's St Crispin's Day speech repeatedly appeals to a collective, English sense of 'we' in an attempt to unite the different regions of Britain represented by Captains Fluellen, Gower, Jamy and MacMorris under a single national banner: 'But we in it shall be remembered, / We few, we happy few, we band of brothers'.[4] Indeed, Henry's declaration that the members of the newly crafted national fraternity will be memorialised and become as 'familiar [...] as household words' is fulfilled in their performance in front of the Globe audience.[5] Yet imagining the nation turns out to be as much of a stumbling block as it is a solution in *Henry V*. Henry's romantic vision of a united England – much less a union between England and France by the end of the play – is imperilled by its uneasy internal fissures, best expressed in the exchange between MacMorris and Fluellen, whose observation of the MacMorris's Irish background leads to the following encounter:

> *Fluellen*: Captain MacMorris, I think, look you, under your correction, there is not many of your nation——
>
> *MacMorris*: Of my nation? What ish my nation? Ish a villain, and a bastard, and a knave, and a rascal? What ish my nation? Who talks of my nation?[6]

Inscribed in MacMorris's reply is a query that asks, just what are *the* nation and *my* nation, and are they different? Evidently, for MacMorris and the other captains, the question of nationhood is a particularly vexed one, as their regional accents and idiolects paradoxically indicate a common linguistic and cultural ancestry, all the while marking their differences.

The answer to 'What ish my nation?' remains as unintuitive today as it was during Shakespeare's lifetime. In fact, the question has increased in complexity and is freshly urgent for nations that find their geographical borders increasingly superseded by what Arjun Appadurai has called the 'ethnoscape, technoscape, finanscape, mediascape, and ideoscape', a web of networks marked by fluid exchanges of cultural and monetary capital.[7]

[4] William Shakespeare, *King Henry V*, ed. T. W. Craik (New York: Arden Shakespeare, 1995), 4.3.59–60.

[5] Shakespeare, *King Henry V*, 4.3.42.

[6] Shakespeare, *King Henry V*, 3.2.121–6.

[7] Arjun Appadurai, *Modernity at Large: Cultural Dimensions of Globalization* (Minneapolis: University of Minnesota Press, 1996), p. 306.

This is not to say that the nation as a category is no longer vital in the twenty-first century; clearly, the imaginative force of the nation in the sense defined by Benedict Anderson remains a potent and durable one, given political events in Britain and the United States in 2016.[8] If the problem of contemporary nationhood can be traced, in part, to the coexistence of transnational networks and state borders, how does MacMorris's question operate in our global landscape? What kind of answers does it generate today, and how might we re-examine our approach to global Shakespeares accordingly?

While a full investigation of these questions is outside the scope of this essay, in what follows I offer Shakespeare's reception in Korea as a case study that can help undo some of the distortions created by previous scholarship on global Shakespeares, and suggest fresh insights into this burgeoning field. As a state defined both by its long national history and its rapid modernisation, Korea is a place where the tensions between nationhood and globalising networks are particularly salient: to elide one or the other would otherwise paint an incomplete picture. Indeed, a long history of foreign invasions and political interventions has resulted in cross-cultural exchanges readily visible in Korea's national fabric. The use of the Chinese writing system until the development of *Hangul* in 1443, the shared lexical heritage with Japan and other Sinophone countries, and the common socio-religious legacies of Confucianism and Buddhism, are just a few examples. These facts are often occluded in Korean studies, and especially Korean Shakespeare studies, in attempts motivated to represent essential 'Korean' qualities against those of China or Japan.[9] Korea, of course, is also comprised of an internal network of the Democratic People's Republic of Korea and the Republic of Korea, one of the last remnants of the Cold War era that pitted western democratic nations against communist ones under the USSR and the People's Republic of China. Because Korea is a product of these internal, regional and global networks, the conversations surrounding its nationhood are especially vibrant right now: how does Korea self-consciously craft, translate and stitch together its nation on the international stage? What are the anxieties involved? Emerging nations like Korea are politically anxious to establish their cultural *bona fides*.

[8] Benedict Anderson, *Imagined Communities: Reflections on the Origin and Spread of Nationalism* (New York: Verso, 2006).

[9] Kim Moran, 'The Stages "Occupied by Shakespeare": Intercultural Performances and the Search for "Korean-ness" in Postcolonial Korea', in Poonam Trivedi and Minami Ryuta, eds, *Re-playing Shakespeare in Asia* (New York: Routledge, 2010), pp. 200–20.

This essay, then, explores Korea's encounter with Shakespeare as a way to suggest how both have mutually remapped each other. I focus, in particular, on two plays with historical and political resonance for Korea: first; *Hamlet*, a 'tragical history' that begins and ends with political turmoil; second, *The Tempest*, a play with a long history of post-colonial appropriations. The first part traces the history of Shakespeare's introduction to Korea by way of Japanese colonisation, and considers the particular importance of *Hamlet* in remembering and, in the process, exorcising the different political spectres haunting Korea's past. If *Hamlet* was used as a dramatic vehicle to memorialise and consolidate Korea's nascent modern nationhood, the second part examines Oh Tae-Suk's *Tempest* (2011), a production that, as we shall see, demonstrates how a response to Shakespeare within a national tradition is at the same time – in fact, better viewed as – a transnational response, which itself inflects the global traditions of the play with new implications and possibilities.

Ghosting Korea: 'Remember me'

Adieu, adieu, adieu, remember me.[10]

The ghost's parting instruction to Hamlet is to remember him, a wish we see fulfilled in Hamlet's restaging of his father's assassination through the play within a play. More broadly, the ghost's command also reminds us that theatre is perpetually involved in the business of memory. Marvin Carlson terms this phenomenon 'ghosting', and defines it as the 'retelling of stories already told, reenactments of events already enacted, the re-experience of emotions already experienced'.[11] Theatre, in other words, is a haunted site of performance that restages, recycles and replays the past. Remarking on the challenges of performing *Hamlet*, the actor Simon Russell Beale observes, 'there has never been a time when there aren't 800 Hamlets [...] You are aware consciously that there is a history about it.'[12] Beale's discussion pertains to the performance history of *Hamlet* in particular, but 'ghosting' as a phenomenon extends beyond the confines of a single play and haunts the stage more broadly as cultural-political praxis.

[10] William Shakespeare, *Hamlet,* eds Neil Taylor and Ann Thompson (New York: Arden Shakespeare, 2006), 1.5.91.

[11] Marvin Carlson, *The Haunted Stage: The Theatre as Memory Machine* (Ann Arbor: University of Michigan Press, 2002), p. 3.

[12] Hal Burton, *Great Acting* (New York: Bonanza, 1967), p. 140.

Indeed, as Carlson suggests, theatre acts, in many ways, as a 'repository for cultural memory'.[13]

As in Hamlet's Denmark, Korea was, and still remains, a 'state […] disjoint and out of frame'.[14] Korea formally gained its independence from Japan in 1945 and rapidly emerged as a global economic force, especially after the 1988 Seoul Olympics. Even so, contemporary Korea continues to be disjointed in its division between North and South, and the Korean peninsula remains a region beset with both domestic and international tensions. Jong-Hwan Kim notes that it was in this perpetually unstable political context that Shakespeare was first introduced to Korea, in 1906, through Japan as '*Saygusbeea*, reflecting the influence of the Japanese way of pronunciation'.[15] The importation of a Japanese *Hamlet* signalled, in many ways, the launch of Japan's political and cultural colonisation, and the subsequent afterlife of *Hamlet* in Korea has uncannily indexed key moments in the shifting geopolitics of the peninsula. For instance, Hyun-U Lee argues that the freedom fighter Duk-Soo Jang's political appropriation of 'To be or not to be' as 'To live or to die' in 1915 was an articulation of a 'fellow-feeling between Hamlet and the Korean people with their painful experience of Japanese colonialism', a camaraderie that continued to exist throughout the twentieth century.[16]

In tracing the different stages involved in the political project of surviving and exorcising the past, Hamlet's own methods of remembering Denmark's political past are instructive guides for us. Immediately following the ghost's departure, Hamlet remarks:

> Remember thee?
> Yea, from the table of my memory
> I'll wipe away all trivial fond records,
> All saws of books, all forms, all pressures past
> That youth and observation copied there
> And thy commandment all alone shall live
> Within the book and volume of my brain[17]

[13] Carlson, *The Haunted Stage*, p. 2.

[14] Shakespeare, *Hamlet*, 1.2.20.

[15] Jong-Hwan Kim, 'Shakespeare in a Korean Cultural Context', *Asian Theatre Journal*, 12.1 (1995), 37–49 (at 38).

[16] Hyun-U Lee, *Glocalizing Shakespeare in Korea and Beyond* (Seoul: Dongin Publishing, 2009), p. 105.

[17] Shakespeare, *Hamlet*, 1.5.97–103.

Here, Hamlet likens his mind to a book in which the ghost's oral account of the past has been inscribed as text. As Hamlet plans the play within a play, this metaphoric inscription of the mind then materialises as actual text in the form of a play script: 'a speech of some dozen lines, or sixteen lines, / which I would set down and insert in't'.[18] In a similar fashion, Korean iterations of *Hamlet* have memorialised within their texts the spectres of a Japanese past. The first full Korean translation by Hyun Chol appeared in 1921, a text based on Tsubouchi Shoyo's Japanese translation of *Hamlet* ten years earlier.[19] The next translation would arrive thirty years later in 1949, by Jung-Sik Sol, a Columbia University graduate: the first version not haunted by the spectre of Japanese influence, and one that perhaps symbolised Korea's formal independence from Japan four years earlier. Since then, Korean scholars have re-examined, revised and retranslated *Hamlet* six additional times as a way to purge any vestigial traces of Japanese Shakespeare.[20] The textual history of Korean *Hamlet*, then, has been intensely national, indeed nationalist, in outlook.

In performance, these political apparitions have been actively embodied. As in the case of the first translation, the first production of *Hamlet* in Korea was Kawakami Otojiro's Japanese adaptation in 1909.[21] The first full-length Korean performance would not be staged until after Korea's liberation, and productions since then have melded the political drama of the peninsula – the 'Korean War, military dictatorship, the IMF monetary crisis' and other scandals – with the volatile politics within *Hamlet*.[22] Articulated in Yun-Taek Lee's *Hamlet*, one of the more recent adaptations (1996–2005), is the urgent need to engage in a Hamlet-esque remembrance, ritualisation and restaging of Korea's maimed past. The most physically salient marker of this reflection is King Hamlet's tomb in the centre of the stage. The grave remains a constant stage device throughout the performance, as the ghost, Ophelia, Laertes, Gertrude and Claudius all occupy the tomb at some point during the production. Hamlet, in particular, lingers around or within the grave and literally breathes the 'rotten' odour of Denmark's past.[23] The grave's presence, as the theatre critic Hye-Jean Chung remarks, '[casts] a lingering shadow of

18 Shakespeare, *Hamlet*, 2.2.477–8.

19 Kim, 'Shakespeare in a Korean Cultural Context', p. 39.

20 Dong-Wook Kim, 'Shakespeare Studies and *Hamlet* in Korea', in Lee, *Glocalizing Shakespeare*, pp. 9–28 (pp. 12, 21).

21 Kim, 'Shakespeare Studies and *Hamlet* in Korea', pp. 11–12.

22 Lee, *Glocalizing Shakespeare*, p. 105.

23 Shakespeare, *Hamlet*, 1.4.90.

[past and imminent] death[s] throughout the whole play',[24] but it also evokes the equally bloody and politically scandalous past of Korea deaths: the Japanese occupation, the Korean War, military dictatorships and the Gwangju massacre (1980). The grave, in other words, is not merely an individual's tomb, but rather a collective one with the capacity to absorb or memorialise domestic and global tragedies that took place in the peninsula.

The final scene of the production expands this notion of a collective tomb by transforming the entire stage into a haunted mausoleum. Hamlet commands Horatio before his death: 'If thou didst ever hold me in thy heart / Absent thee from felicity awhile / And in this harsh world draw thy breath in pain / To tell my story'.[25] In Lee's production, the narrative told by Horatio is translated into a ghostly performance. The scene lasts over three minutes without dialogue: the whole stage is covered by a single expansive sheet of white cloth, and undead characters slowly emerge one by one from the tomb by ripping through the fabric. After circling around the stage, they exit one by one; Hamlet, however, remains on stage a while longer and gazes at the audience before exiting. Just as his father's ghostly gaze initially prompted Hamlet's journey of remembering, the final moment of the production imparts to its audience a similar instruction: 'adieu, adieu, adieu, remember me'.[26] Remember what or whom, we might ask? As in the case of *Hamlet,* Lee's production suggests that the spectres haunting the Korean peninsula both domestically and globally are obvious: the seamless white sheet is Lee's nostalgic gesture towards an unadulterated Korean past before its colonial occupation, and its destruction overtly marks Korea's current disjointed state. Yet the ways in which the audience might not only remember, but also exorcise or manage such past spectres remain unclear at best in Lee's *Hamlet.* Part of the problem is the genre of the play itself – a tragedy, or, as the subtitle of the second quarto reminds us, a 'tragical history', a literary form that requires as its denouement calamity, whether personal or political: 'Of carnal, bloody and unnatural acts, / Of accidental judgments, casual slaughters, / Of deaths put on by cunning for no cause'.[27] The play ends with Horatio's promise to recount the past of Denmark, a kingdom whose political misfortunes are not met with reprieve, but foreign occupation by the opportunistic Fortinbras.

[24] Hye-Jean Chung, *Korea Times* (2001), 21 March.

[25] Shakespeare, *Hamlet*, 5.2.330–3.

[26] Shakespeare, *Hamlet*, 1.5.91.

[27] Shakespeare, *Hamlet*, 5.2.365–7.

In order to imagine the aftermath of national tragedy, we might turn instead to another popular early modern genre – tragicomedy – that is structured to explore possible responses to tragedy. Tragicomedy, to use Shakespeare's contemporary John Fletcher's oft-cited definition, 'is not so called in respect of mirth and killing, but in respect it wants deaths, which is inough to make it no tragedy, yet brings some neere it, which is inough to make it no comedie'.[28] Several of Shakespeare's plays fit this category – *Pericles*, *The Winter's Tale*, *Cymbeline* and *The Tempest* – but it is unsurprising that director Oh Tae-Suk chose *The Tempest* to dramatise the repercussions of colonisation in Korea and reimagine different possibilities for a brave new world, or, more accurately, peninsula.

The Tempest, of course, has a long history of being associated with colonialism and post-colonialism. Indeed, by the turn of the twentieth century, the play had been reimagined everywhere from Latin America (José Enrique Rodó, 1900); through Anglo-America (Sydney Lee, 1898); to the Caribbean (Rudyard Kipling, 1898). While, as Virginia and Alden Vaughan note, Prospero was initially read as a 'benign imperialist, the conduit of language, learning, refinement and religion – the uplifter of uncivilized man', and Caliban as that uncivilised individual, a number of revisionist interpretations of the play emerged in the middle of the twentieth century.[29] Octave Mannoni's *Psychologie de la colonization* was one of the first texts to theorise the colonial relations between the play's principal characters, however problematically.[30] Subsequent publications, including George Lamming's *Pleasures of Exile* and Aime Césaire's *Une Tempête*, have explored the costs of colonialism through Caliban's perspective.[31] In the twentieth century, post-colonial interpretations have become the de facto standard. Yet, as Anston Bosman remarks in his review of Janice Honeyman's *Tempest* – a collaboration between South Africa's Baxter Theatre Centre and the Royal Shakespeare Company in 2009 – there is a sense of 'exhaustion of *The Tempest* as a vehicle for that [colonial]

[28] John Fletcher, *The Faithful Shepherdess*, ed. Cyrus Hoy, in Fredson Bowers, gen ed., *The Dramatic Works in the Beaumont and Fletcher Canon,* vol. III (Cambridge: Cambridge University Press, 1976), pp. 483–612 (p. 497).

[29] Virginia Mason Vaughan and Alden T. Vaughan, 'Introduction', in Virginia Mason Vaughan and Alden T. Vaughan, eds, *The Tempest* (New York: Arden Shakespeare, 2001), p. 102.

[30] Translated as Octave Mannoni, *Prospero and Caliban: The Psychology of Colonization* (Ann Arbor: University of Michigan Press, 1990).

[31] George Lamming, *The Pleasures of Exile* (Ann Arbor: University of Michigan Press, 1992); Aime Césaire, *Une Tempête* (Paris: Editions du Sieul, 1969), translated as *A Tempest*, trans. Richard Miller (New York: TGC Translations, 2002).

allegory and the urgent need for South African theater, now fifteen years into democracy, to appropriate Shakespeare in freshly imaginative ways'.[32] Indeed, while productions like Honeyman's *Tempest* have continued to register the colonial aftermath for both local and global audiences, they also illustrate our relative inattention to other social conflicts and collusions within the play.

Oh Tae-Suk's *Tempest* (2011), in a sense, stands at two separate but intersecting crossroads: how can the production reimagine Shakespeare's late play for the twenty-first century, and how can it also usher in a renewed sense of Korea that comes to terms with and moves beyond its colonised past? As I will suggest, the most immediately apparent directorial decision is Oh's refusal to stage a neat allegory that presents Japan as colonialist Prospero and Korea as enslaved Caliban. Indeed, the production is much richer in its adaptation of *The Tempest* than its initial reviews – which have reflexively flattened the production into a national narrative – suggest. *The Telegraph*'s critic Paul Gent has indicated that Oh's *Tempest* is 'thoroughly Korean in flavour', and notes the following: 'The biggest change of all […] is that Caliban is a monster with two heads in constant disagreement. In the final scenes, Prospero grants them their freedom by splitting them – undoubtedly a reference to North and South Korea.'[33] In a similar vein, *The Guardian*'s critic Michael Billington shares with Gent an instinct to homogenise Oh's production as one 'with its Brookish bamboo canes, Shakespearean plot and Korean music and dance […] an eloquent testament to the fusion of the best of east and west'.[34] In these reviews, we can readily observe the ways in which a national framework distorts and limits our critical understanding of a global Shakespeare production. Indeed, Gent – in his eagerness to read the two-headed Caliban and the subsequent liberation of the heads from each other as an allusion to Korea – manages to err even in simple political awareness; if Oh, in fact, were to stage a national allegory, it would make more sense to stage an eventual *union,* rather than division, between the two Koreas. Likewise, Billington's hackneyed suggestion that the production is a neat fusion

[32] Anston Bosman, 'Cape of Storms: The Baxter Theatre Centre – RSC *Tempest,* 2009', *Shakespeare Quarterly,* 61.1 (2010), 108–17 (109).

[33] Paul Gent, 'Edinburgh Festival 2011: *The Tempest*, King's Theatre, review', available at http://www.telegraph.co.uk/culture/theatre/edinburgh-festival-reviews/8701748/Edinburgh-Festival-2011-The-Tempest-Kings-Theatre-review.html, accessed 16 May 2017.

[34] Michael Billington, '*The Tempest* – Review', available at: https://www.theguardian.com/stage/2011/aug/15/the-tempest-review (accessed 10 May 2017).

between 'the best of east and west' participates in a similarly simplistic rhetoric that sees the merits of global productions primarily in their exotic aesthetics.[35]

This is not to say that Oh's *Tempest* is not Korean, both in its narrative context and its visual language. The play takes place in fifth-century Korea during the Three Kingdom era, with Naples as *Shilla* and Milan as *Garak*, the smaller state of the two. We also immediately get a taste of Oh's Korean aesthetics in the opening scene where Prospero orchestrates a tempest to the rhythmic beats of his traditional drums: the long, white sleeves of the drowning sailors' Korean costumes ripple and flow to mimic the waves of the storm. Yet we risk overlooking the larger questions surrounding the production of Oh's *Tempest* if we stubbornly seek to force the production into a preconceived national box. Indeed, the central query that sustains the production is how characters with harrowing pasts might accept, to borrow Shakespeare's words, 'what's past is prologue' and begin to explore different social possibilities for their future.[36] After all, as Oh reminds us, every character in Shakespeare's *Tempest,* with the potential exception of Ariel, is a migrant or refugee. In so doing, the Korean *Tempest* takes seriously the oft-elided motifs of seemingly miraculous reconciliation and forgiveness that are central to the genre of tragicomedy, yet seem jarringly out of place in post-colonial *Tempest* adaptations.

Appropriately, in Oh's production, there are no epic battles or confrontations that pit the master against the slave. Instead, Oh invites us into the ordinary lives of the characters stranded on the island: Miranda, who, as an immigrant, struggles to fit in with her similarly aged peers – an addition in the Korean *Tempest* – who are seen poking fun at her; the two-headed Caliban who figuratively and literally butts heads far more often with himself than Prospero; Ariel, who is less a slave than a mother figure who serves as a bridge between the teenage Miranda and her single father Prospero; Alonso, who as an aging king frets about the future of his kingdom in light of the perceived drowning of Ferdinand; and more. The fullest treatment of grief and acceptance, however, is best captured in Oh's portrayal of Prospero, who is preoccupied with managing his periods of mental breakdown rather than ruling over the island. Indeed, one of our earliest impressions of Prospero is a poignant scene in which he attempts and fails to utter words to curse those who exiled him to the island. Prospero continues to recount the traumatic

35 Billington, '*The Tempest* – Review'.

36 Shakespeare, *The Tempest,* 2.1.251.

conditions of his journey to the island – navigating for thirty days a *jjokbae,* a small boat made by carving out the insides of a single piece of wood, with 'seawater gushing out from every rat hole as the rain pours down in the middle of the stormy sea'.[37] Prospero's language here is a loose translation of Shakespeare's *Tempest*: 'A rotten carcase of a butt, not rigged, / Nor tackle, sail, nor mast – the very rats / Instinctively have quit it'.[38] Not unlike Hamlet, Prospero is haunted by this memory and attempts to exorcise or manage it by reperforming the past – a play within a play – that marks Oh Tae-Suk's most liberal adaptation of Shakespeare's *Tempest*: the entire stage turns dark save a narrow circular light on Prospero, a visual dramatisation of both his constricted space on a small boat and his limited vision as he navigates through a tempest. And we see him repeatedly remark while hyperventilating, 'thirty days on a tiny boat with a baby [...] how could they?' and 'here, here, here, bail the water'.[39]

How, then, Oh Tae-Suk's production asks, might Prospero – and to a lesser degree, the other characters – move away from trauma and learn the art of reconciliation and forgiveness? If magic has enabled Prospero to draw his enemies to him, conjure a tempest and orchestrate the events of the play, Oh suggests with Shakespeare that Prospero must learn how to relinquish his control over the narrative of the play. In Shakespeare's *Tempest,* this occurs in the Epilogue where Prospero admits, 'now my charms are all o'erthrown, / And what strength I have's mine own, / Which is most faint', a neat metatheatrical gesture to ask his audience to release him from the confines of the stage with their applause, or 'the help of your good hands'.[40] Oh's production subtly changes the idea of renouncing to sharing his magic and weaves it throughout the play: Prospero is seen teaching his magic to Ferdinand, granting the two-headed Caliban's long-standing wish to exist as two and, finally, bequeathing his magic fan to an audience member. In doing so, Oh imagines, perhaps in a rather sentimental way, a mutually collaborative future not only among the different residents of the island but also between the cast and the audience. As in Shakespeare's play, the reconciliation between Prospero and Alonso, Sebastian and Antonio seems, in many ways, to be artificial, particularly

37 Tae-Suk Oh, '*The Tempest*: Full Video', *Global Shakespeares Archive*, 2011, available at: http://globalshakespeares.mit.edu/tempest-oh-tae-suk-2011/ (accessed 10 May 2017).

38 Shakespeare, *The Tempest*, 1.2.146–8.

39 Oh, '*The Tempest*'.

40 Shakespeare, *The Tempest*, 5.1.319–21, 328.

in the highly ritualised bows exchanged among all parties. Yet the bigger point of mutual collaboration in Oh's *Tempest* is a reminder to its Korean audience that Korea need not be haunted by its traumatic experience of colonisation. In addition, it is a reminder that *The Tempest* offers rich narrative possibilities beyond Prospero and Caliban's colonial relationship, such as Miranda as a second-generation immigrant and Prospero as a political exile and single father.

More broadly, Oh Tae-Suk's *Tempest* also serves as a reminder that the creative process of adapting Shakespeare is a collaborative one that reshapes both the contemporary agent and the play itself. A nuanced exploration of the different cultural, political, historical and aesthetic dimensions of the projects of global Shakespeares, then, requires us to develop appropriately suited frameworks rather than attempt to examine all productions under the lens of nationhood. Of course, productions like Lee's *Hamlet* yield their richest interpretative possibilities when seen as a dramatic allegory for nationhood. Yet, as Oh's *Tempest* and its reviews by *The Telegraph* and *The Guardian* demonstrate, the national model is not invariably apt and, in fact, reduces the production to a caricature of itself. Alexa Huang and Anston Bosman have recently begun discussions surrounding the critical need for new frameworks: Huang demonstrates the benefits of 'locality criticism', or the meticulous interrogation of 'the cultural coordinates of a work, including the setting of a play, its performance venue, and the specificities of the cultural location of a performance [e.g. a Confucian temple in rural China]' that resists reading performances as broad, national allegories; at the other end of the spectrum, Bosman prompts us to investigate 'three global networks: a theatrical network made up chiefly of performers and directors; a textual network comprising writers, editors and translators; and a digital network deploying a range of media and devices'.[41] As global Shakespeare productions continue to be staged, new critical frameworks that register unforeseen connections, dimensions and networks will need to be developed. My brief treatment of Shakespeare in Korea has offered a critique of the ostensibly stable concept of national Shakespeares, and suggests that the study of global Shakespeares can no longer be delimited to inquiries that exclusively see national boundaries. Instead, it is tasked with exploring a

[41] Alexa Huang, *Chinese Shakespeares: Two Centuries of Cultural Exchange* (New York: Columbia University Press, 2009), pp. 25, 27; Anston Bosman, 'Shakespeare and Globalization', in Margreta de Grazia and Stanley Wells, eds, *The New Cambridge Companion to Shakespeare: Second Edition* (Cambridge: Cambridge University Press, 2010), pp. 285–301 (pp. 286–7).

landscape that is neither fully localised, nationalised nor globalised. It is my hope that this essay has provided a rubric for future work not just on Korean Shakespeares, but also on other Shakespeares in hybrid contexts now emerging or not yet imagined.

Dictionary Distortions

SARAH OGILVIE

Early on a sunny morning in Oxford in June 2005, I rode my bicycle to work at the offices of the *Oxford English Dictionary* (*OED*), and at the gates there was a large crowd blocking my way. They were protesters with megaphones and placards. The local television cameras were there, and some of the protesters had set up sofas on the sidewalk. They were potato farmers and members of the British Potato Council who were protesting against the *OED* for our definition of *couch potato* (a person who spends leisure time passively or idly sitting around, especially watching television). They wanted us to replace the phrase *couch potato* with their own invented term *couch slouch* because they felt that 'couch potato' was negatively distorting the image of the potato. As Kathryn Race, spokesperson for the British Potato Council, explained: 'We are trying to get rid of the image that potatoes are bad for you.'[1] In other words, they believed the *OED* was giving the potato a bad name and they wanted us to fix it.

Lexicography has a rich history of people objecting to a dictionary's contents, be it the exclusion of a word, the inclusion of a word, or the definition of a word. A dictionary is seen as an authoritative text that holds the power to standardise language and prescribe its meaning, spelling, pronunciation and usage. Lexicographers may strive to *describe* actual usage; but the public, especially lobbyists, often wants them to *prescribe* and to present a sanitised version, or distorted version, of usage that suits their agenda. Both of these expectations are doomed to failure of course: the public, governments or lobbyists will always want more than the lexicographer can give; and, because lexicography is a human activity and inherently subjective, the lexicographer will almost always fail in objective description. Distortion in some form will always exist.

There are many examples of dictionaries being petitioned to present a sanitised version of culture and reality. In May 2016, an online petition called for the removal of the derogatory Singapore English term *Chinese helicopter* (a Singaporean whose schooling was conducted in Mandarin

[1] For press coverage at the time, see, for example, *The Guardian*, available at: https://www.theguardian.com/uk/2005/jun/20/ruralaffairs.foodanddrink (accessed 10 May 2017).

Chinese and who has limited knowledge of English), which had been added to the *OED* earlier that year. Despite written evidence showing the word's use from 1981 to 2006, the Singaporean journalist Goh Beng Choo gathered hundreds of signatories in a petition calling for the word's removal from the dictionary.[2] 'I am against the addition of Singlish terms to the *OED* because to me', she told the *Straits Times*, 'Singlish is colloquial English, not standard English, just like [how] there are colloquial terms in many other languages.'[3] As supported by the petitioners, she wrote:

> The term 'Chinese helicopter' uses punning to tease Chinese-educated people in Singapore. It is highly disrespectful and if it stays in the dictionary, it will give the impression that it is an acceptable term. It is actually insensitive and highly derogatory and will hurt millions of elderly Chinese-educated citizens. It will pollute the language learning of young generations of Singaporeans.[4]

The notion that certain words pollute or corrupt a language, and the belief that a dictionary has the power to distort the image of a language by either sanctioning that corruption or defending the purity of a language, can be found throughout history. The nineteenth-century editors of the first edition of the *Oxford English Dictionary* faced similar criticism when reviewers chastised them for including too many 'outlandish' words; that is, words from languages outside Europe and words from varieties of English spoken outside Britain. In 1889, a reviewer of the *OED*'s first volume lamented:

> [T]hey have been far too liberal in admitting to the columns of an English dictionary a multitude of words that form no part of the English language […] In our eyes the first duty of those who devote themselves to philological studies is not only to trace the origin of language and the history of its evolution, but to defend its purity, for a corrupt and decaying language is an infallible sign of a corrupt and

2 See https://www.change.org/p/singaporeans-get-petitions-to-have-a-derogatory-term-removed-from-the-oxford-english-dictionary-87408ff4-ef43-4a7a-bb18-85cbd036ddfe (accessed 10 May 2017).

3 See http://www.straitstimes.com/singapore/education/moe-no-penalty-for-using-singlish-appropriately (accessed 10 May 2017).

4 See https://www.change.org/p/singaporeans-get-petitions-to-have-a-derogatory-term-removed-from-the-oxford-english-dictionary-87408ff4-ef43-4a7a-bb18-85cbd036ddfe (accessed 10 May 2017). Alas, the petition was one signature short of its desired goal of five hundred signatures after six months.

> decaying civilisation. It is one of the gates by which barbarism may invade and over-power the traditions of a great race.[5]

Then, as now, the public often assumes that the role of a dictionary is to shape or control reality, rather than reflect or mirror it. For some engaged readers, the dictionary has a moral duty to save society and civilisation from decay. In January 2015, a group of prominent authors protested the *Oxford Junior Dictionary*. Twenty-eight authors, including Margaret Atwood and Andrew Motion, expressed outrage that the children's dictionary had deleted words pertaining to nature and, instead, included words pertaining to computers and the internet. The actual dictionary had been published in 2007, but it took them eight years to notice that *bramble*, *clover* and *willow* were out and *blog*, *chatroom* and *database* were in. Their petition said they were 'profoundly alarmed' by the 'shocking and poorly considered' dictionary policy. They believed that the link between children and the countryside was 'in danger of becoming unraveled, to the detriment of society, culture, and the natural environment'. This group of protesters felt that the dictionary was presenting a negatively distorted view of children's worlds, and they wanted the dictionary to fix it. They wrote: 'The Oxford Dictionaries have a rightful authority and a leading place in cultural life. We believe the *Oxford Junior Dictionary* should address these issues and that it should seek to help shape children's understanding of the world, not just to mirror its trends.'[6]

Mirroring trends and describing words and cultural practices is exactly what good dictionaries strive to do; such aims are inherent to the descriptive method. A lexicographer's role is not to shape people's understandings of the world, but rather to describe them. As Robert Burchfield, chief editor of the *OED* from 1957 to 1986, put it: 'it is the duty of lexicographers to record actual usage, as shown by collected examples, not to express moral approval or disapproval of usage; dictionaries cannot be regulative in matters of social, political, and religious attitudes; there is no question of any animus on the part of lexicographers against the Jews, or the Arabs, or anyone else'.[7]

[5] 'The Literature and Language of the Age', *Edinburgh Review* (April, 1889), p. 349.

[6] Margaret Atwood et al., 'Reconnecting Kids with Nature is Vital, and Needs Cultural Leadership', email attachment sent to Oxford University Press, 12 January 2015, available at: http://www.naturemusicpoetry.com/uploads/2/9/3/8/29384149/letter_to_oup_final.pdf (accessed 10 May 2017).

[7] R. W. Burchfield, *Unlocking the Language* (London: Faber & Faber, 1989), p. 113.

Burchfield was referring to an incident in the early 1970s in which a wealthy Jewish businessman had noticed that the *OED* included a derogatory sense of the verb 'to jew', meaning 'to drive a hard bargain', which had been used in the English language from 1824 to 1972. The businessman brought an action against Oxford University Press, claiming that the definition was 'derogatory, defamatory and deplorable'. The word may have been all those things but the definition was not. The businessman lost the case in July 1973, but not before it went all the way to the high court. After the case, Burchfield received death threats, and there exists a letter in the OED Archives with cut-out newspaper letters glued onto a page of foolscap saying 'you will die'.

Getting complaints about definitions goes with the territory of being a lexicographer. Usually it is just that some people do not like the way the definition has reflected the changing use of a word. But just occasionally the lexicographer gets it plain wrong in a controversial context. This was the case in 1951 when the fourth edition of the *Concise Oxford Dictionary* was published with 'Pakistan' defined as 'A separate Moslem State in India, Moslem autonomy; (from 1947) the independent Moslem Dominion in India'. Names of countries do not normally qualify for entries in non-encyclopaedic Oxford dictionaries, so the entry should not have been there in the first place, but it certainly should not have described the country of Pakistan as part of India. When India had gained its independence from Britain in 1947, the country was partitioned. Pakistan became a separate country for the Muslim majority population of what had been British India. Getting the meaning of this word wrong was a political landmine.

The definition lay unnoticed for eight years until suddenly the Pakistani government called for a ban on the *OED* and confiscated it from all public schools, colleges and offices. Police raided the Oxford University Press offices in Karachi, and seized the final copy of the dictionary, which lay in the drawer of a typist. The British Consulate became involved and Oxford University Press apologised, issuing a correction slip to be inserted in all copies of the dictionary. The Pakistan government lifted the ban in November 1959.

These examples may seem frivolous but the point is a serious one: on one hand, the dictionary, like the Bible, is seen as an authoritative text that never changes and does not distort, and throughout history it acquired that reputation by playing a powerful role in the standardisation of language. But on the other hand, the dictionary is expected to distort, in fact is petitioned to distort, when and if the public deems it morally or ideologically necessary. It is precisely because of its authoritative status that lobbyists want to influence the contents of a dictionary for their own agenda. It is also one of the reasons why lexicographers strive to provide accurate definitions, but in the case of 'Pakistan' they failed.

Hence, there is often a tension between the general user who trusts that the content of a dictionary is never skewed, corrupted or false, and the lexicographer who may strive for such objective precision while being acutely aware that, as with any human activity, lexicography is a subjective process open to a myriad of distortions. The lexicographer nonetheless perseveres in their quest to describe the world as proficiently as they can. Dictionaries have always attracted controversy, and the controversy is always connected to issues of distortion either on the part of the lexicographer or on the part of the public's reception of the dictionary. For the public, there will be a desire for a particular distortion that suits their political agenda. For the lexicographer, on a micro level there will be distortions in definitions or in coverage of words or semantic domains across the alphabet (alphabet fatigue); on a macro level, there will be distortions in transmission across revised editions of the same dictionary text.

The history of lexicography shows that this tension has always existed. In 1607, there was an outcry when the Cambridge scholar John Cowell (1554–1611) published his law dictionary, *The Interpreter*. Cowell's dictionary is now seen as one of the best of its day, but, in seventeenth-century England, his definitions of the words 'King', 'Parliament' and 'Prerogative' resulted in him being sentenced to death. Royal power was a controversial issue and the House of Commons objected to the wording of Cowell's definition of 'King': 'he is above the Law by his absolute power', and his definition of 'Parliament', which stated that 'either the king is above the Parlement, that is the positive lawes of his kingdome, or els that he is not an absolute king'. The definition of 'Prerogative' indicated that the King 'hath a prerogative above the law'. Cowell's dictionaries were confiscated and burnt and eventually Cowell was pardoned, but he was forced to resign his Cambridge professorship, and died four months later.[8]

Transmission across versions of the same dictionary creates its own unique type of dictionary distortion. An example of distortion of this type involves a discovery I made while working as an editor on the *OED* and includes an interesting epilogue in which my own discoveries of the distortion were in turn distorted by the media; that is, a case of distortion

8 The controversy did not go away. Four decades later, there was a civil war and James's son Charles I was executed for trying to rule without Parliament and exercise his 'prerogative'.

of the description of distortion, or a case of (as I like to call it) 'distortion squared'.

After working on dictionaries in Australia for ten years, in 2000 I went to work on the *OED* in Oxford. My role was to work on the third edition of the *OED* and to edit the words coming into English from 'World Englishes' (varieties of English around the world) and from languages outside Europe – whether that was Sanskrit or Arabic or North American Indian languages. The first edition of the *OED* was started in 1857 and finally published in 1928. Its four main editors were James Murray, Henry Bradley, Charles Onions and William Craigie. In 1933, the *OED Supplement* was published by the two still-living editors, Charles Onions and William Craigie, and it comprised all the words and meanings that had been missed during the compilation of the first edition. The dictionary lay in abeyance until the 1950s, when Robert Burchfield revised the 1933 *Supplement* and published a four-volume supplement in 1972, 1976, 1982 and 1986. Burchfield's supplement was merged with the first edition and published as the *OED* second edition in 1989.[9] The second edition of the *OED* was not strictly a 'second' edition, in the sense that it was not a revision of the contents of the first edition, but rather merely a compilation of the first edition with the addition of Burchfield's *Supplement* plus a few thousand extra new words. So, when I started as an editor on the third edition of the *OED* in 2000, which was to be a true third edition (that is, a revision of all the entries in the second edition), most of the entries I worked on had been untouched for over a hundred years since they initially appeared in the first edition. Most of the entries had been written by Murray, Bradley, Onions and Craigie, though some had been written by Burchfield.

When I started working there, I came to the task with the same understanding about the history of the *OED* that most might have: that the early editors in the nineteenth century were particularly Anglocentric and had deliberately kept out foreign words, words from World Englishes and swear words, but that those distortions in the coverage of the lexicon had been fixed by Robert Burchfield, the New Zealander mentioned earlier,

[9] On this, see R. W. Burchfield, and H. Aarsleff, *The Oxford English Dictionary and the State of the Language* (Washington: Library of Congress, 1998). See also W. A. Craigie and C. T. Onions, eds, *A New English Dictionary on Historical Principles. Founded on the Materials Collected by the Philological Society. Edited by James A. H. Murray, Henry Bradley, William A. Craigie, C. T. Onions. Introduction, Supplement, and Bibliography* (Oxford: Clarendon Press, 1933); and J. A. H. Murray, ed., *A New English Dictionary on Historical Principles, Part I. A-ANT* (Oxford: Clarendon Press, 1884). See further, notes 13 and 14 below.

who had come to Oxford as a Rhodes Scholar in the 1950s and later became the first non-British chief editor of the *OED* from 1957 to 1986. The consensus at the time can be summed up by Bailey and Görlach: 'while the initial editors of the OED virtually excluded words not in general use in Great Britain and the United States, their successors have recognized the international dimension of English by what the editor [Robert Burchfield] calls "bold forays into the written English of regions outside the British Isles, particularly that of North America, Australia, New Zealand, South Africa, India, and Pakistan"'.[10] However, the more I started editing these words, the more I got to know the men whose work I was editing, and the more this picture did not make sense. I started to identify patterns in the *OED* entries that contradicted this story of 'progress' from imperialism to post-colonialism in which coverage of foreign words improved in the *OED*.

The early editors seemed to be including far more words from outside Britain than we had been led to believe. There were thousands of them. From the first page of the dictionary, published in 1884, James Murray had put in words from all over the world: South African animals such as *aardvark* and *aardwolf*; words from the West Indies and South America such as *agouti*, a guinea pig, *alouatte*, a howling monkey and *albacore*, a fish found in the West Indies and the Pacific; Australian plants and animals such as *adansonia*, 'the Cream of Tartar Tree, or Sour Gourd of N. Australia'; *adder*, 'Death Adder of N. Australia'; and *ant-eater*, 'the aculeated, or Porcupine Ant eater (*Echidna)* of the order *Monotremata*, found in Australia'; and words from Indian English such as *aal*, a red dye; *abkari*, the sale of alcohol in India; *adjutant*, a species of stork in India; *amah*, a wet-nurse; and *amildar*, 'a native factory manager, or agent, in India'. And when they did include these words, they dealt with them brilliantly, in a very open way for the late nineteenth century. I was constantly amazed by how much and what the Victorian editors had included.

Materials in the archives revealed that the early editors did this in the face of pressure not to do so. Letters in the archives show that consultants (such as the anthropologist E. B. Tylor) advised them to exclude 'outlandish words'; the Delegates of Oxford University Press pressured them to save space and delete words that 'have no place in an English Dictionary'; and reviewers (as we have seen) urged them to stop corrupting the English language with 'barbarous' and 'peculiar' vocabulary. '[T]here is no surer or more fatal sign of the decay of a language than in the interpolation of

10 Richard Bailey and Manfred Görlach, eds, *English as a World Language* (Ann Arbor: University of Michigan Press, 1982), p. 4.

barbarous terms and foreign words; if a great dictionary is to be regarded as a treasury of the language it should give no currency to false and fraudulent issues', bemoaned the *Edinburgh Review*.[11]

But Murray and his team ignored the critics and kept putting in not hundreds but thousands of loanwords and World Englishes. As I went through the dictionary word by word and entry by entry, it seemed that rather than Burchfield being portrayed as the saviour who opened the pages of the *OED* to words from outside Europe, the credit should go to the early editors who actually did include them in the first place. But this was merely a hunch and, to see if it was true, I needed to compare two versions of the same text: one written by the early editors and one written by Robert Burchfield. The 1933 *Supplement* and Burchfield's *Supplement* provided the perfect comparative sources, as one was based on the other; that is, the 1933 *Supplement* was the base text for Burchfield's *Supplement*. Both texts shared the same aims and remit – to supplement the first edition of the *OED*, and therefore, they shared potentially the same balance of vocabulary.

By comparing over nine thousand dictionary entries (10 per cent of each dictionary) across nineteen parameters, I discovered that the editors of the 1933 *Supplement* included loanwords and World Englishes in higher proportions than their successor, Burchfield, who did two unusual things: he reinstated tramlines (two parallel lines beside headwords indicating that a word is 'alien and not yet naturalized') and he deleted 17 per cent of loanwords and World Englishes in the 1933 *Supplement*. Usually a word is never deleted from the *OED*: if it becomes obsolete, a dagger symbol is placed beside the headword but it is never deleted.[12]

The comparison revealed that the 1933 *Supplement* included proportionally more (5.4 per cent) loanwords and World Englishes than

[11] See Sarah Ogilvie, *Words of the World: A Global History of the Oxford English Dictionary* (Cambridge, Cambridge University Press, 2013), pp. 74–80; and Anon, 'The Literature and Language of the Age', *Edinburgh Review* (April, 1889), p. 348.

[12] At first, I thought Burchfield probably deleted entries without much evidence (one or two quotations) but this is not the case: there are examples of words with plenty of evidence, which would easily qualify them for inclusion. For example, *shape*, *n*[2] a Tibetan councillor, appears in the 1933 *Supplement* with three quotations from a variety of sources; and *boviander,* the name in British Guyana for a person of mixed race living on the riverbanks, appears with four quotations taken from a selection of sources (books, newspapers and traveller's tales) showing the word used in full English contexts. See more on the dictionary policies and practices of Robert Burchfield in Ogilvie, *Words of the World*, pp. 165–209.

Burchfield's *Supplement*. Of the 10 per cent sample of each dictionary, 25.8 per cent of Burchfield's *Supplement* was loanwords and World Englishes, as compared with 31.2 per cent of the 1933 *Supplement*. This study also revealed that Burchfield was not the *OED* editor who included the most World Englishes and loanwords; proportionally, Charles Onions included more World Englishes and loanwords than both Burchfield and Craigie. Clearly the early editors were not as Anglocentric as scholars and readers thought. In fact, these early editors were criticised in their day for being too inclusive. So when in the twentieth century did readers start to think the opposite was true? Where and when had this distortion taken place? I started hunting for the source of this misrepresentation and, quite unexpectedly, all paths eventually led back to Robert Burchfield.

Burchfield had written in the preface to the first of the four volumes of his *OED Supplement*, published in 1972: 'Readers will discover by constant use of the Supplement that the written English of regions like Australia, South Africa, and India have been accorded the kind of treatment that lexicographers of a former generation might have reserved for the English of Britain alone.'[13]

In the fourth volume of his *Supplement*, Burchfield criticised his predecessors for what he called 'Murray's insular policy':[14]

> The main departure from the policy of Murray was my decision to try to locate and list vocabulary of all English-speaking countries, and not merely that of the United Kingdom. For the most part Murray preferred to fend off overseas words until they had become firmly entrenched in British use. Words more or less restricted to North America, Australia, New Zealand, South Africa, the West Indies, and so on, were treated almost like illegal immigrants. All that has been changed and, as far as possible, equality of attention has been given to the sprawling vocabulary of all English-speaking countries. At a time when the English language seems to be breaking up into innumerable clearly distinguishable varieties, it seemed to me important to abandon Murray's insular policy and go out and find what was happening to the language elsewhere.[15]

Tracing the reception of Burchfield's writing, one discovers that scholars, the popular media and reviewers all echoed him, without ever checking

13 R. W. Burchfield, *A Supplement to the Oxford English Dictionary*, I (Oxford: Clarendon Press, 1972), p. xv.

14 R. W. Burchfield, *A Supplement to the Oxford English Dictionary*, IV (Oxford: Clarendon Press, 1986), p. xi.

15 Burchfield, *Supplement*, IV, p. xi.

the work of his predecessors. For example, Charlotte Brewer highlighted that Burchfield was 'determined to include as much non-English English as possible' and John Simpson repeats the story in his entry for Burchfield in the *Oxford Dictionary of National Biography*: 'Burchfield's New Zealand background made him particularly conscious that the *Supplement* should enhance the *OED*'s coverage of international varieties of English, and the achievement of this remains one of his legacies to the dictionary.'[16] The *Globe and Mail* in Canada explained that: 'Mr. Burchfield, in his preface to the final supplement, said the dictionary's original editors resisted including foreign words "until they had become firmly entrenched in British use," and that some words were treated "almost like illegal immigrants".'[17] Philip Howard in *The Times* noted that '[Murray's] successor, born and educated at Wanganui, New Zealand, has a more liberal and realistic attitude to overseas Englishes and loanwords from foreign languages'.[18] Alas, this was exactly the message that Burchfield had given about his own lexicographic practice, and it was echoed widely in popular newspapers and scholarly articles alike, all of which painted a distorted picture of the work of the early and later *OED* editors.[19]

This prompts three questions: why did Burchfield distort the image of the early editors as Anglocentric when they were not? Why did he distort the picture of the first edition of the *OED* as excluding words from outside Britain when it did not? And finally, why did he present a distorted image of himself as the champion of these words when, in fact, his policy and practice could be judged as more conservative than his predecessors?

The answer to all these questions is that we do not know. Burchfield died in 2004, and he left no record that would suggest his distortion was deliberate. In fact, I believe that his practice was *not* deliberate. He was one of the most notable lexicographers of the twentieth century, and my suggestion is that he was typical of the tendency of the 1960s and 1970s to present a history and story of 'progress': that is, a smooth story from

[16] Charlotte Brewer, 'The Second Edition of the *Oxford English Dictionary*', *Review of English Studies*, 44 (1993), 313–42; John Simpson, 'Burchfield, Robert William (1923–2004)', *Oxford Dictionary of National Biography* (Oxford: Oxford University Press, 2008), available at: http://www.oxforddnb.com/view/article/93833 (accessed 8 November 2016).

[17] *The Globe and Mail* (Canada), 9 May 1986, p. 9.

[18] *The Times,* 8 May 1986, p. 12.

[19] See Ogilvie, *Words of the World*, pp. 165–205, for more on the writings and speeches by Burchfield that detail his lexicographic practice, and the ways in which his message was repeated in popular newspapers and scholarly articles alike.

imperialism to post-colonialism in which coverage of words of the world improved in the *OED*. Burchfield sincerely believed that the early *OED* editors who lived and worked at the height of the British Empire were conservative in their policy and practice relating to words of the world, and I think he genuinely believed that he was the post-colonial hero who opened the pages of the dictionary to these words for the first time. Because Burchfield told this story not only as chief editor of the *OED* but also as a New Zealander, no one questioned it and no one noticed the distortion. Another reason is that, in the scholarly world of linguistics, the 1970s was when the first work on varieties of English started to come about. Perhaps he wanted to be seen as part of that new emerging field.

I am very mindful in this not to ascribe mendacity to Burchfield: I can only believe that he believed he was doing what he said he was doing. But it reminds us crucially that a lexicographer's practice may not match his or her policy or rhetoric, and it demonstrates the value of combining quantitative analysis with qualitative. I first discovered these findings in 2004, while working as an editor on the *OED* and, while my colleagues and I were all surprised, we just got on with the job and immediately began the task of putting the missing words back into the dictionary. I gave a conference paper about it and published an article about it in a refereed journal, and no one made any fuss.[20]

However, the story does not end there. In 2013, I published a book on the *OED* called *Words of the World*, which primarily focused on the pioneering work of the early editors of the *OED*, showing how they went out of their way to include words from all over the world, in spite of pressures to exclude them. One chapter documented Burchfield's exclusion of the World English words from the 1933 *Supplement*. Interestingly, it was this section of the book that the popular press chose to target and, consequently, distort. Indeed, my attempt to tell a 'good news' story about the early editors was ignored and instead the journalists honed in on Burchfield, implying that he was xenophobic and insisting that his deletion of entries from the *OED* was intentional, covert and surreptitious, none of which I had stated or implied.

The front page of *The Guardian*, the British newspaper, led with 'Former

[20] Sarah Ogilvie, 'From "Outlandish Words" to World English: the legitimisation of global varieties of English in the Oxford English Dictionary', in G. Williams and S. Vessier, eds, *Proceedings of the 11th EURALEX International Conference* (Lorient, Universite de Bretagne-Sud, 2004), pp. 651–8; and Sarah Ogilvie, 'Rethinking Burchfield and World Englishes', *International Journal of Lexicography*, 21.1 (2008), 23–59.

OED Editor Covertly Deleted Thousands of Words, Book Claims', and explained it thus:

> An eminent former editor of the *Oxford English Dictio*nary covertly deleted thousands of words because of their foreign origins and bizarrely blamed previous editors, according to claims in a book published this week.[21]

The public responded vehemently in the Comments section of the newspaper website. 'I never liked Burchfield', wrote madcom, 'His version of *Fowler's English Usage* was didactic and he had taken all the character and wit from the original. He was too dour to have been given charge of a dictionary.' Godburn asked: 'Does that mean we nearly ended up being as xenophobic as the French?' Despite the fact that nowhere in the book had I attributed mendacity to Burchfield, nor implied that he secretly or surreptitiously deleted the words, *The New York Times* insisted on calling it a 'Dictionary Dust Up', and reported that 'Word guardians have been up in arms this week over claims in a new book about the *Oxford English Dictionary*, which asserts that one of its former editors, Robert Burchfield, surreptitiously expunged hundreds of words with foreign origins.'[22] 'Who the devil did he [Burchfield] think he was? Certainly no scholar', commented ACW from New Jersey, 'He moved from descriptive to prescriptive, and I think most users of the *OED* expect the former.' I tried to defend Burchfield and correct what was being unfairly said about him, but I am not sure I was successful.

What started as an academic uncovering of a persistent distortion about the content and creation of the *OED* throughout the twentieth century ended up as an emotional and vitriolic distortion in newspapers and social media. This was no doubt because of the persistent belief that dictionaries are immutable – they must never change and must always tell the truth and must be comprehensive – rather than appreciating that lexicography is a human endeavour, prone to subjectivity, partiality, error and distortion, like any other human pursuit. An engaged reading public will often complain that a dictionary includes or excludes certain words, or defines them one way rather than another, and will continue to put pres-

[21] Alison Flood, Review, available at: https://www.theguardian.com/books/2012/nov/26/former-oed-editor-deleted-words (accessed 20 February 2016).

[22] Leslie Kaufman, Review, available at: http://www.nytimes.com/2012/11/29/books/sarah-ogilvie-on-deletions-from-the-oxford-english-dictionary.html (accessed 20 February 2016).

sure on dictionary makers to change what is 'wrong'. Dictionary makers will always resist this because they are aiming to *describe* language usage rather than prescribe it. Doomed to failure, there will always be a tension between both sides.

Wherever there is controversy there is distortion of some kind. Whether the distortion pertains to definitions of the word 'King' in the seventeenth century or 'Pakistan' in the 1950s, or the inclusion of foreign words in the *OED* in the nineteenth century, or derogatory terms for 'to jew' in the 1970s, or 'couch potato' in 2005, or nature words in children's dictionaries in 2015, or the phrase 'Chinese helicopter' in 2016, or my own experience of trying to clarify the distortion of my discovery of a distortion, we see that the public, the popular press and governments thrive on distortion, and where dictionaries are involved I suspect they always will.

Where Do Indigenous Origin Stories and Empowered Objects Fit into a Literary History of the American Continent?

TIMOTHY POWELL

For all of the changes that American literature has been through since the Culture Wars – African American, Asian American, Latina/o studies, feminism, queer theory, post-colonialism and transnationalism, to name just a few – perhaps the least understood part of American literary history is its very beginnings, rooted in Indigenous origin stories passed down as part of the oral tradition. If we return for a moment to the benchmark for measuring the increasing diversity of the canon of American literature, *The Norton Anthology of American Literature*, this distortion comes clearly into focus. As of this writing, the current eighth edition of the *Norton Anthology*'s opening section, 'Stories of the Beginning of the World', contains just two origin stories – Navajo and Iroquois – before Columbus and the conquistadors claim the continent and colonise American literary history.[1]

How can one measure such a massive distortion? First, the temporal distortion: recent archaeological excavations at San Bartolo revealed Maya glyphs in murals dating to around 300 BCE, nearly two millennia before Columbus wrote in his journal, 'With fifty men we could subjugate them all and make them do what whatever we want.'[2] The Kwakwaka'wakw of British Columbia are still recounting stories performed as dances, with magnificent carved masks, and songs accompanied by a huge drum made out of a hollowed-out cedar log. The Kwakwaka'wakw say these stories are six thousand years old and very much alive. Second, the cultural distortion: in the Unites States alone there are currently more than 540 federally recognised tribes, each with their own distinct origin stories; to include only stories from two cultures thus grossly diminishes the cultural diversity hidden behind the term 'Native American'. Third, the formal

[1] Nina Baym and Robert S. Levine, eds, *The Norton Anthology of American Literature: Eighth Edition* (New York: W. W. Norton & Company, 2012).

[2] Howard Zinn, *A People's History of the United States* (New York: Harper & Row, 2016), p. 1.

distortion: as the folklorist Barre Toelken points out, the term 'oral tradition' can inadvertently oversimplify a more holistic approach that could be more fully described as 'performance of arts, crafts, foods, stories, songs, and dances' enlivened by an 'emotional commitment in the form of body movement, breathing, use of vocal cords, tasting, and hearing the resultant "texts", better understood as "constellations of meaning"'.[3] And yet, because American literary scholars do not, generally speaking, do field work, most encounter origin stories primarily in print form. As Nora and Richard Dauenhauer, distinguished anthropologists of Tlingit culture, observe: 'The writing down of oral literature, no matter how well-intentioned or how well carried out, petrifies it [...] A petrified log may look like wood, but it is actually stone.'[4]

Rather than going a mile wide and attempting to survey the hundreds of Indigenous cultures across the continent, this analysis endeavours to go a mile deep by studying very carefully one particular origin story told by one very special Ojibwe elder, my *we'eh*, Larry Aitken from the Leech Lake reservation in northern Minnesota. More specifically, I want to focus on a videotape recording made at the University of Pennsylvania Museum of Archaeology and Anthropology, where Larry told an origin story accompanied by the playing of a drum from the museum's collection. In keeping with this essay's intent to situate such holistic expressions within the context of American literary history, the story is meant to trouble the categories of 'author', 'title', 'publication date' and 'genre' that implicitly structure chronological representations of American literary history. My method for doing so will be to treat Larry Aitken's teachings, which I have recorded over the course of our fifteen-year friendship, with the same respect given to academic scholarship in the field of early American literature.

Bizindan ['Listen']

'If you work with us', Larry Aitken explains, '*bizindan* ['listen'], you accept the body of Ojibwe knowledge and infuse it into your own work.'[5] The ultimate goal of this essay is to accept what scholars call Anishinaabe ontology and epistemology, or what Larry would call cosmology, as a

[3] Barre Toelken, *Anguish of Snails: Native American Folklore in the West* (Boulder, CO: University Press of Colorado, 2003), p. 13.

[4] Julie Cruikshank, *Social Life of Stories: Narrative and Knowledge in the Yukon Territory* (Vancouver: University of British Columbia Press, 2000), p. xiii.

[5] Larry Aitken in discussion with the author, 15 October 2008.

viable way to interpret a video that Larry and I made at the Penn Museum in 2009, with the assistance of Lucy Williams (Jeremy A. Sabloff Keeper of the North American collections) and David McDonald (videographer and editor of DMcD Productions). The video, though very short, provides a remarkable insight into the spiritual relationship between a drum from the Penn Museum's collection and Larry Aitken in his traditional role of *oshkabewis*, or what might be roughly translated as a 'spiritual translator'. As a former professor of American literature now teaching in a Religious Studies department, restoring the spiritual dimensions of the origin story is important to me, as it most definitely is to Larry. The challenge, plainly stated, is to take seriously Larry Aitken's perspective that the drum as an empowered object tells the origin story and he, with great humility, simply translates. 'Our human shortcoming', Larry explains, 'is to have animate objects [e.g. drums] not known to the academy as storytellers and wisdom keepers.'[6]

One of the fundamental tenets of anthropology, dating back to the teachings of Franz Boas, is the notion of cultural relativism or the idea that cultures should be studied from the perspective of those within the circle of traditional knowledge, not judged from without by the standard of 'objectivity' derived from western science. It may be helpful to scholars of American literature to come at the interpretation of the story I'm calling 'The Heart Beat of Mother Earth' through the work of anthropologists such as Tim Ingold and Colin Scott. Ingold, for example, writes of Indigenous storytellers 'seeing into' a world where Indigenous songs, stories and designs serve to conduct the attention of performers into the world, deeper and deeper, as one proceeds from outward appearance to an ever more poetic involvement. At its most intense, the boundaries between person and place, between the self and the landscape, dissolve altogether.[7]

In 'Rethinking the Animate, Re-Animating Thought', Ingold writes of objects like a drum: 'animacy is not a property of persons imaginatively projected onto the things with which they perceive themselves to be surrounded. Rather [...] it is the dynamic, transformative potential of the entire field of relations within which beings of all kinds, more or less person-like or thing-like, continually bring one another into existence.'[8]

6 Larry Aitken in discussion with the author, 15 October 2008.

7 Tim Ingold, *The Perception of the Environment: Essays on Livelihood, Dwelling and Skill* (London: Routledge, 2000), p. 56.

8 Tim Ingold, 'Rethinking the Animate, Re-Animating Thought', *Ethnos*, 71.1 (2006), 9–20 (10).

To translate back into more practical terms, in the course of this very short video, Larry Aitken is 'nudged' by the drum, an animate being in the Ojibwe cosmology, to tell an origin story and then to play the drum, thus 'dissolving' the 'boundaries' between the elder and the drum, or what Ingolds calls the 'performer' and 'beings of all kinds'. This allows us to see 'deeper and deeper' into Ojibwe cosmology and perhaps American literature. It should be noted that the 'dynamic, transformative potential of the [...] field of relations' cannot be accessed by anyone who, in this case, visits the Penn Museum. To activate this dynamic relationship, requires an elder like Larry Aitken, who has spent his life working with traditional knowledge keepers from his community in the Ojibwe language, learning a specific skill-set not readily accessible to scholars of American literature.

Having said that, anthropologists such as Colin Scott, who works closely with Cree hunters and wisdom keepers in northern Canada, are coming closer to describing the kind of interactions we will see in the video. Larry Aitken's understanding of Anishinaabe cosmology, for example, connects the drum back from the academic confines of the Penn Museum to the animals and environment of the Anishinaabe homelands. 'Humans are so anthropomorphic', Larry told me later, 'that we struggle to believe the drum is a living being. When we get over ourselves we will realise the drum was once the hide of an animal, the drum was once a tree that transformed itself into the instrument of a wisdom keeper.'[9] Colin Scott effectively translates this traditional knowledge into academic prose when he writes: 'In the interaction of a human with a tree, intelligence lies not "inside the head of the human actor" [...] Rather, it is immanent in the total system of perception and action constituted by the co-presence of the human and the tree within a wider environment.'[10] Scott writes of his own personal experience hunting bear with Cree people: 'I was inducted, as a matter of personal biography, into the gravity of my responsibility to the bear, and by extension, to all for whom the bear has responsibility, including less powerful animals and, of course, properly behaving humans.' And yet while he advocates for 'taking seriously Cree premises about the world and our actions in it', he admits that such principles 'are surely beyond scientific proof or refutation'.[11]

Interestingly, theorists working outside the context of Indigenous culture have begun to construct new critical paradigms that express ideas

[9] Larry Aitken in discussion with the author, 15 October 2008.

[10] Colin Scott, 'Spirit and Practical Knowledge in the Person of the Bear among Wemindji Cree Hunters', *Ethnos*, 71.1 (2006), 51–66 (53).

[11] Scott, 'Spirit and Practical Knowledge', p. 60.

known to Indigenous people for millennia. Jane Bennett's *Vibrant Matter: A Political Ecology of Things* (2010), for example, sets out to 'focus on the task of developing a vocabulary and syntax for, and thus a better discernment of, the active powers issuing from nonsubjects', thus breaking down the 'onto-theological binaries of life/matter [...] organic/inorganic'.[12] In this 'ontological field', Bennett continues, '*all* forces and flows (materialities) are or can become lively, affective, and signaling. And so an affective, speaking human body is not *radically* different from the affective, signaling nonhumans with which it coexists, hosts, enjoys, [and] serves.'[13] Bennett, Bruno Latour and other theorists working on rethinking materiality deserve a great deal of credit for expanding the philosophical imaginary. As we will see, the drum in the video functions as what Bruno Latour calls an 'actant' – 'a source of action that can be either human or nonhuman; it is that which has efficacy, can *do* things [...] produce effects'.[14] In other words, the drum communicates with Larry Aitken, compelling him to tell an origin story and subsequently to play the drum. As Larry explained to me afterwards: 'The drum can recognise a wisdom keeper and knows how to talk to them. The wisdom keeper is startled, surprised by the force nudging them, trying to contact the wisdom keeper to do something.'[15]

Where this analysis departs from Bennett's concept of *vital materiality* is in terms of the role that spirituality plays in the interaction between the drum and the wisdom keepers. Bennett writes that 'what I am calling personal affect or material vibrancy is not a spiritual supplement or "life force" added to the matter said to house it [...] This vibrant matter is *not* the raw material for the creative activity of humans or God.'[16] To strip away spirituality risks also stripping away cultural specificity, a problem too often found in the abstractions of theoretical writings in an academic context. As we will see in the close reading of the video under discussion, Ojibwe spirituality plays a crucial role in awakening the drum ceremonially, empowering what Larry calls 'the head spirit of the drum' to share the traditional knowledge it has kept faithfully for 'eons of time'.[17]

12 Jane Bennett, *Vibrant Matter: A Political Ecology of Things* (Durham, NC: Duke University Press, 2009), p. x.

13 Bennett, *Vibrant Matter*, p. 117.

14 Bennett, *Vibrant Matter*, p. vii.

15 Larry Aitken in discussion with the author, 15 October 2008.

16 Bennett, *Vibrant Matter*, p. xiii.

17 'The Heartbeat of Mother Earth', *YouTube*, uploaded by Timothy B. Powell, available at: https://youtu.be/HA3XWz2iIdE (accessed 10 October 2016).

I want to argue here that literary scholars can play a meaningful role in productively expanding current understandings of vibrant matter. Spirits and magical thinking, as we all know, have been an essential part of literature, from Odysseus's descent into the underworld to consult with Tiresias, to Hamlet's confrontation with his father's ghost on the ramparts of Elsinore Castle, to Harry Potter's power to mesmerise a generation with feats of magic. I will return to the role that literary scholars can play in revealing new insights into a holistic approach to Indigenous origin stories at the end of the essay, but first I want to turn to a close reading of the video to explain exactly how it is that a drum comes to tell an origin story.

A Drum Speaks

My goal in this section is to provide a richly nuanced visual and cultural context for a very short origin story that, standing alone on the white page, translated into English, would barely merit attention from a literary scholar. The story, very simply, could be rendered as:

> A drum is *dewe'igan.* It means drum, *dewe'igan.* When you hit the drum, it awakens. They say that the first sound ever, in the beginning, was the sound of the drum. And the sound of the drum was the beginning of the heartbeat of mother earth. When you first heard the drum it was the heart starting on this earth. And that's why the old ones say, the first sound ever heard for all time was boom, boom, boom. [Ojibwe] which means the drum awakens the earth, *niimaamaa-aki*, our mother earth. Boom, boom, boom.[18]

The simplicity of the English transcription, however, belies the role of vibrant matter like the drum that Larry Aitken holds in his hand as he tells this story. Within Ojibwe cosmology, the drum is considered to be an animate being, or what Latour would call an *actant*, and that plays a complex role in the way that the story works to transport the attentive listener all the way back to the very beginnings of life on this planet. Stories like this, I will argue, possess the power to teach us to see anew the distorted origins of American literary history in ways that may yet prove to be transformative.

To get there, we need to think about the cultural work that Indigenous stories do within the communities where they are told. As Julie Cruikshank notes of her work with Angela Sydney, a Deishseetaan (Crow) woman of

[18] 'The Heartbeat of Mother Earth'.

both Tagish and Tlingit ancestry, 'She demonstrates first what a story *says* and then what it can *do* when engaged as a strategy of communication. Her use of narrative suggests that oral tradition is better understood as a social activity than as a reified text, that meanings do not inhere in a story but are created in the everyday situations in which they are told.'[19] This insight will prove helpful as we begin to move through the video slowly and to see the difference between the reified text in the paragraph above and the spontaneous creation of a story as a social activity resulting from the interaction between the spirit of the drum and an Ojibwe *oshkabewis*, trained to act as a go-between or translator for the drum.

The video begins, tellingly, with an invocation of the spirit of the birchbark objects – a winnowing basket, a large maple-syrup basket, miniature canoes, and drums – that Larry requested the museum staff to bring out for his visit. 'All these things [...] have spirit', Larry explains. 'There is spirit in the drum.'[20] The video's editor, David McDonald, then cuts away to a video of Larry at a powwow in the gymnasium of the Itasca Community College Powwow, where Larry taught at the time. The juxtaposition serves to provide a visual metaphor for the relationship that connects Larry to his people and a vibrant, ongoing system of knowledge. Wearing his traditional regalia, Larry leads a processional around the dance drum, carrying the American flag. The image, in this context, encourages Americanists to feel connected to places such as the Leech Lake reservation, where Larry lives. As the Pomo scholar Greg Sarris stated in his important book *Keeping Slug Woman Alive: A Holistic Approach to American Indian Texts*: 'I am not privileging an Indian's point of view regarding the texts and topics considered. I am not interested in pitting Indians against non-Indians [...] Instead, these essays try to show that all of us can and should talk to one another, that each group can inform and be informed by the other.'[21] While I agree with Sarris's generous spirit of collaboration, I would add that in this case I am privileging Larry Aitken's point of view in the sense that, at a place like the University of Pennsylvania, traditional wisdom keepers' voices are rarely heard. I do agree with Sarris, though, that academic scholars and the keepers of traditional knowledge can forge mutually beneficial relationships like the one seen in 'The Heartbeat of Mother Earth'.

By setting the origin story quoted above in relation to the interaction

19 Cruikshank, *Social Life of Stories*, pp. 25, xv.

20 'The Heartbeat of Mother Earth'.

21 Greg Sarris, *Keeping Slug Woman Alive: A Holistic Approach to American Indian Texts* (Berkeley: University of California Press, 1993), p. 7.

between a traditional Ojibwe wisdom keeper and a drum 'enlivened' by Larry's presence, new dimensions of the story begin to come into view, adorning the bare text. Nurit Bird-David explains such interactions as a form of 'relational epistemology': the 'study of how things-in-situations relate to the actor-perceiver'.[22] More specifically, the drum in the museum [things-in-situation] reacts to an actor-perceiver who recognises *dewe'igan* as an equally, if not greater, wisdom keeper. Together, they work to tell the story of the precise moment when the Earth came into being, a primordial setting that also contributes to the story being told. Interestingly, the story does not really exist as text at all, but rather as what Cruickshank calls a 'social activity' in which the meanings 'are created' by the interaction between the different kinds of vibrant matter that come together spontaneously.

One way to metaphorically 'see' the invisible spirit of the drum interacting with the wisdom keeper is to note what linguists call the act of 'code switching' or, simplistically stated, those moments in which Larry shifts from English to *Ojibwemowin* ('the Ojibwe language'). I say 'simplistic' because, as we will see, each instance of code switching has its own unique semantic valence. Immediately upon finishing the story quoted above, for example, Larry switches into Ojibwe, which he then translates as: 'the drum awakens the earth, *niimaamaa-aki* (Mother Earth)'. As Margaret Kovach observes, when reconstructing 'tribal epistemologies and Indigenous research frameworks, one must first assert the interrelationship between Indigenous language structure and worldview'.[23] In keeping with Kovach's insight, I want to suggest that the linguistic shifts also indicate epistemological shifts, wherein the storyteller enters into an increasingly complex relationship with what Larry calls the 'invisible forces' or *manidoog* (spirits) that can only be understood in relation to Ojibwe cosmology.

In this instance, Larry speaks Ojibwe to the spirits of his elders, 'the old ones', who taught Larry as a boy about traditional knowledge. Having summoned the spirits of *chi-aah ya agg* (wisdom keepers), Larry invokes a traditional way of knowing the world through the Ojibwe language. 'What we do whenever we hit the drum is to awaken something ceremonially. It might mean to awaken [...] a being or objects that are

22 Nurit Bird-David, '"Animism" Revisited: Personhood, Environment, and Relational Epistemology 1', *Current Anthropology*, 40.S1 (1999), S67–S91 (79).

23 Margaret Elizabeth Kovach, *Indigenous Methodologies: Characteristics, Conversations, and Contexts* (Toronto: University of Toronto Press, 2010), p. 59.

here.'[24] He then switches for a second time into Ojibwe, but instead of recalling the voices of elders he begins to address the vibrant objects around him: 'Attention, attention, birch bark vessels. Attention, we're about talk. And they're all listening.'[25] As Larry will explain later, he has 'awakened' the animate beings surrounding him by invoking *Anishinaabe gashki'ewiziwin* (traditional forms of 'knowledge' or 'power'). As Maureen Matthews writes in her trenchant analysis exploring the agency of Ojibwe drums, extremely gifted and powerful Ojibwe medicine men used drums as a way to invoke 'spirit helpers, his *'wiikaana' e-gii-dazhimaad epenimod ina*, his ritual relatives upon whom he depended'.[26] 'Like an underground river', Matthews continues, these spirit helpers 'emerge from time to time, flowing and active, causing some of the abrupt shifts in register which we have seen in the narrative'.[27] I would like to suggest that something similar happens in the video where Larry Aitken summons the spirits of these birch-bark vessels. In doing so, we witness an abrupt shift in the narrative that I thought would structure the interview. Again, the shift reveals itself through code-switching: this time, just before Larry plays the drum, he again invokes the 'elders' to share a song about ricing. Larry's decision to pick up the museum's drum and to play it came as quite a shock to me. Having only worked at the Penn Museum a short time, I was unsure of the protocols regarding Native people playing the 'artefacts'.[28] After the fear of being fired finally subsided, I became fascinated by this moment wherein the drum becomes an active participant in telling the story.

To borrow a tool from the digital humanities, creating tags that indicate the shift in 'languages' helps to make the 'invisible forces' discernible, albeit with a certain degree of distortion resulting from translating spirits into tags. Nevertheless, the code switching in this sequence wherein Larry prepares to play the drum might look something like this: <English> <Ojibwe> <English> <Ojibwe> <Voice of the Drum>. It is quite a remarkable feat that Larry Aitken accomplishes here, for he simultaneously awakens the drum ceremonially by switching in and out of Ojibwe, while translating into English. Finally, the drum speaks in its own voice

24 'The Heartbeat of Mother Earth'.

25 'The Heartbeat of Mother Earth'.

26 Maureen Matthews, *Naamiwan's Drum: The Story of a Contested Repatriation of Anishinaabe Artifacts* (Toronto: University of Toronto Press, forthcoming), p. 226.

27 Matthews, *Naamiwan's Drum*, p. 230.

28 A special thank you to Lucy Williams who was happy to have Larry play the drum.

with Larry accompanying it by singing the ricing song. The spontaneity of the drum's action and its profound effect upon Larry can be heard in the moment after he finishes the song. 'And just like that…' Larry says, his voice cracking with the amazement of what he later recalled as the 'force' of the drum that 'surprises the wisdom keeper'. Recovering, Larry affirms the spiritual interaction by saying, 'And this drum, *dewe'igan*, is the one that helped to do this.' He then immediately offers tobacco to the drum, the proper way to thank a 'spirit helper' for their guidance. 'And so I need to make sure that because I used this drum that I offer tobacco to this drum for letting me use it again.'[29] He then speaks directly to the drum in Ojibwe in the form of a prayer.

In the 1930s, the anthropologist A. Irving Hallowell documented a similar instance of a drum being ceremonially awakened by a very powerful medicine man named *Naamiwan*, or Fair Wind. As Hallowell notes: 'The more deeply we penetrate into the world view of the Ojibwa the more apparent it is that "social relations" between human beings… and other-than-human persons are of cardinal significance.' 'Other-than-human persons' are, according to Ojibwe cosmology, animate objects like a drum or a bear or a thunderbird that share their knowledge or look after the Anishinaabe people. As an example of Fair Wind's relationship with the spirit of the drum, Hallowell writes that certain outcomes 'can be determined, by consulting the drum'.[30] With remarkable cultural sensitivity, Hallowell explains: 'the drum is the medium of this information; and only Fair Wind and [his son] Angus […] understand the messages which come through the drum'.[31] During a break between songs, 'Angus talked to the *djibaiyak* ("spirits of the dead") that were reputed to be speaking through the drum […] The words were uttered by Angus in a low tone, with his head partly bent over the drum, which he gave slowly timed blows with his drumstick at fairly regular intervals. It appears that Angus, while listening carefully to the drum, was at the same time repeating certain questions which were being asked, and then answering them.'[32] Here, *relational epistemology* comes to life, as it does in the video, such that the drum and the wisdom keeper communicate directly.

As Larry says in the video, in order to induce this spiritual relationship,

[29] 'The Heartbeat of Mother Earth'.

[30] Alfred Irving Hallowell, 'Spirits of the Dead in Saulteaux Life and Thought', in Jennifer S. H. Brown and Susan Elaine Gray, eds, *Contributions to Ojibwe Studies: Essays, 1934–1972* (Lincoln, NE: University of Nebraska Press, 2010), p. 430.

[31] Hallowell, 'Spirits of the Dead', p. 430.

[32] Hallowell, 'Spirits of the Dead', p. 428.

one must know how to 'ask correctly'. Once the vibrant matter has been awakened ceremonially, the 'birchbark vessels […] are going to give the breadth of their knowledge that they've stored for eons of time', Larry says.[33] Here again, we witness a masterful example of epistemological code switching, albeit much more profound. Note, for example, that when Larry talks of the drum sharing a 'knowledge' that has been 'stored for eons of time', he is no longer speaking to this one particular drum made at the end of the nineteenth century. The temporal breadth and depth of this traditional knowledge implicitly indicates that Larry is now speaking to the 'head spirit of the drum'. Maureen Matthews, working with Ojibwe linguist Roger Roulette, does a magnificent job in her book, *Naamiwan's Drum*, of demonstrating how this way of knowing is encoded in the language. The Ojibwe translation of what Larry calls the 'head spirit of the drum' is, Matthews writes, '*Debinim* […] a way of referring to the spirit-beings as owners of particular animals [or drums]. The name for the most powerful force in the world, *Gaa-dibendjiged*, the owner of all comes from the same root.' *Gaa-dibendjiged*, Matthews continues, is considered to be 'the source of all life', which is 'not anthropomorphized […] In the cascading kinship of power in the Ojibwe world, the spirit-entities [head spirit of the drum] act as intermediaries' to *Gaa-dibendjiged.* 'Medicine men who "know" spirit-entities act as further conduits, channeling', in this case, the origin story from the spirit world to this world.[34]

As Larry concludes, 'It's about time that we return to those things [museum artefacts] that are kept for us, so we can learn from them and appreciate each other as partners.' Here, I want to thank Larry for his partnership over the years and for teaching us about a new way to understand origin stories. Speaking only for myself, nothing in my training as a scholar of American literature prepared me to see the 'birch bark vessels' as 'friends that have been sleeping for a while. If not sleeping, dormant. And in the right way we can wake them up and bring them home so they are of use to our people.'[35] As Larry observes, when this very old form of traditional knowledge is paired with digital technology, 'It can invigorate and enliven and inspire knowledge and wisdom and learning.'[36] About a year after making this video, Larry and I took a long drive from the Leech Lake reservation to Mille Lacs reservation, affording us hours to discuss what had happened that day in the Penn Museum. I told him I hoped to

33 'The Heartbeat of Mother Earth'.

34 Matthews, *Naamiwan's Drum*, p. 105.

35 'The Heartbeat of Mother Earth'.

36 'The Heartbeat of Mother Earth'.

write an article one day to try to help American literature scholars understand the vital role of what Larry calls 'invisible forces' at play in this this traditional form of storytelling:

> In the old days, the written word was only one form of meaning. Actually, it is the invisible forces speaking to the wisdom keeper [...] The human imagination thinks this cannot be. [The problem is] not self-doubt as much as human insecurity about this higher level of thinking that goes beyond writing or the visual [...] This can be a great good for teachers of American literature.[37]

In the next section, I will endeavour to explain how the 'higher level of thinking' can be utilised to lessen the distortion that currently surrounds understandings of Indigenous stories. So too, I believe that American literature can play a crucial role in helping scholars and theorists in other fields to understand how this kind of *vibrant storytelling* works in ways that can deepen current understandings of time, history and being.

Re-Animating the Origins of American Literature

To explore the question of how an origin story told by a drum and an *oshkabewis* creates the opportunity to rethink the epistemological underpinnings of the field, I want to briefly review four works on the subject that have helped me to understand how contemporary critical narratives situate Indigenous orations, sermons and performances as part of American literary history: Craig Womack's *Red on Red: Native American Literary Separatism*; Carolyn Eastman's *A Nation of Speechifiers: Making an American Public after the Revolution*; Sandra Gustafson's *Eloquence is Power: Oratory and Performance in Early America*; and Lisa Brooks's *The Common Pot: The Recovery of Native Space in the Northeast*.[38] By way of conclusion, I want to consider how the vibrant materiality explored in the preceding sections also compels us to rethink the periodisation of American literary history. As we will see, trying to situate Indigenous

[37] Larry Aitken in discussion with the author, 15 October 2008.

[38] Craig Womack, *Red on Red: Native American Literary Separatism* (Minneapolis, MN: University of Minnesota Press, 1999); Carolyn Eastman, *A Nation of Speechifiers: Making an American Public after the Revolution* (Chicago: University of Chicago Press, 2009); Sandra Gustafson, *Eloquence is Power: Oratory and Performance in Early America* (Chapel Hill, NC: University of North Carolina Press, 2000); Lisa Brooks, *The Common Pot: The Recovery of Native Space in the Northeast* (Minneapolis, MN: University of Minnesota Press, 2008).

origin stories within the chronological-based paradigm of American literature grossly distorts the *dynamic temporality* of 'The Heartbeat of Mother Earth'. Again, this step forward will prove challenging, so again we approach by traversing terrain already mapped by scholars in the field.

One of the first critical questions to arise is whether chronology, or what might be termed *temporal colonisation*, so distorts the Native tradition that its stories should be studied separately. As Craig Womack (Creek/Muscogee) famously declared in *Red on Red*: 'Let Americanists struggle for *their* place in the canon. (Understand this is not an argument for inclusion – I am saying with all the bias I can muster that *our* American canon, the Native literary canon of the Americas, predates *their* American canon. I see them as two separate canons.)'[39] Taking this criticism to heart, my goal is to argue *both* that Indigenous origin stories function in completely different ways that need to be theorised in culturally specific terms, but that the unique sense of temporality and materiality of origin stories can make an important contribution to American literary studies.

An example of the distortion that occurs by subordinating Indigenous cultures to chronological narratives of 'American history' can be seen in works such as Caroline Eastman's *A Nation of Speechifiers*. Although the book is not a literary analysis, Eastman nonetheless devotes a chapter to Native American oratory, focusing on 'Logan's Lament,' a document written by John Logan (Cayuga/Mingo) in the oratorical style of his people at a negotiation during Dunmore's War on the western Pennsylvania frontier in 1774. Historians have debated the accuracy of the text, but nevertheless it went on to become one of the most famous examples of Indigenous oratory, reprinted in colonial newspapers, elementary school text books and Thomas Jefferson's *Notes on the State of Virginia* in 1782. Eastman does an impressive job of tracking the use of Native oratory in nearly one-third of more than two hundred schoolbooks, showing how these orations were held up in admiration. The focus on how this Indigenous form fits into the culture of the dominant white society, however, leads Eastman to the conclusion that the editors of these texts mediated the oratory 'in a manner that gradually silenced real Indians'.[40] Rather than restoring those voices and studying the unique properties of Indigenous oratory, the focus on print culture inadvertently contributes to silencing the voices yet again.

Sandra Gustafson's *Eloquence is Power* more effectively situates Native

39 Womack, *Red on* Red, p. 7.

40 Eastman, *A Nation of Speechifiers*, p. 99.

American oratory within an Indigenous continuum that includes Samson Occom (Mohegan), Hendrick (Mohawk) and, especially, Canassatego (Onondaga). Rather than depicting 'real Indians' as being 'silenced', Gustafson demonstrates, for example, the degree of control that Canassatego wields over colonial administrators at the Lancaster Treaty of 1744. The analysis self-consciously avoids studying Native oratory within a single cultural paradigm, advocating instead for more 'heterogeneous and mutually influential traditions of oratory within the colonies and the early republic'. This model allows her to call attention to Euro-American performance and oratory 'in relation to native American diplomatic eloquence', such that the 'public culture of the Revolution can be seen as a form of "playing Indian", as well as playing Greek or Roman'.[41] Gustafson also does a fine job of situating Native oratory in relation to Indigenous traditions that predated European conquest: 'Treaty protocol had its basis in the Iroquois Condolence Council, a ritual with roots in the founding of the League' that dates back to an era before the continent was colonised by chronological time.[42] Gustafson deserves a great deal of credit, too, for significantly expanding the opening section of the forthcoming ninth edition of *The Norton Anthology of American Literature* to include a greater selection of Indigenous origin stories and orations, such as that of Canassatego at Lancaster.

For all of its significant contributions, *Eloquence is Power* remains confined within the temporal borders of 'Early American' periodisation and the corresponding limitations of studying the oral tradition mediated by print culture. In other words, all of the texts considered date from the colonial and early republic era, which necessitates isolating them from contemporary recitations of, for example, the Iroquois Condolence Ritual, a living tradition performed yearly with wampum belts at the Haudenosaunee Long House at Onondaga, which cannot be definitively situated on a chronological timeline.

Lisa Brooks's (Abenaki) examination of early Indigenous literature in relation to 'Native space in the northeast', in *The Common Pot*, takes Gustafson's work a step further by thoughtfully examining the oratorical and written works of Samson Occom, William Apess and Cannassatego in relation to Indigenous epistemology, language and landscape. Like Gustafson, Brooks concentrates primarily on texts published during the colonial period. Brooks makes an important contribution to the field,

41 Gustafson, *Eloquence is Power*, p. xix.

42 Gustafson, *Eloquence is Power*, p. 122.

however, by reconstructing a new/old paradigm based on the traditional knowledge encoded in the Abenaki language (which, like Ojibwe, derives from the Algonquin language family). She writes that the Abenaki 'root word *awigha-* denotes, "to draw," "to write," "to map." The word *awikhigan*, which originally described birchbark messages, maps, and scrolls, came to encompass books and letters.'[43] Brooks goes on to note that the birch-bark scrolls inscribed with pictographs that the Ojibwe kept were always accompanied by oral recitations, suggesting a new model using the Indigenous metaphor of the three sisters: squash, corn and beans, which grew together in a symbiotic relationship. Brooks writes:

> The oral and written traditions have become interrelated and intertwined, not in a contest between two brothers diametrically opposed but in a manner that reflects the relationship between the three sisters of the northeastern tradition, each contributing to the sustenance and growth of the other and reliant on their interdependence for the continuance of the whole.[44]

To continue Brooks's metaphor, I would like to suggest that the third sister to the intertwined oral and written traditions is animate objects, whether they be a drum, a rock art painting, a medicine bundle, or wampum belts whose beads remember the words spoken over them.

Another important insight that I want to build upon is Brooks's emphasis on 'Native space'. Brooks quotes Winona Wheeler, who writes, 'The land is mnemonic, it has its own set of memories and when the old people go out on the land it nudges or reminds them, and their memories are rekindled.'[45] Wheeler's description of the land 'nudging' the old people to tell their stories is precisely the same word choice that Larry Aitken uses when he describes being 'nudged' by the drum to tell an origin story. Brooks goes on to suggest a new paradigm for interpreting stories and memories set within 'the context of their whole environment. This has entailed an evolving process of mapping relationships between people, places, rivers, words, and the plethora of beings who inhabit any place-world.'[46] Inspired by Wheeler's notion of land interacting with storytellers and Brooks's view of the environment populated by a 'plethora of beings', I want to conclude by considering how to include a

43 Brooks, *The Common Pot*, p. xxi.

44 Brooks, *The Common Pot*, p. 254.

45 Quoted in Brooks, *The Common Pot*, p. xxiv.

46 Brooks, *The Common Pot*, p. xxiv.

similarly animate sense of time as the fourth dimension of what Brooks calls 'Native Space'.

In the close reading of 'The Heartbeat of Mother Earth' above, the metaphor of tagging was used to identify code switching related to shifts in both language and worldviews. Expanding upon this notion, one might also mark up the transcript to identify temporal shifts in the story. The video begins, for example with a profound switch from the present moment to 'the first sound ever [...] the sound of the drum', which was 'the heartbeat of Mother Earth'. Here the story transports the listener back to the exact moment when the earth comes into being, not as an impossibly distant historical moment – 4.35 billion years ago according to chronological time – but as an event unfolding in what might be called the *storied present.*

Oddly, humanists have not fully come to terms with Einstein's proof, published more than a century ago, that what Newton called 'absolute time' has no basis in scientific reality as described by physicists.[47] I would suggest, in passing, that a great deal more work needs to be done on the intersections between relational epistemology and Einstein's theory of relativity. A glimpse of what such a study might reveal, in terms of Indigenous storytelling, can be seen in Keith Basso's justifiably famous *Wisdom Sits in Places: Landscape and Language among the Western Apache.* Working with Apache elders, Basso describes what could be termed the fourth dimension of Brooks's conception of 'Native Space'. In the passage below, Basso describes listening to an Apache elder, Charles Henry, telling stories while standing at the very place where the story occurred in pre-chronological time:

> Now they are coming! They are walking upstream from down below. Now they are arriving here [...] It looked to them then as it looks to us now. We know that from its name – its name gives a picture of it, just as it was a long time ago.[48]

Basso, to his great credit, allows his marvel at the event to shine through when he responds: '"That was great!" I exclaim. "It's like we

[47] Brian Greene, *The Fabric of the Cosmos: Space, Time, and the Texture of Reality* (London: Vintage, 2004), p. 139, quotes Einstein: 'For we convinced physicists, the distinction between past, present, and future is only an illusion, however persistent.'

[48] Keith H. Basso, *Wisdom Sits in Places: Landscape and Language Among the Western Apache* (Albuquerque: University of New Mexico Press, 1996), p. 12.

were *there,* watching them when they came!"'[49] And indeed, this is exactly what it feels like to be in the presence of such a powerful origin story: a quality, unfortunately, not captured in the video but electrifying to behold when such a story spontaneously reveals itself to a wisdom keeper.

Such a profound temporal shift – from the Penn Museum to hearing the heartbeat of Mother Earth just before creation – radically calls into question whether the chronological periodisation of early American literature should be abandoned altogether in describing Indigenous origin stories. Note that the underlying structures of the field break down altogether due to the forces of this seismic shift. Larry Aitken, or even the drum at the Penn Museum, cannot be accurately attributed as the 'author' of the story. Accepting Ojibwe cosmology as a viable hermeneutic framework for interpreting the story, the other-than-human being who 'owns' the story, following Matthews and Roulette, would be the *debinim* or 'the spirit-being that owns', in this case, *dewe'iganag* (drums). Ultimately, the 'spirit-entities' are mere conduits to *Gaa-dibendjiged*, which Roger Roulette translates as 'the source of all life'. Because *Gaa-dibendjiged* exists outside of chronological time, the notion that the story can be dated or periodised also breaks down. Certainly the print-culture metaphor of 'publication date' loses all meaning in terms of interpreting the story in the context of Ojibwe cosmology. The temporal distance between the date the video was created (2007) and the date the drum sounded as the heartbeat of Mother Earth (4.35 billion years ago) collapses such that these two moments intersect.

In this sense, the origins of American literary history are reanimated. Time, free of temporal colonisation, thus functions such that 'The Heartbeat of Mother Earth' can be appreciated as one of the many origins of American literary history. This presents literary scholars with a compelling challenge to theorise Indigenous origin stories as powerful entities that can transport us through time, such that we stand as witness to what might be thought of as the Ojibwe Big Bang theory, spoken in the voice of the drum: 'boom, boom, boom'. When I spoke to Larry later, he was fully cognisant of the power of the story to accomplish this: 'I wanted to take you there', to the moment when the heartbeat of Mother Earth reverberated, 'so that you could understand a little better what I mean by Ojibwe cosmology'.[50]

[49] Basso, *Wisdom Sits in Places*, p. 13.

[50] Larry Aitken in discussion with the author, 15 October 2008.

When I told him that I wanted to write an article explaining what this means to American literary scholars, Larry noted that 'academaniacs' were too enamoured with writing (meaning alphabetic writing). Larry explained that the Ojibwe had a writing system that predated European colonisation. When the Ojibwe lived on the East Coast, a prophecy warned that white people were coming and would destroy the cultures of those living on the land. The Ojibwe, as the keepers of the sacred scrolls, therefore began a westward migration, taking the pictographic scrolls with them, until they came to the land where food grows in the water (wild rice). Ojibwe wisdom keepers can still read this pictographic form of writing today. Thus Larry explained:

> In the old days, the written word was only one form of meaning. Actually, it is invisible forces speaking to the wisdom keeper. Object knows a wisdom keeper and how to talk to them [...] The human imagination thinks this cannot be [...] [The problem is] not self-doubt as much as human insecurity about this higher level of thinking that goes beyond writing or the visual [...] This can be a good thing for teachers of American literature.[51]

What, then, does all this mean for scholars of American literature? An important first step would be to radically decolonise the origins of the field so that one day, perhaps, the entire first volume of *The Norton Anthology of American Literature* will be devoted to Indigenous stories from across the continent, from the Maya to the Inuit, from the Kwakwaka'wakw to the Seminoles. The Ojibwe call these ancient stories *aadizookaan*. As Maureen Matthews observes, 'bringing a good life, *bimaadiziwin*, into being is possible only with the help of *aadizookannag*'.[52] The recovery of these Indigenous stories is ultimately about health, healing the wounds inflicted by the epistemology and ontology of colonisation that have been passed down in the form of intergenerational historical trauma manifested, in the field of American literature, in the severe distortion of the remarkable powers of Indigenous origin stories.

To restore a state of *bimaadiziwin* to the field, we must accept elders like Larry Aitken as equal to writers such as Herman Melville or scholars such as F. O. Matthiessen. We must break free of the tyranny of print culture and recognise the three sisters of oral, written and material traditions as being constitutive of ancient and modern American literature.

[51] Larry Aitken in discussion with the author, 15 October 2008.

[52] Matthews, *Naamiwan's Drum*, p. 115.

Digital technology, in this case the video, provides a unique opportunity to rethink American literary history in relation to the values of Indigenous cultures, and as this essay has suggested, there is so much more work that needs to be done.

Distortion in Textual Object Facsimile Production: A Liability or an Asset?

GIOVANNI SCORCIONI

The aim of this essay is to analyse the concept of distortion in relation to the transmission of textual objects through the creation of facsimiles. The general claim of the essay is that, paradoxically, the process of distortion is itself an essential means to get rid of distortion; this concept will become clearer as we explain the different kinds of distortion that we encounter in the process of producing a facsimile edition of a medieval manuscript. Each type of distortion comes from a specific stage of the facsimile-making process.[1]

As we retrace the process from start to finish, the four main stages of production will be described; namely, the photo-setting, pre-press, printing and binding stages. Each stage will be discussed in relation to the type of alteration it deals with or causes. With reference to practical examples, it will be argued that distortion can be either positive or negative depending on context, use and aim. A sequence of manuscripts will be taken into consideration to further demonstrate how distortion plays a main role in the art of facsimile making.

Starting from the definition of perception as the means by which we determine alteration, there will be a discussion of how the use of different colour systems can lead to different outcomes, in terms of perception and distortion. This discussion will take place in the context of the pre-press and printing stages. The latter will allow us to talk about how perception is fundamental in the creation of a facsimile; although based on science and technology, it can be safely stated that the process of facsimile making is far from being an exact science and it involves technical skills, art and craftsmanship in almost equal measure. For example, the process of colour proofing is a testament to such abilities and it relates to the concept of distortion, for its purpose lies in limiting distortion to create a printed facsimile as close as possible to the original document.

One last aspect of distortion – the 'commercial' or exogenous – will

[1] For more on this subject, and for useful images of facsimile production, see Giovanni Scorcioni, *Facsimile Finder*, at https://www.facsimilefinder.com/articles/distortion-facsimile-production/ (accessed 15 July 2017).

also be evaluated. With this terminology we are indicating nothing less than the alteration of facsimiles to the point where they can no longer be considered as such. They gain new features and lose some old ones, all with the aim of making the product more attractive to the general public and to buyers, but to the detriment of historical and stylistic accuracy.

Finally, the essay will come to a conclusion claiming the complementary nature of printed facsimiles and digital scans. It will be stressed how the former, because of its etymology (meaning 'made similar'), needs to be as close as possible to the original, as opposed to the digital image – a ground-breaking scholarly tool – which, however, cannot make up for the lack of physicality that can only be conveyed by the tangible object.

How Does Distortion Positively and Negatively Affect the Facsimile-Making Process?

Depending on the context, use and aim, distortion can present itself as positive or negative. Negative distortion affects the perception of the object of interest in a way that impedes the knowledge of that object. Positive distortion is a set of actions put in place by the makers of a facsimile in order to rectify negative distortion. In extreme cases, negative distortion can, for various reasons, be deliberately applied by the makers of the facsimile.

I focus on three main types of distortion: endogenous, digital and exogenous – each belonging to specific stages of the making process. The endogenous distortion belongs to the photo-set stage; the digital one to the pre-press and printing stages; and the exogenous one to the printing and binding stages. The discussion will highlight each step in order to understand whether it affects positively or negatively the textual object and/or its making process, specifically in the context of facsimile production.

Endogenous Distortion

The first stage of facsimile making is the photo acquisition; in other words taking photos of the object. This is the stage where we are to deal with 'endogenous' or 'material' distortion: it means that the alteration is caused by factors within the object itself. It is essential to keep in mind, though, that the scope of this essay is to analyse the inherent defect in relation to the process of duplication of a manuscript, and in no way represents a critique to the object's nature per se. Thus, the aim of photo acquisition is to obtain images that will be used to produce the facsimile. Such images must be compliant with several technical requirements to allow the process of facsimile production to be successful. In the context at hand this type of distortion, which can prove to be potentially problematic, is yet still manageable and controllable.

To clarify, by factors within the object itself I mean features (alterations), depending on the material and the state of the writing support, that inherently distort the original that is being replicated. Often the writing support being dealt with is not the standard modern book; it could be a codex, a scroll, or even papyri, and all of these present an innate level of distortion. Particularly in this field, hand-made physical objects such as manuscripts bear several points of inherent distortion: at the gutter, for example, pages are bending inwards; parchment is usually wrinkled, with holes and defects; at times, single folios may have been sewn in, leaving a stub that by partly covering the following page hinders the photographing process. One could argue that these alterations should be eliminated in order to produce a defect-free replica: however, the purpose of a facsimile is not to improve the original but to replicate it with all its flaws and defects. To do this, the team involved in such a process has first to normalise some of the complexities, in order to then re-create them.

Endogenous Distortion in the Structure and Format of the Manuscript

A practical example can illustrate this. All readers have come across books that are particularly difficult to keep flat and open, due, for example, to a tight binding. Taking photographs of a manuscript that cannot be forced flat open is challenging and results in images that represent the pages in a distorted format. To minimise this type of distortion, specialists use several means: among others, custom-built stands that keep the manuscript folios as flat as possible in order to limit the distortion, while keeping the binding safe. Images obtained from an 'undistorted' object will allow, at the end of the process, the replica to have, if not the same, then a similar endogenous distortion. This is ultimately the aim of every good replica: to give the beholder a similar experience of the original object.

The *Oxford Menologion*, with its series of miniatures revealing an extensive use of gold leaf, represents a good case study of another instance of endogenous distortion. Oxford, Bodleian Library, MS. Gr. th. f. 1[2] was made for Demetrios I, ruler of Thessaloniki in Greece in the later fourteenth and earlier fifteenth centuries. This small manuscript contains

[2] Digitised in full at the Bodleian Library's website: http://bodley30.bodley.ox.ac.uk:8180/luna/servlet/detail/ODLodl~8~8~59163~132133:Menologion (accessed 17 September 2016); produced in facsimile by AyN Editions in 2007.

elaborate illuminated images celebrating saints' feasts throughout the church year. Indeed, when dealing with manuscript facsimiles, more often than not we come across illuminated books. The term 'illuminated' comes from the Latin *illuminare*, 'to enlighten or illuminate', which means to embellish a manuscript with the use of luminous colours (especially gold and silver).[3]

When faced with these valuable decorations, specialists must come to terms with the issues they bring along with their beauty. The gold leaf, which is gold hammered into thin sheets,[4] poses special problems while capturing photos of the manuscript. The light coming from the powerful lamps used to illuminate the manuscript reflects on the golden features of the miniature, leading to an undesirable shimmering that damages the quality of the photos. This 'negative' distortion is usually rectified by taking more shots of the same page from different angles, giving the digital artist the means to accurately reconstruct the gold patterns in the facsimile edition to obtain a good representation of the original manuscript. Both parchment cockling and gold leaf shimmering are negative to begin with, for they can potentially hinder the facsimile-making process; however, they can be controlled and managed, leading to a product that undergoes a 'counter-distortion'. Counter-distortion is usually obtained through manual (as in the case of flattening a folio with cockling) or digital processes (as in the case of gold reconstruction).

Digital Distortion

Once the photographs of the manuscript are shot, the following step is to digitally work the images in order to obtain printing files. At this stage the second type of distortion occurs; namely, the digital one. Digital distortion may be described as negative or positive depending on the context: positive digital distortion is the use of tools to manipulate digital information in order to achieve a result; digital distortion becomes negative when, due to its inherent technical limitations, it affects the final printed product, distancing it from the original.

The tools employed to create the positive distortion are, in themselves,

[3] Michelle Brown, *Understanding Illuminated Manuscripts: A Guide to Technical Terms* (Los Angeles: The J. Paul Getty Museum in association with The British Library, 1994), p. 69.

[4] On the preparation and use of gold leaf, see Katherine Scarfe Beckett's calligraphy website: http://www.calligraphy-skills.com/gold-leaf-technique.html (accessed 17 September 2016).

neutral. The positive aspect of digital distortion consists in the technical skills and craftsmanship that specialists and experts apply to produce a facsimile that is as close as possible to the original. When managing this type of distortion, we are dealing with the struggles specialists have to face to avoid a misrepresentation of the item. Misrepresentation is very possibly an inherent feature of digital-imaging software, as will be discussed later, when comparing facsimiles and digital scans.

The standard definition for the word *perception* is 'awareness of the elements of environment through physical sensation'.[5] Thus depending on our senses perception can be positive or negative; if we take the definition a step further, we may consider it as the means by which we determine alteration between two things, and it has a leading role when comparing a facsimile to an original manuscript. In the facsimile-making process perception is fundamental, especially at certain stages such as pre-press editing: what eventually gets printed depends on the perception of the individual operating the machines. In this context, the role of perception is discussed in relation to the way colour systems have a leading role in the pre-press and printing processes, potentially resulting in a distortion originating in digital technology.

Colour Systems Explained

Knowledge of colour systems is useful in understanding the substantial differences between looking at a digital scan on a screen and looking at an object such as a manuscript or a facsimile. The technology underlying digital photography or printed/painted objects determines the perception we have of the physical object when examined on a screen in digital format or in real life. There are two main colour systems: the additive colour system and the subtractive colour system.

Computer screens, cameras and televisions use the additive colour system: in this system, the creation of images is based on the emission of light. Indeed, computers use backlit screens, composed of millions of tiny lamps made in three colours – red, green and blue. Each lamp can turn from completely off to fully bright. Millions of lamps (or pixels) together, seen at a proper distance, create the illusion of images on the screen.

Keeping in mind that in the additive system it is the screen that emits light, we shall proceed on to the second system, the subtractive colour system. In comparison to the additive colour system, the subtractive

[5] Merriam-Webster's Collegiate Dictionary, s.v. 'Perception', *Merriam-Webster's Collegiate Dictionary*, 11th edn (Springfield, MA: Merriam-Webster, 2003): http://www.merriam-webster.com/.

system is to be considered a steady and unvaried system, in that since the beginning of time it has always been used by artists to paint a manuscript, or presses to print colours, and, in general, by whomever created an image using colour on a surface. This system – based on a clear support and, in the case of a manuscript, clean parchment – creates images by adding layers of colours onto the support itself. The substantial difference between the two colour system is that, while in the additive system light comes from within the emitters, in the subtractive system light comes from an external source, rebounds off the painted support and is reflected upon our eyes. The source of light affects our perception of colours – and the idea is that the products of these two different systems are ultimately unparalleled, offering two different experiences.

Awareness of such systems allows us to understand the role that distortion plays in the making of a facsimile. In fact, in the production of a manuscript facsimile there are at least two major changes of colour system: the procedure starts from a painted manuscript, which is an object made in the subtractive system; images of the specific object are taken using a digital camera, which works in the additive system; then, the digital information is post-produced on the computer, which we know is an additive system; finally, when the facsimile is printed, the digital information is converted back into the subtractive system.

Moving back and forth between different colour systems tends to create 'negative distortion', specifically distortion of the textual object and its representation in both the digital format and the printed format of the facsimile. The only means of contrasting such distortion is through the technical and artistic skills of printmakers (that is, positive or counter-distortion). When technology falls short, specialists and their know-how come to the rescue and make up for the negative effects caused by the inherent limits of technology.

Negative and Positive Examples of Digital Distortion

The best example of specialist knowledge that solves an unwanted distortion is the expert use of imaging software such as Adobe Photoshop. This software allows the manipulation of digital information to obtain printable files, suitable to be used to produce a facsimile that is as close as possible, in shape and colour rendering, to the original manuscript.

An example of positive distortion is the use of digital-imaging software to correct the original manuscript folio's distortion. As it is not always easy to physically flatten wrinkled parchment during the photo acquisition and the photos of distorted folios would not be usable for facsimile production, digital software is used to solve such problem. The process could be defined as controlled distortion, and hence can be thought of as positive, for by means of digital distortion applied to the photos, the printmakers are able to obtain printable files in order to produce a facsimile as close as possible to the original manuscript.

The *Peterborough Psalter* (Brussels, Royal Library, MS 9961-62)[6] is a beautiful fourteenth-century Gothic manuscript produced in the Peterborough scriptorium by three unidentified artists. The text is laid out in columns and written in blue ink and gold leaf with elaborate illuminations and historiated initials illustrating the Psalms and Calendar.[7] Photos of the manuscript are not sufficient to produce a facsimile edition of the gold features: gold leaf replica is in fact printed using special machines that apply the material following a specific, predetermined pattern; the photos alone represent the unified view of the page, and not only the gold text. The printing pattern is determined by the technician who redraws by hand the gold text and/or illustration onto the screen, creating the stencil to reproduce the original. The result of the technician's work is a printing plate that will be used to apply the gold leaf replica to the facsimile.

This art is taken one step further when dealing with shell gold, which is trickier not only to redesign but also to identify on the original manuscript. In some cases, in fact, this kind of gold can be barely perceptible in the context of the painted image: to create proper printing plates, curators and facsimile technicians carry out an extremely careful analysis of the original manuscript, trying to identify every smallest stroke of shell gold on the manuscript.

Colour Proofing and Digital (Counter-)Distortion

It is worth noticing that the pre-press stage is not the only step where perception plays a relevant part, for the printing process is mainly based on it, both from an artistic and a technological point of view. Although art and technology can often be at odds, one claiming superiority over the other, in the field of facsimile making they are much more allies than enemies, being ultimately complementary. One expression of this is the process of colour proofing, when both the technical and artistic skills of printmakers are truly put to a test. This painstaking process entails, at least initially, duplicating the most significant pages and details from the

[6] Available digitally on the repository website, http://belgica.kbr.be/nl/coll/ms/ms9961_62_nl.html (accessed 17 September 2016).

[7] See Lucy Freeman Sandler, 'Peterborough Abbey and the Peterborough Psalter in Brussels', *Journal of the British Archaeological Association*, 3rd series, 33 (1970), 36–49.

original manuscript and assembling them together in a proofing page. The page is then printed and closely compared with the original manuscript. As there is no exact or numerical way to measure the difference in colouring between the facsimile and the original manuscript, every printmaker evaluates the quality of the proofing page according to their own perception and knowledge. When the printmaker notices that there is an inconsistency between the original manuscript and the proofing page, he or she works out the changes that need to be applied to the digital information in order to print a new and more faithful proofing page. This process is repeated several times to achieve a proofing page that is as close as possible to the original manuscript and that will be the base for the production of the entire facsimile. This process is another example of controlled distortion applied to digital information: at some point in the process, colour information gets altered, and the only way to remedy this is to digitally distort it back. This process is thus an expression of how perception of the individual technician plays an important part in the detecting of shade differences between the original and the facsimile.

Exogenous or 'Commercial' Distortion

After the photo-set, pre-press and printing steps, the last stage of production of a facsimile closely resembles the traditional bookbinding process. This process includes techniques such as cutting to shape, folding, gathering and binding the book. This final technique makes the case for the last type of distortion one may encounter in the process of facsimile making, that is, the exogenous or 'commercial' distortion.

In the past, luxury covers were sought after by wealthy sponsors to decorate their manuscripts. In present times, human beings have not changed much and aesthetic appearance is still where the attention is most concentrated, which means focusing on producing a beautiful binding. A large majority of facsimiles are sold to private collectors in Europe and, in order to increase sales to this type of customer, some less scrupulous publishers opt for the production of fake or counterfeit bindings. Producing a facsimile with something substantially different from the original manuscript is, as already stated, a voluntary distortion that alters the quality of the final product.

Commercial distortion of the binding can unfold in three different ways: first, some publishers research and reconstruct what they believe could have been the original binding, with varying degrees of success in achieving a good result; second, some publishers take a coeval binding from a similar manuscript (perhaps from the same author or workshop) and use it for the facsimile. Needless to say, the binding they choose is often much nicer than the one being replaced, looking to make it more pleasant to the eye. The third and final scenario, possibly the worst of all, involves publishers having a 'dress to impress' moment: they design an elaborate and deluxe binding, usually with a lot of gold and stones, simply to impress customers and sell more. Luckily, the third group of the 'fake binding' distortion is quite rare and mostly occurs with minor, unskilled publishers.

Digital Images and Facsimiles: Friends or Foes?

This section will provide a comparison between two important tools: facsimiles – discussed at length – and digital scans. To do this, a personal experience by Roger Wieck, curator of medieval and Renaissance manuscripts at the Morgan Library, will provide our case study.

The Morgan Library is in possession of a tiny and beautiful illuminated manuscript known as the *Prayerbook of Claude de France* (New York, Morgan Library and Museum, M. 1166). Less than 3in tall and 2.5in wide, it is a testament to the skills of the artists who produced this small and delicate item.[8] This prayer book is dated around 1517 and was made for Claude, a woman who had married François de Angouleme in 1514, just a couple of years prior to his coronation. At the time this manuscript was made, Claude was struggling to conceive her first male heir, having already had two girls. As this manuscript was a very personal object of devotion, we can picture Claude carrying it during this time of trouble in her purse or dress pocket, in very close proximity to her body. Functionally, the object is very small, and this, combined with a tight binding, makes it difficult to keep the manuscript open for proper analysis and, of course, for good image acquisition. Since the miniatures go all the way to the borders, such a fragile manuscript should never be handled more than is absolutely necessary. To avoid excessive handling and, at the same time, encourage scholarship on the manuscript, it became imperative that good copies, both digital and printed, should be made.

In 2010, a facsimile publisher took the initiative and produced an accurate facsimile edition of this delightful work of art.[9] The shooting of the manuscript was not an easy process: with it being so tiny and with

[8] See the description of the manuscript at http://www.themorgan.org/collection/Prayer-Book-of-Claude-de-France (accessed 14 July 2017).

[9] For details, see https://www.facsimilefinder.com/facsimiles/prayer-book-of-claude-de-france-facsimile (accessed 15 July 2017).

such a tight binding, publisher and curator had to get really creative in order to keep the manuscript open without invasive tools such as fingers or polystyrene strips. The result of the shooting is a set of digital scans of exceptionally high quality, which can be enjoyed for free online by anyone, anywhere, at any time. Being fully accessible from any internet access in the world is one of the great, ground-breaking advantages of online digital repositories of images. The same scans were used by the publisher to produce the charming facsimile that can now be found in many public and private collections.

Roger Wieck was asked to write the commentary for the facsimile, and he stated that both the digital scans and the printed facsimile played an invaluable role in his work. As curator of the library, Wieck was entitled to visit the vault, home to the manuscript, as often as he wanted in order to peruse the original for his analysis; at the same time, being concerned with the conservation of the object, he was well aware that handling it more than absolutely necessary would have conflicted with his role as conservator, and would put the manuscript at risk. As he wrote the commentary he was constantly in the presence of the printed facsimile; he kept it on his desk while working, as a sort of 'muse', a pleasant substitute of the original. He claimed that the daily companionship of the facsimile was inspiring, and gave him the opportunity to live with the manuscript almost as Claude de France had done. At the same time, the digital scans allowed him to explore details of the manuscript that could never have been visible to the naked eye. High-quality scans can be zoomed to high levels and a close analysis of the miniatures revealed a detail that until then had gone unnoticed. Indeed, Wieck observed the presence of an almost undetectable halo that completely changed the meaning of a painted scene. It is a single, very small stroke of painted gold, so small and blended with other light colours that Wieck never noticed it during his time with the original manuscript. On the Morgan Library's website it is possible to view all the openings of the manuscript, with a short caption describing the miniatures. Before the website was updated just after the new discovery, the caption of folio 39v read: 'St. René resuscitating a dead child' – the meaning that Wieck ascribed to that scene at that time, before observing the halo. After spotting the almost undetectable feature, the Morgan Library's curator has changed that caption to 'The Infant St. René Resuscitated by St. Maurilius'. Thus, a small detail was overlooked because of the understandable anxiety to preserve the manuscript and this essential element might have gone unnoticed, preventing us from having a clear and complete understanding of the scene. It is thanks to the analysis of a digital reproduction that this new discovery was made possible.

The conclusion of this story is both simple and fascinating: even for scholars with direct access to the original manuscript, both printed facsimile and digital scans are exceptional tools for researching a work of art. Art and technology have complementary features: digital images are ideal for close analysis that is sometimes impossible with the manuscript itself; printed facsimiles give us the opportunity to live with the object, to witness its physicality, to experience what our predecessors – from the creator, to the commissioner of the book, to the subsequent owners – might have experienced with that manuscript in their hands.

Having discussed the advantages that these two tools bring along with them, as with all things, nothing is perfect and some drawbacks are to be expected. I shall now examine the disadvantages of printed facsimiles and digital images.

Can the High-Pricing of Printed Facsimiles Be Avoided?

The greatest shortcoming of printed facsimiles is certainly the price, which usually limits potential library customers to only the wealthiest academic institutions. However, the cost of production almost always justifies the high sale price: facsimiles are limited editions; every manuscript poses specific replication problems that need to be solved with creative solutions; and finally, the process of production is almost never standard or industrial, thus increasing the final cost of the facsimile.

A good example is the production of the noteworthy *Très Riches Heures of the Duke of Berry* facsimile, made in 2010 by Franco Cosimo Panini (Italy). The facsimile was printed on a Heidelberger Druckmaschinen's SpeedMaster XL 105, a $2 million press produced in Germany. It takes more than three hours to set it up in order to produce excellent-quality facsimile pages and print a run of 1,000 copies of a single printing sheet. The same machine would be able to print 8,000 copies of a regular book in a much shorter time, due to the less demanding set-up time needed for a normal publication versus a high-quality facsimile.

A manuscript such as the *Très Riches Heures*, 8in x 11in and two hundred folios, usually fits on twenty-five printing sheets. In normal conditions, one could calculate three hours for each side of the twenty-five folios, making a total of 150 billable hours of two skilled specialists and the SpeedMaster. However, the specific case of the Chantilly manuscript speaks volumes: in fact, several printing sheets needed to be run through the SpeedMaster more than once. The most intricate of the pages are so rich in colours and decoration that the facsimile version needed to go through the press up to twelve times to properly replicate all the shades of the beautiful work of art. Including drying times, that single printing sheet containing eight folios of the manuscript took over two weeks to be successfully completed. This is just one example of the many that one could consider to explain why facsimiles may be very expensive to the final buyer. Moreover, the printing part is only one of the steps of the process, which may take up to eighteen months from photos of the manuscript to actual delivery of the facsimile.[10] Printed facsimiles, despite their cost and relatively limited availability, though, are very possibly the next best thing after original manuscripts, for they allow us to experience the objects in their physicality – they give the best experience of the original work of art they represent.

Digital Images: a New Era?

Digital images carry some advantages that make them one of the most ground-breaking tools for the study and diffusion of manuscript history. The first and most obvious advantage is that, when publicly shared on the internet (through proper websites or even through social networks), digital images allow the widest access to information that until a decade ago were accessible only through physical movement of the object, or of the user.

The second important advantage is that digital images, when properly produced, allow levels of analysis that the naked eye simply cannot achieve, as we noted in the *Prayerbook* example above. However, digital images cannot be considered facsimiles: despite the large amount of information that they are able to convey, they lack important elements of the original object and can mislead one's perception and knowledge of that object. One caveat is important here: that is, when talking about distortion this essay has paid attention to choice of words. Indeed, the expression 'digital facsimile' has not been used, because using the word 'facsimile' for digital images would itself be a *distortion* of the truth. The word 'facsimile', from Latin, means 'made similar'. Consistency with the etymology of the word prevents digital images from being considered facsimiles. Since a facsimile is something that is as close as possible to the object it represents in all its aspects, the idea of a 'digital facsimile' would defy such definition. There is no doubt that digital scans are a spectacu-

[10] The most recent example that comes to mind is the Voynich manuscript, which, as claimed by the publisher, was in production for about eighteen months. See El Manuscrito Voynich (Burgos: Siloé, arte y bibliofilia, 2018) at https://www.facsimilefinder.com/facsimiles/voynich-manuscript-replica-facsimile

lar tool for teaching and research, but can we truly say that they can be manuscripts' facsimiles?

The manuscript *Hours of Jeanne d'Evreux* is a case in point.[11] The manuscript originates from the fourteenth century and was the first major French work to display delicate miniatures in the so-called demi-grisaille technique. The detailed precision of the miniatures is all the more impressive when considering that this codex is one of the smallest books of hours in existence, measuring a mere 3.5in x 2.3in. Yet, if one were to look at its digital scans on a big screen, one would not be able to realise its size, and as such would not be able to appreciate it in all its delicacy. The digital scan would not convey all the aspects required by a facsimile, running the risk of misrepresenting the manuscript. Hence, albeit complementary, facsimiles and digital scans are not interchangeable. This argument encourages the quest for a different term to express the use of digital images in manuscript studies, so as to appropriately define this powerful, yet sometimes limited, tool. Ultimately, digital scans might convey to someone who has never seen a manuscript the distorted idea that an image on a screen is enough to appreciate the majestic beauty of illuminated manuscripts: yet, all who had the privilege to experience a real illuminated manuscript know that the entirety of the object is as important as the beautiful images painted on the pages.

Facsimiles, then, despite their limits and flaws, can truly enhance the field of manuscript studies, granting people with no access an unprecedented artefactual experience; indeed, they partially fill in the void left by the absence of the manuscript. Digital scans, on the other hand, give wide and easy access to images of manuscripts but run the risk of misrepresenting the physical object. Both are essential to the world of manuscript studies and both share a leading role in the field; each provides a different experience but ultimately they are the paramount tools that allow scholars and amateurs to appreciate both the obscure and illuminated past.

[11] For a full description see http://www.metmuseum.org/toah/works-of-art/54.1.2/ for a full description (accessed 14 July 2017).

The Uncanny Reformation: Revenant Texts and Distorted Time in Henrician England[1]

GREG WALKER

In this essay I look at a group of texts written in the late fourteenth and early fifteenth centuries, which were initially circulated in manuscript as contributions to the 'Lollard' debates about church wealth and clerical morality in that period. They were then printed in the early 1530s (and reprinted in the 1560s and 1570s) as contributions to similar debates a century and more later than their origin. These texts, Lollard writing re-presented for Reformation reading, offer an interesting case study of chronological and epistemological distortion, as they might be argued to distort conceptions of time and history around them both 'positively' and 'negatively' – if those terms have any meaning – but always powerfully and provocatively. The texts present challenges to our definitions of how they might be categorised, what they might suggest about the communities that produced and received them, and what they imply about our own sense of their relationship to time and the creation of historical narrative.

Late medieval works printed in the Tudor period have generally been read, explicitly or implicitly, in terms of the posthumous or the undead, as examples of the 'afterlives' of medieval writings.[2] But I want to consider them here not only as revenants, things not quite dying, but also as things not quite new-born, as contributions to the work in progress of the never entirely achieved project of English religious Reformation. So, in so far as they might be distortions of late-medieval authorial intentions,

[1] I am very grateful to Professor John J. McGavin for his comments on an early draft of this essay.

[2] See, for example, Ann Hudson, '"No new thyng": The Printing of Medieval Texts in the Early Reformation Period', in Douglas Gray and E. G. Stanley, eds, *Middle English Studies Presented to Norman Davis in Honour of his Seventieth Birthday* (Oxford: Clarendon Press, 1983), pp. 153–74; David Matthews, 'The Spectral Past: Medieval Literature in the Early Modern Period', in Robert DeMaria Jr, Heesok Chang and Samantha Zacher, eds, *A Companion to British Literature: Vol. II: Early Modern Literature 1450–1660* (Chichester: John Wiley and Sons, 2014), pp. 1–15; and Wendy Scase, 'Antifraternal Traditions in Reformation Pamphlets', in Nicholas Rodgers, ed., *The Friars in Medieval Britain*, Harlaxton Medieval Studies XIX (Donington: Shaun Tyas, 2010), pp. 239–64.

disinterred and reanimated by Tudor printers, they are also elements of a new reformed typology of protest, fresh texts offered to new readers as part of a campaign to free hearts and minds allegedly long-manacled by the old lies of catholic deception. As we shall see, both their novelty and their antiquity were central to their presentation and reception.

To begin very simply: these texts certainly distort modern readers' perceptions of the terms of debate in the early exchanges of Henry VIII's Reformation, with polemical claim and counter-claim clouding any clear sense of the facts at issue. Just how much wealth did the Tudor Church possess? How much did the clergy earn in tithes, how much in offerings for masses and trentals? How many souls were there in purgatory, how many poor laymen were ruined by how many sturdy begging friars, monks and nuns?[3] But they also, and more interestingly, distort our sense of chronology itself, of the role of chronology in the Reformation debates, and the taxonomies we deploy to understand the history of the Reformation. Texts from one period that claim to comment on the debates of a later one are self-evidently paradoxical, distorting common-sense thinking in the same way that Persse McGarrigle does in David Lodge's *Small World* when he announces that his thesis topic is the influence of T. S. Eliot on Shakespeare. But these (pre-)Reformation texts do this both more urgently and more earnestly, warping productively our sense of the linearity of book history, offering instances of what the art historians Alexander Nagel and Christopher S. Wood have termed the *anachronic artefact*: the art work that blurs, folds and crumples time in each iteration of its performance.[4]

However we try to understand time and space, it seems we are irresistibly drawn to the problematic, fuzzy margins, the grey areas where things are uncertain, anomalous, stateless and migrant. Just as we are attracted to the dirty pleasures of matter out of place, so are we drawn to that which is seemingly out of time, and to the questions and apparent paradoxes that it throws up. Conventionally, for a text or idea to be exemplary of a period or a *zeitgeist*, to be definitively 'of its moment', implies that once that moment has passed, it will be literally 'out of time' – belated, redundant, finished. But, as the shift in critical thinking from notions of anachronism to a sense of the 'untimely' or the anachronic reminds us, timeliness is never quite that simple. The 'anachronic turn' recalls

[3] See, for example, the claims made in Simon Fish, *A Supplication for the Beggars* (Antwerp: J. Grapheus, 1529?), and the counter-claims in Thomas More, *The Supplication of Souls* (London: William Rastell, 1529).

[4] Alexander Nagel and Christopher S. Wood, *Anachronic Renaissance* (New York: Zone Books, 2010).

the ways in which bodies, texts, artefacts and artworks can be of, and in more than one moment, indeed in many 'moments', part of many events, moving through time and distorting and reconfiguring chronology around them as they move.[5] To be out of time in this sense does not rule out the capacity to do new, often startlingly powerful contemporary work, to work in and with time, to draw alternative, rival timelines and histories into new conjunctions, to unsettle our sense of what is original and what is derivative, translated or transplanted. As Jonathan Gil Harris observes, Nietzche's notion of the untimely or *unzeitgemässe*:

> [D]oes not simply connote the persistence of the past in the present; it also has a critical dimension. By resisting absorption into a homogeneous present, it brings with it the difference that produces the possibility of a new future even as it evokes the past.[6]

In this essay I want to look briefly, as I have suggested, at a clutch of texts that were (and are) seemingly out of time. Created in one century, they were reproduced in print in the next, first in an intense period following the opening of the Reformation Parliament in October 1529, and then again around fifty years later. These texts problematise notions of original creativity and transmission, and disrupt ideas of chronology and periodisation by being of no period and of several simultaneously. They are, arguably, possibly simultaneously, exiles, migrants and revenants: old books cut loose from their informing contexts, seemingly lost, then brought back to do new work in a particular cultural moment. How we label them, of course, has a profound effect on how we think about them, and how we think of *using* them. But, whatever we name them, they are texts with a power to address their new moment that comes precisely from their being simultaneously both old and new, strange yet familiar, in ways that Freud famously associated with the idea of the uncanny – that distortion of time and space that is also a manifestation of a disrupted psyche and disturbed cognition.[7] Indeed these texts and the situation that gave them new life in

[5] See Nagel and Wood, *Anachronic Renaissance*, pp. 9–10 and 14; and Jonathan Gil Harris, *Untimely Matter in the Time of Shakespeare* (Philadelphia: University of Pennsylvania Press, 2009).

[6] Gil Harris, *Untimely Matter*, p. 11.

[7] Sigmund Freud, *The Uncanny* (London: Penguin Books, 2003). See, for example, p. 368 ('It may be true that the uncanny [*unheimlich*] is something which is secretly familiar [*heimlich–heimisch*] which has undergone repression and then returned from it, and that everything that is uncanny fulfils this condition') and pp. 363–4 ('[the] uncanny is in reality nothing new or alien, but something which is familiar and old-established in the mind which has become alienated

the turbulent early years of the English Reformation strike me as precisely uncanny, subject to the paradoxical energies that generate the revenant and the self-destructive compulsion to repeat, as well as Harris's capacity to generate possible new futures.[8] The acts of distortion they perform are powerfully performative both in their present moments and also in both the past and future, seeking to redefine what was and what yet might be in the moment of their repetition.

But first some history. The opening session of the parliament summoned by Henry VIII in 1529 provided a forum for the voicing of discontents with the English Church, its wealth and practices that had been gathering momentum over the previous decade. But the parliament also provided a catalyst, indeed a shot of adrenalin, that energised those criticisms and focused the early stirrings of confessionalism that were beginning to be voiced at that time in London and elsewhere. What provided that catalyst, and ensured that the name 'the Reformation Parliament' was no anachronistic imposition, was Sir Thomas More's remarkable opening speech to the members of both Houses, in which the new Lord Chancellor condemned his recently fallen predecessor, Thomas, Cardinal Wolsey, as a gross, castrated ram, a 'great wether', who had deceived and manipulated the King through lies and juggling. 'Diverse great enormities' had been allowed to develop in Church and state under Wolsey's legatine regime, More suggested, and anyone who felt that they had been the victim of these vaguely defined but clearly portentous offences should present their petitions to the King, who promised to give them hearing.[9]

from it only through the process of repression'). For modern readings, see Anne Williams, *Art of Darkness* (Chicago: University of Chicago Press, 1995), and Nicholas Royle, *The Uncanny* (Manchester: Manchester University Press, 2003) (note the suggestion on p. vii that the uncanny is 'something strangely familiar [...] a flickering moment of embroilment in the experience of something at once strange and familiar').

8 See Royle, *The Uncanny*, p. 2 ('[the uncanny] would appear to be indissociably bound up with a sense of repetition or "coming back" – the return of the repressed, the constant or eternal recurrence of the same thing, a compulsion to repeat') and p. 84 ('To repeat: the uncanny seems to be about a strange repetitiveness. It has to do with the return of something repressed, something no longer familiar, the return of the dead'); Lawrence Kramer, 'Revenants: Masculine Thresholds in Schubert, James, and Freud', *Modern Language Quarterly*, 57 (1996), 449–77, 450–2; and Freud, *The Uncanny*, p. 369 (the uncanny involved 'the unintended recurrence of the same thing [...] apparent death and reanimation of the dead have been represented as most uncanny themes').

9 Edward Halle, *The Union of the Two Noble Families of Lancaster and York (1550)*, Scolar Press facsimile (Melton: Scolar Press, 1970), p. clxxxiii–(v).

This speech, and what followed in the first parliamentary session, with prominent courtiers speaking in the Commons against clerical fees and impositions, effectively declared open house for discussion of Church governance, jurisdiction and religious reform. And the political nation responded to the call with alacrity, bringing in complaints, draft bills and petitions for redress to Parliament and the royal council, and generating debates involving all shades of opinion, from conservative senior churchmen anxious to dismantle the centralising machinery of Wolsey's legatine office and reclaim the former prerogatives of the bishops and their diocesan courts for themselves, to evangelical reformers eager to push for the disestablishment of church property, an end to heresy trials, and reform of traditional beliefs and practices such as pilgrimages, image worship, good works, and belief in purgatory.[10] At Henry's urging, More had made the acknowledgement and discussion of 'enormities' at the heart of Church and state an acceptable practice. In the terms set out by the social anthropologist James C. Scott, he had written that discussion into the public transcript of the reign,[11] thereby encouraging anyone with a view to air or an axe to grind to channel them through the medium of a discussion of rottenness at the heart of the ecclesiastical order. It was a bold, even reckless gesture, and one that both More and the King, albeit for different reasons, were to regret for the rest of their lives. But it energised and traumatised contemporary political culture in roughly equal measure.

The winter of 1529–30 was thus a period of unprecedented turbulence and contention in the experience of most if not all English men and women then living. The striking nature of More's speech, and the rancorous divisions of the parliamentary debates, resonate through the correspondence of contemporary ambassadors, statesmen and more humble observers alike, and echo through the writing of the following years. For what followed was a remarkable outpouring of the literature of complaint and petition.[12] And one current in that literary torrent was provided by evangelical writers anxious to emphasise that their complaints were no modish contemporary innovations, opportunistically borrowed from

[10] See Greg Walker, *Reading Literature Historically: Drama and Poetry from Chaucer to the Reformation* (Edinburgh: Edinburgh University Press, 2013), pp. 36–41.

[11] See James C. Scott, *Weapons of the Weak: Everyday Forms of Peasant Resistance* (New Haven and London: Yale University Press, 1985) and *Domination and the Arts of Resistance: The Hidden Transcript* (New Haven and London: Yale University Press, 1990).

[12] See Greg Walker, *Writing and Tyranny: English Literature and the Henrician Reformation* (Oxford: Oxford University Press, 2005), *passim*.

Luther and his allies (as their conservative critics alleged), but long-standing grievances, frequently voiced by patriotic Englishmen in the past. To this end they sought out the opinions of a previous generation of critics of church governance and doctrine, principally later Lollard writings (including, as we shall see, works spuriously attributed to Chaucer), and revised and adapted them for a modern readership. As a result, old texts were unearthed, collated, rewritten and printed, the unfinished business of the previous century was revisited, the exiled and the repressed returned, and the Wycliffite dead walked and spoke again in Tudor England.

To name only a handful of these texts: in 1530, two Lollard tracts were published by the Antwerp printer Johannes Hoochstraten (under the pseudonym 'Hans Luft of Marborow'). A substantial section of 'an old treatise made about the time of King Richard II' against clerical ownership of property and holding of secular offices was printed as part of a modern text, *A Proper Dialogue between a Gentleman and a Husbandman, each complaining to Other their Miserable Calamity through the Ambition of the Clergy,* probably written by Jerome Barlow.[13] A second text, *A Compendious Old Treatise Showing how that we ought to have the Scripture in English,* written c.1400 by the Lollard John Purvey, was also printed by Hoochstraten the same year. Later in 1530 both of these texts were republished together in a single volume, again by Hoochstraten, and two texts claiming to be the testimony of Lollard martyrs under persecution, the *Examinations* of William Thorpe and Sir John Oldcastle, were also published in Antwerp for the English market. A year later, *The Prayer and Complaint of the Ploughman unto Christ* (supposedly written 'not long after the year of our lord 1300', but provided with a modern preface dated 'the last day of February 1531'), printed by Martinus de Keyser in Antwerp, and reprinted in the same year by Thomas Godfrey in London, introduced a slightly more literary sensibility into the debate, while in 1532 Godfrey printed *The Plowman's Tale,* a polemical fifteenth-century dream vision with a complex history that claimed to be the 'lost' contribution of the Ploughman to Chaucer's *Canterbury Tales.*[14] Finally, around 1536, a still more nakedly polemical late-medieval tract, *Jack Upland,* was printed by the reformer John Gough, as 'compiled by the famous Geoffrey Chaucer'.

[13] The *Dialogue* was also known as *An ABC of the Clergy,* as it is prefaced by a verse text of that name. For the detail here, see Margaret Aston, 'Lollardy and the Reformation: Survival or Revival?', *History,* 49 (1964), 149–70; Hudson, '"No new thyng"', pp. 153–74.

[14] See '*The Plowman's Tale* and the Politics of 1532: A Cautionary Tale?', in Walker, *Reading Literature Historically,* pp. 121–68.

What all these texts had in common was that they offered venerable precedents for the arguments of the evangelicals of the early 1530s. They thus, as Ann Hudson and Margaret Aston have shown, seemed to provide a concrete refutation of the charge that such arguments were the inventions of a few modern heretics ('a sect newfangled, / With execrable heresies entangled'[15]) inspired by Luther. As the Husbandman in *A Proper Dialogue* asserts, he can prove that charge to be 'a stark lie' on the evidence of the Lollard tract, 'which [...] I dare be bold /[...] is above an hundred year old, / As the English [it]self doth testify' (Biii(v)):

> Lo now, by this treatise may ye well see
> That aforetimes against the spirituality
> Men did inveigh, showing their vices. (Civ)

To this the Gentleman replies:

> If such annoyant things might come to light,
> That noble men had once of them a sight,
> The world yet would change, peradventure.
> For here-against the clergy cannot bark,
> Saying as they do, 'This is a new work,
> Of heretics contrived lately'.
> And by this treatise it appeareth plain
> That before our days men did complain
> Against the clerks' ambition so starkly. (Cv)[16]

15 *A Proper Dialogue*, Biii(v). For criticism of this sort, see, for example, the mockery of the 'new-named brethren' in Sir Thomas More, *Letter Against Frith*, in *Letter to Bugenhagen, Supplication of Souls, Letter Against Frith*, in Franks Manley, Germain Marc'hadour, Richard C. Marius and Clarence H. Miller, eds, *The Complete Works of St Thomas More*, 7 edns (New Haven and London: Yale University Press, 1990), pp. 233 (and following); and, regarding 'new-fangled fantasies' and 'these new fathers of the new brethren' in More, *The Apology of Sir Thomas More, Knight*, in J. B. Trapp, ed., *The Complete Works of St Thomas More*, 9 (New Haven and London: Yale University Press, 1979), pp. 9 and 168.

16 See also *The Prayer and Complaint of the Plowman unto Christ*, which aimed to show that the clergy's criticism of evangelical preaching as 'a new learning' was 'no new thing but an old practice of our prelates' (Aiii(v)). The author claimed that Christ and the apostles 'taught nothing that was not taught in the Law and the Prophets more than a thousand years before [...] Yet all this notwithstanding, the Scribes, the Pharisees, the bishops, the priests, the lawyers, and the elders of the people cried always, "What new learning is this? These fellows teach new learning. These be they that trouble all the world with their new learning", etc [...] And so with a vain name of new learning, and with their authority of old

Such texts provided Henrician evangelicals with the necessary proof that they were indeed God's chosen, ordained to do Christ's work as part of predestined eschatological history. They were part of a reformist typology, pointing forward from the Plantagenet and Lancastrian past to the Tudor time of revelation. As Luther put it in the preface to the 1528 edition of the Lollard *Opus Arduum*, John Wyclif was no anomalous dissenter of merely historical interest, but 'a witness preordained by God so many years before us, for the confirmation of our doctrine'.[17] He had, though, like Gildas before him, been as a voice crying in the wilderness, destined to see his views defeated – or rather forestalled – by the ignorance of his times. As Tyndale argued in the preface to *The Prophet Jonas* (?1531):

> Wyclif preached repentance unto our fathers not long since, they repented not, for their hearts were indurate and their eyes blinded with their own pope-holy righteousness, wherewith they made their souls gay against [i.e. *in preparation for*] the receiving again of that wicked spirit that bringeth vii worse than himself with him and maketh the latter end worse than the beginning.[18]

As both Tyndale here and the author of *A Proper Dialogue* elsewhere suggested, the Lollard moment had been only one of many abortive attempts to spread the vernacular gospel or reclaim the wealth of the Church for lay use. Henry V had tried it, but been distracted towards French wars by his self-interested bishops; Kings Stephen, John, and Henry II had tried before him, as had Louis of Bavaria, all without success.[19]

learning and ancientness of the church, they so blinded the same people that heard Christ's doctrine of his own mouth [...] that the next day after they cried, "hang him on the cross! Hang him on the cross!"' (Aii). 'Even now after the same manner [...] our holy bishops with all their ragman's roll be of the selfsame sort, the very children of their fathers the Pharisees' (Aii(v)), responsible for the litany of persecutions from that of 'Stephen the first martyr to the blood of that innocent man of God, Thomas Hytton, who William Warham, bishop of Canterbury and John Fisher, bishop of Rochester, murdered at Maidstone in Kent, anno 1530, for the same truth' (Aiii).

17 Hudson, '"No new thyng"', p. 174; Aston, 'Lollardy and the Reformation', *passim*.

18 William Tyndale, *The prophete Jonas with an introduccio[n] before teachinge to vndersto[n]de him and the right vse also of all the scripture...* (Antwerp : M. de Keyser, 1531?), Biii(v). In Tyndale's account, Gildas 'preached repentance unto the old Britons that inhabited England; they repented not and so God sent in their enemies on every side and destroyed them' (ibid). See also, Aston, 'Lollardy and the Reformation', 152–5.

19 Tyndale, *The Prophete Jonas*, Cvi(v)–Cvii; *A Proper Dialogue*, Bii(v).

For these reformers, the medieval period was thus a long, dark, backward abysm of time, an age of superstition in which kings and people alike were blinded and repeatedly misled by the impostures and juggling of the clergy.[20] Yet it was also, crucially, a period that generated a clutch of writers who anticipated – and indeed sometimes went significantly further than – the reforming initiatives of the Henrician period.[21] The reformers' version of English history was thus the story of God's repeated attempts to bring the people to repentance and conversion through the teaching of his prophets, a history that was repeating itself with still greater urgency in the Tudor present:

> And now Christ to preach repentance is risen yet once again out of his sepulchre in which the Pope had buried him and keepeth him down [...] And as I doubt not of the examples that are past, so am I sure that great wrath will follow, except repentance return it back again and cease it.[22]

The *Compendious Old Treatise* also used history as the basis of a seemingly prophetic account of the success of biblical translation and vernacular evangelism in the Tudor period that was also a warning of the dire consequences of failure:

> It lieth never in Antichrist's power to destroy all English books, for, as fast as he burneth, other men shall draw, and thus the cause of heresy and of the people that dieth in heresy is the frowardness of bishops that will not suffer men to have open communing and free in the law

[20] See Thomas Betteridge, *Tudor Histories of the English Reformation, 1530–83* (Aldershot: Ashgate, 1999), pp. 1–86, and Glanmor Williams, *Reformation Views of Church History* (Cambridge: John Clarke and Son reprint, 2004), p. 15.

[21] In addition to the examples cited below, see Robert Crowley's observation in his preface to the first printed edition of *Piers Plowman* that at the time of its writing, which Crowley dated to the reign of Edward III, 'it pleased God to open the eyes of many to see his truth, giving them boldness of heart, to open their mouths, and cry out against the works of darkness, as did John Wicklefe'. Robert Crowley, 'The Printer to the Reader' (1550), p. 1. See Matthews, 'The Spectral Past', p. 5. The idea would come to fruition in John Foxe's *Acts and Monuments...*, ed. G. Townsend and S. R. Cattley, 8 vols (London: R. B. Seely and W. Burnside, 1837–41), II, p. 796, where Wyclif is described thus: 'in these so great and troublous times and horrible darkness of ignorance, what time there seemed in a manner to be not one so little a spark of pure doctrine remaining [...] by God's providence sprang and rose up [one] through whom the Lord would first waken and raise up the Word'.

[22] Tyndale, *The Prophete Jonas*, Biv.

of God, and now they turn His law by their cruel constitutions into damnation of the people. (sig, Avi(v))

Texts such as the *Treatise* and *A Proper Dialogue* confidently predicted that, once exposed, the frauds and corruption of the clergy would provoke such a furious reaction from the laity – the commons, lords and sovereign alike – that they would be swept away forever. And the medium of such exposure would be these texts themselves. As we have seen, the Gentleman declared in *A Proper Dialogue*, 'if such ancient things might come to light, / That noble men had once of them a sight, / The world yet would change, paradventure'. The *ABC concerning the Spirituality* and the editor of Thorpe's *Examination* (perhaps Tyndale), put it more confidently, the clergy's 'disguised madness in the latter end, / As Saint Paul to Timothy doth prophesy, / Shall be known to all men manifestly' – 'the lord of light shall lighten thee with the candle of his grace to see the truth', 'For their [the clergy's] clotted lies could never have continued so long in the light as they have done in corners'.[23] Once the people had the Bible in English before them, they would see the glaring difference between the lifestyles of the apostles and those of the clergy nowadays, *A Proper Dialogue* declares, and they would take action.[24]

The *Proper Dialogue* author, indeed, had a more pragmatic suggestion of how this truth might be revealed, having his Husbandman propose that he and the Gentleman 'get us to London incontinent' to protest to the Reformation Parliament itself in accordance with Henry VIII's invitation, 'the constraint of our misery to declare, / Under a meet form of lamentation' (Aiii(v)). And when the Gentleman objects that their voices would surely be drowned out by those of 'the marvellous great multitude' of clerics in Parliament, his interlocutor replies:

[23] *An ABC*, in *A Proper Dialogue*, Ai(v); 'Unto the Christian Reader', in *The Examinacion of Master William Thorpe, preste…* (1530), Aii(v) and Ai(v); and Aston, 'Lollardy and the Reformation', p. 155. Likewise *A Compendious Old Treatise* promised, 'Although I am old, clothed i' barbarous weed, / Nothing garnished with gay eloquency, / Yet I tell the truth if ye list to take heed' (*A Proper Dialogue*, Cviii), citing John 3:20 ('For every one that doth evil hateth the light, and cometh not to the light, that his works may not be reproved.'), while *The Prayer and Complaint of the Plowman* confidently predicted that 'As for the truth, when they [the bishops] have slain and put to silence all the preachers of the same and laid it to sleep, doubtless God, after his old fashion, shall thereby them and those means that they doubt least, rise up the truth again, to the utter confusion of his enemies' (Aiii(v)).

[24] *A Proper Dialogue*, Avii(v). See also *An ABC*'s apparent certainty that 'were their [the clergy's] faults detect manifestly' 'men should see their seeking / Is to confound Christ's gospel utterly' (*An ABC* in *A Proper Dialogue*, Aii).

Their tyranny is great, without fail,
Nevertheless, if we would them assail
With arguments of the holy Gospel,
They should not be once able to resist,
For the words of our saviour Christ
Should stop them, were they never so fell. (Bii)

God, truth and history were thus on the reformers' side, they claimed. But the conclusive evidence that these claims were true came in the paradoxical form of proof, as we have seen, that all of this had happened before. Other good men and women had seen through the clergy's frauds, and exposed and denounced them before. This was indeed 'no new thing', no fresh fantasy dreamed up by Luther and Tyndale to unsettle the ancient, unbroken traditions of the Church, but part of an equally venerable tradition of truth-telling. The old authentic texts printed in the early 1530s provided in and of themselves a categorical refutation of the allegation that contemporary reformers were rootless, newfangled fantasists.

And yet, such texts offered at the same time a tacit acknowledgement of their own impotence. Their proof of authenticity was bought at the price of their acceptance of a place in a long history of unresolved and, by definition, fruitless repetition. In order for it to succeed, that is, the Reformation must already have happened. But to have already happened, it must also always already have failed. Reform's contemporary success was thus predicated on the demonstrable failure of the self-same thing in the past: and the more often the better. True men, the argument runs, have always spoken out against the usurpations and corruptions of the clergy, and the Church has always reacted violently to that criticism, seeking to destroy both the texts and the witnessing bodies of its critics. The dark, dirty secrets of the clergy were thus continually being unearthed and exposed, only to be reburied again to be re-exposed by later generations. Indeed, evangelical history relied precisely upon those secrets repeatedly *being* rehidden in order that they might be repeatedly represented *as* hidden, and re-exposed for fresh scandalised scrutiny. Such repression of the truth was thus the basis of the evangelicals' own truth claims, an idea grounded in Christ's words recorded in Matthew 10:34: 'Do not think that I came to send peace upon earth: I came not to send peace, but the sword. [I came to set a man at variance against his father, and the daughter against her mother.]'[25] Contention and division of the

[25] See Thomas More, *Dialogue Concerning Heresies*, ed. M. C. Lawler, Germain Marc'hadour and Richard Marius, *The Complete Works of St. Thomas More*, 6

kind that characterised the period of the Reformation Parliament were thus the necessary proof of the reformers' claims to be the true disciples of Christ. If they were not persecuted, met with violent denial and suppression whenever they appeared, they could not be who they claimed to be.

The reformers of the 1530s could indeed prove they were telling the truth, then, because others before them had said the self-same things. They stood in a line stretching back to Christ himself, and indeed beyond, for *The Prayer and Complaint* argued that Christ was persecuted by the Pharisees and elders for doing 'no more than preach what the law and the prophets had declared a thousand years before [him]'.[26] But, like their Plantagenet predecessors, they could only claim that this time they would succeed, because their arguments were so shockingly compelling and incontrovertible. Once the people – once the King, the nobles – saw the truth, the whole corrupt edifice of clerical tyranny would come tumbling down. The light of the gospel would scatter the shadows and banish all trace of centuries of darkness. How could they be sure it would do this? Because it was always happening – or rather it would have been, had it not always been prevented. The spectre of repeated failure thus haunted the early Tudor reformers, as their anxious warnings about God's wrath – should they fail 'yet once again' to do his work in the unique, yet uncannily familiar circumstances of the 1530s – seem to suggest.

For opponents of evangelical reform, such as Thomas More, 'heresy' was also a matter of repetition, part of the *longue durée* of Christian history, the equivalent of the ship of Theseus described by Nagel and Wood, a paradoxical, anachronic object whose identity and 'ontological stability' were, despite the fact that it was finally constituted of none of its original timbers, 'sustained across time by the stability of its name and the tacit substitution of its parts'.[27] All of the component parts were new,

(New Haven and London: Yale University Press, 1981), pp. 124–5, the claim made in the Tudor part of the *Compendious Old Treatise*, attributed to the voice of the text itself, that 'Enemies I shall have many a shaven crown… / Yet to showeth verity one may be bold / As though it be an proverb daily spoken: / 'Who that telleth truth his head shall be broken' (in *A Proper Dialogue*, Cii), and Tyndale's *The Obedience of a Christian Man* (Antwerp: Hans Luft [i.e. J. Hoochstraten], 1528), Bi(v): 'it is a plain earnest that there is no other way into the kingdom of life than through persecution and suffering of pain, and of very death, after the ensample of Christ'.

[26] *The Prayer and Complaint*, Ai(v)–Aii.

[27] Nagel and Wood, *Anachronic Renaissance*, pp. 8–9. In More's version of divine history it was also tradition and history, the unbroken continuity of the Church in faith from the time of the Apostles to the present, that was the absolute guarantee

but the ship itself nonetheless somehow remained authentic and original. In More's view, Luther, Tyndale, John Frith and Thomas Bilney were just the modern names given to the roles once played by the heretics of the third to the fifth centuries, Arius, Pelagius, Manichaeus and Faustus, all of whom were in turn but limbs of the devil and Antichrist, distinct in their specifics but interchangeable in their motivation and their places in ecclesiastical history:

> And surely the thing that made Arius, Pelagius, Faustus, Manichaeus, Donatus [...] and all the rabble of old heretics to drown themsel[ves] in those damnable heresies was nothing but high pride of their learning in scripture, wherein they followed their own wits and left the common faith of the catholic church, preferring their own gay glosses before the right catholic faith of all Christ's church. (*Dialogue*, p. 153)

Thus, just as Wyclif:

> [B]egan again the old heresies of those ancient heretics whom and whose errors the church of Christ had condemned and subdued many diverse ages before, so doth Luther again began to set up his. For all that he hath in effect he hath of him [Wyclif]. Saving that, lest he should seem to say nothing of his own, he added some things of himself of such manner sort as there was never heretic before his days. (*Dialogue*, p. 315)

And the same act of proud, repetitive, wilful innovation, More argued, characterised the Tudor heretics, such as Thomas Bilney (who 'whatsoever himself listed to take for good, that thought he forthwith approved by God. And so framed himself a faith, framed himself a conscience, framed himself a devotion, wherein him list, and wherein him liked he set himself a liberty') and John Frith (who, More claimed, had merely drunk the dregs of Oecolampadius, Tyndale and Zwingli).

For More, the return of these literally repressed heresies marks a distinctive case of the revenant. Just as Bilney, Frith and Tyndale were recognisable as new examples of the eternal heretic, so the resurrected Lollard texts are also both strange and familiar, both worryingly new and

of its righteousness. For in a point to which he returned repeatedly in *Dialogue Concerning Heresies*, it was unthinkable that the Christ who had promised that he would always be with true believers (Matthew 28:20, 'behold I am with you all days, even to the consummation of the world') would not allow the Church to err so badly or for so long in any matter vital for salvation.

wearisomely old, the latest cases of a history of haunting that could only be met and challenged by a yet further case of repetition – the detailed rehearsal and refutation of their claims point by point, line by line, by the true believer.[28] As More feared, this heretical tradition could – given fallen, fallible human nature – never be fully exorcised, but each new generation of the orthodox must take up yet once again the challenge afresh, concede to the urge to repeat themselves, both certain that God would not allow them to fail, and resigned to the prospect of continued frustration.

The Anachronic Reformation

The period of the Reformation Parliament was, then, a moment that, even as it seemed to many to exemplify terrifying, even apocalyptic, novelty, also seemed to live again other moments of English history. Indeed, it was a moment that declared vociferously its own belated place in a long history of such moments of potential revolutionary spiritual and social renovation, as one in a series of haunting, uncanny repetitions. It was a moment of profound chronological distortion in which history folded in upon itself and declared its own indecisiveness, even as those involved most actively in the folding process claimed both the familiarity and the absolute decisiveness of what was happening, whether they thought it was for good or for ill.

In Nagel and Wood's account of the anachronic in art they observe that, 'the work of art, when it is late, when it repeats, when it hesitates, when it remembers, but also when it projects an ideal, is "anachronic"'. '[T]he ability of the work of art to hold incompatible models in suspension, without deciding is the key to art's anachronic quality, its ability to "fetch" a past, create a past, perhaps even fetch the future.'[29] In these senses the revenant texts of 1530–35 are precisely anachronic. Both belated and prophetic, they bend and fold time, suggesting how the past foreshadowed and predicted the present and also how the present repeats the same prophetic act, echoing the past and projecting a further reformist future to their present and future Tudor readers. They folded the 'premature reformation' of the 1400s into the Henrician Reformation

[28] For More's strategy of 'leav[ing] not one syllable out' in his rehearsal of his opponents' arguments, see, for example, More, *The Apology*, p. 6; and More, *The Debellation of Salem and Bizance*, in John Guy, Ralph Keen, Clarence H. Miller and Ruth McGugan, eds, *The Complete Works of St Thomas More*, 10 (New Haven and London: Yale University Press, 1987), p. 7.

[29] Nagel and Wood, *Anachronic Renaissance*, pp. 13, 18.

of the 1530s, bringing the too early and the belated into provocative juxtaposition. The future moment of the fulfilment of the gospel that those Lollard writers prophesied was the now of their Tudor successors, but the work of fulfilment was still to be done if the present was not simply to pass into history as yet another lost opportunity. And that, of course, is precisely what it would do when the longed-for Henrician Reformation proved to be too little and too slow to meet the more committed reformers' demands, prompting John Fox to reprint *Jack Upland*, the *Compendious Old Treatise* and *The Prayer and Complaint* in his *Acts and Monuments* in the 1560s and 1570s, as part of the campaign to promote further reformation in the reign of Henry's daughter Elizabeth, thereby adding yet another level of compulsive repetition and typology to reformist historiography.

More specifically, perhaps, the 'Chaucer' resurrected in *The Plowman's Tale* and *Jack Upland* was a definitively anachronic figure, uncanny in his mixing of the familiar and the strange, of the just possibly plausible and the utterly impossible. To write like Chaucer, to write *as* Chaucer in the fifteenth century, or to pass off this writing as Chaucer's in the 1530s, these were audacious, unsettling acts. And some attempts were more convincing than others. *The Plowman's Tale* (seemingly the work of a number of hands through the early fifteenth century)[30] makes a plausible attempt to reproduce Chaucerian form and tone at the start of the text at least, through a brief frame narrative in which 'our host' invites the eponymous Ploughman to 'come near and tell us some holy thing'. But the ensuing tale is a distinctly un-Chaucerian account of a 'sermon' that the narrator claims to have witnessed, which 'sermon' turns out in turn to be a third-person account of a one-sided dialogue between two beasts – a pelican sympathetic to religious reform and a griffon representing the clergy – over the sins of the Church. The tale did not make it into William Thynne's 1532 edition of Chaucer's *Works*, suggesting there were doubts about its authenticity at the time (a possibility seemingly confirmed by the testimony of Thynne's son Francis, who recalled in his *Animadversions*, printed in 1599, that the tale was 'supposed, but untruly, to be made by old Sir Thomas Wyatt [...] and not by Chaucer').[31] But it did sneak into the expanded edition of 1542. *Jack Upland*, a rather more straightforward polemic against the friars, made it into neither edition and

30 Walker, 'The *Plowman's Tale*', pp. 154–6.

31 F. J. Furnivall, ed., *Animadversions uppon the Corrections of some Imperfectiones of Chaucer's Workes…sett down by Francis Thynne*, Early English Text Society, original series, 9 (London: Kegan Paul, Trench and Trubner, 1865), p. 10.

would not be incorporated into the canon until the seventeenth century, and then only briefly.

These texts were thus paradigmatic instances of the revenant (in both the medieval sense of an unquiet spirit bound to the earth by unfinished business, and the Freudian sense of a manifestation of anxiety, of that which has been repressed returning).[32] For the uncanny, paradoxical power of the revenant resides, as Lawrence Kramer usefully describes it, specifically in the impossibility of its own existence. The revenant unnerves and distorts precisely because its observers are aware, even as they stare at it, that it cannot actually be real. It is, in Kramer's words, 'there, right there, precisely insofar as it can't possibly be there at all'.[33] The thought that Chaucer, the urbane father of English poetry, who so rarely intruded specific contemporary commentary into his works, and habitually avoided controversy, might have written a text as sharply contentious and unnuanced as *The Plowman's Tale*, still less the list of bludgeoning, anticlerical, rhetorical questions that make up *Jack Upland*, was practically unthinkable. But that knowledge was no doubt tempered and held in productive tension in the minds of the printers and evangelical readers of these texts with an equal and opposite zealous desire that he might actually have done so – that the poet was really 'one of us' after all, a member of the hidden true church of Christ. Could the Geoffrey Chaucer who wrote *An ABC*, *The Parson's Tale* or the 'Retraction' also have written *Jack Upland*? It was an impossible thought. But to prove it, there was *Jack Upland*, right there, claiming on its title page that it was 'compiled by the famous Geoffrey Chaucer'.

It was not only, then, that, as Nagel and Wood's model suggests,[34] these revenant texts allow the past to participate in the present, disrupting its certainties, but that through them the present reaches back into the past and seeks to rewrite part of it in the cultural memory, reconfiguring Chaucer as the proto-Protestant, the 'right Wyclifian' that he would be received as by his Elizabethan editors. Adding the poet to the file of

[32] For the medieval tradition of the spirit bound to the earth by unfinished business, see Nancy Caciola, 'Wraiths, Revenants and Ritual in Medieval Culture', *Past and Present*, 152 (1996), 3–45.

[33] Kramer, 'Revenants', p. 453. Kramer's point is a development of Freud's suggestion that the uncanny involves 'things which seem to confirm our deep-seated irrational beliefs', the example cited being the existence of revenants ('so the dead *do* live on and appear on the scene of their former activities'). Freud, *The Uncanny*, p. 371. See also Royle, *The Uncanny*, p. 84 ('something comes back because in some sense it was never properly there in the first place').

[34] Nagel and Wood, *Anachronic Renaissance*, p. 32.

restless spirits returning to admonish their Tudor descendants to attend to the still-to-be-reformed Church, these texts rewrite the past in the attempt to influence the present and determine the future, exemplifying Nagel and Wood's suggestion that, an 'artwork functioned as a token of power in its own time, precisely by complicating time, by reactivating prestigious forebears, by comparing events across time, by fabricating memories'.[35] As I have suggested, the revenant Lollard and pseudo-Chaucerian texts of the 1530s do – or seek to do – all of these things.

The 'early' Reformation of the 1530s was thus at once early, belated and forestalled, a return to and of old things and an aspirational pointing forward to things not yet achieved but always already imagined. It was thus, like the texts that drove it, precisely, disruptively, untimely. To borrow a phrase from Jonathan Gil Harris, it was 'out-of-time, inhabiting a moment but also alien to it and out of step with it'.[36] That untimeliness created both its cultural power – its capacity to confront critics and would-be supporters alike with the shock of the old, the authenticity of the revenant returned to complete its work, and its internal contradictions – and its distorting, disruptive bifurcation between reassuring age and startling, uncertain novelty.

What these texts provide is one specific, local instance of the much wider paradigm shift that distorted and remade the early modern sense of time and history, and individuals' relations to those notions, in the course of the sixteenth-century Reformations. They play out in microcosm the clash between the idea of history as legible and repeatable and the sense of unprecedented, unsettling novelty that must have been the experience of many if not most politically engaged subjects in the period. The mobilisation of society as never before by the demands, both collective and individual, of confessionalisation, the need to take sides in an increasingly evident religious schism, involved many more citizens in the politicised religious disputes of the moment. These disputes were at once national and international and played out in the hearts and homes of every individual believer. Citizens of sixteenth-century England were prompted to think, feel and believe things about their own history, and their place in that history, in ways that previous generations had not been. The landscape was shifting before their eyes as familiar landmarks were erased or reinterpreted, old stories retold with new meanings and new lessons applied to them. English subjects were asked to think of King

35 Nagel and Wood, *Anachronic Renaissance*, p. 18.

36 Harris, *Untimely Matter*, p. 11.

John not as a tyrant but a champion of a premature royal supremacy,[37] and of Thomas Becket not as a martyr but a traitor. They saw Chaucer rewritten not as a pilgrim but an opponent of pilgrimage, the father not only of English letters but also of English reform. All of this was part of the grand project to rethink the previous millennium not as one of continuity and progress but of Babylonian captivity, an enslavement under a popish antichrist. Some of those touched by these arguments evidently saw them as a liberation, an enfranchisement to think and speak in new ways and so become new selves. Others just as clearly saw them as a threat, a sign of truths corrupted and things falling apart. What they shared, I would argue, was a new, and as yet not fully acknowledged, sense of time and history distorted and unmade, of the present moment as different in kind from the past yet at the same time uncannily like it. Even as they claimed the repeatability of history, they simultaneously attested to its difference from their 'now'. For the reformers, the difference was evident in the unique opportunity to redeem and fulfil the past in the present.[38] For More and his allies it opened up a terrifying prospect, should heresy prevail, of the unshackling of the present from history – the loss of the continuity that joined them to the church fathers in uninterrupted witnesses to the truths of the faith.

If the humanist scholarship of the Renaissance rested on the notion of history as a scrutable sequence in which events could be dated and texts securely located (or their provenance disputed) on the basis of linguistic or contextual analysis and reason – a sense of reading the past as a different country, but one where different things were done in logically explicable ways – so the early Reformation, through revenant texts such as those we have considered, confused the picture and distorted the sense of sequentiality. At the same time as they acknowledged the difference of the past (as in the assertion in *The Proper Dialogue* that one could tell the age of the text by the antiquity of its language – 'as the English [it]self doth testify' (Biii(v))), so they also suggested, or indeed asserted, how the past might repeat itself in the present, might prefigure or pre-empt it. And, they

[37] See *Proper Dialogue*, Bi(v) and Tyndale, *Obedience of a Christian Man*, Vv(r–v).

[38] See, for example, Walter Lynne, *The Beginning and Ending of all Popery, or Popish Kingdom* (London, Aldgate Street: John Herforde, 1548), Cii, where it is claimed that 'many old and faithful fathers' saw that the Pope was antichrist, 'yet durst they not clearly set it forth, except only by figures. Trusting always that through the mercy of God a time should come when they might be brought to light. And so clearly set forth that it were impossible more sightly [sic] to pain them.' That time, for Lynne, was evidently the Tudor present.

implied, it might do so not as a storehouse of exempla to be studied and understood but as a more confused, troubling memory or echo of paths not taken, journeys pursued only so far and then forestalled.

On the other side of the argument, that melancholic nostalgia that looked back from the 1590s at a Catholic England by then seemingly irretrievably lost – accessible across the gulf created by mid-Tudor reform only in the architectural traces of bare-ruined choirs and half-remembered traditions recalled in street names, folk practices and the failing memories of the old – was, of course, not yet established in the 1530s. But in More's writings there are hints of it, and surer signs of another kind of melancholy, another nostalgia prompted by weariness at the demand to repeat, of the sense that nothing is really over. Heretics will repeatedly challenge true belief with ever-more subtle weapons, and men of good will must repeatedly oppose and refute them.

A sense of the distortion and confusion of chronologies is suggested by the charges each side levelled against the other. For More, the heretic's prime need was to claim novelty for his or her opinions, while the reformers, as we have seen, were desperate to claim exactly the reverse. More claimed so because, for him, heresy was above all things an act of will, an assertion of the individual's own pride in themselves, of the ego's need to be admired and adored. Hence, every heretic was secretly convinced of his or her own uniqueness, even while he or she slavishly repeated the errors of their predecessors, driven ultimately by the timeless malice of the devil. For the reformers, the rewriting of history proved that they were not alone but part of a long tradition, but at the same time uniquely privileged to live in the lord of light's time of revelation, both echoing and also completing the story of Christian history. Yet in that sense of repetition, of the 'yet-once-again-ness' of Reformation historiography we see the distorting, generative power of the revenant at work, and gain a sense of the paradoxical nature of this new reformed typology – of folk living, not in the clarity of God's will fulfilled in and through history, but in a time of uncertain revelation, of potentially infinite regress, of distorting, uncanny repetition. (We might note here the unsettling claim in *The Prayer and Complaint* that even Christ and the apostles were not innovators but repeaters, teaching 'no new thing which was not taught in the law and the prophets more than a thousand years before [them]' (Ai(V)–Aii).) The idea that history was shared and knowable was falling apart, to be replaced by a sense of fragmented, contested histories, multiple, rival, uncertain and unfinished. The past was being rewritten as contested territory, distorted and remade by the confessionalism of the present, just as the present was being remade from the claims made in and about the past. A sense that history and its texts were never finished and done with, but always simultaneously both out of and working *in* time was perhaps the most powerfully distorting, transformative consequence of the debates generated by the Reformation Parliament.

Just as historians have come to think not of a single, decisive, revolutionary Reformation, but of a whole series of reformations, variously progressive, reactionary, magisterial or popular, with varying implications for what followed, and varying degrees of success, so perhaps these texts help us to see this lengthy process of reform not as marking, however haltingly or fragmentarily, a break with the past, but as performing an ongoing re-evaluation of relationships with a set of rival pasts, a paradoxical series of repetitive breaks and new beginnings that presented themselves as continuity, and continuities that presented themselves as unique moments of dislocation and rupture. In this sense the cultural work of these revenant texts distorted not simply the certainties of their own moment in time, but the early-modern sense of time and history more generally.

The Presence of the Book

CLAUDE WILLAN

When Harold Bloom wrote that all reading was misreading, that all prision was in fact misprision, and that poets learned from and imitated their forerunners by misreading them, he inaugurated a now well-established school of literary aesthetics.[1] For Bloom, the material means by which a text was transmitted from a writer to a reader was in itself apparently unproblematic. He happily reified mediation in his impatience to delineate the shaping force of literary history. In fact, the study of distortion shows that, in a sense, Bloom is exactly wrong. All reading is correct reading, because each textual artefact is unique.

Distortion is the moment at which the physical means of transmitting a text irrupt into a reader's experience of it. I will discuss distortion here as a phenomenon occurring in printed materials, but I do not wish to exclude other recognisable instances such as static in a radio signal, or white noise on a cathode-ray-tube television screen. To speak of distortion as an impairment, however, is to confirm the Platonic priority of another book-object. As textual scholars have shown, locating this authoritative *ur*-text can be, to say the least, difficult.[2] Distortion is not a condition befalling individual textual artefacts ('book-objects') here and there: there is no non-distorted reading. In fact, a belief in non-distorted reading amounts to believing in pure, transparent mediation that leaves no trace of itself on the mediated.[3] Leaving aside for the purposes of this essay the

[1] Harold Bloom, *The Anxiety of Influence: A Theory of Poetry* (Oxford: Oxford University Press, 1997).

[2] See Stephen Orgel, 'What is an Editor', *Shakespeare Studies*, 24 (1996), 23–30. Brian Vickers's *The One King Lear* (Cambridge, MA: Harvard University Press, 2016) sought to reconstruct an *ur*-text for Shakespeare's play; Holger Syme argued for the folly of such an attempt, and for Vickers's approach to it, first on Twitter and then in 'The Text is Foolish: Brian Vickers's "The One King Lear"', *Los Angeles Review of Books*, 6 September 2016, available at: https://lareviewofbooks.org/article/text-foolish-brian-vickerss-one-king-lear/ (accessed 22 February 2017).

[3] For an excellent set of recent approaches to mediation and its historical forms, see the essays collected in the section 'Mediation: A Concept in History', in Clifford Siskin and William Warner, eds, *This is Enlightenment* (Chicago: University of Chicago Press, 2010), pp. 37–137.

profound political implications of placing the labour of mediation under erasure, I will offer here a heuristic of distortion. Absent such a heuristic, 'distorted' book-objects and their texts will always be treated as degraded derivatives. The corollary of that treatment is to elevate an unknown, possibly non-existent *ur*-text to a position of unimpeachable authority, and to degrade both the experience of reading and of the embodied text and reader. We can solve the problem of distortion by placing the irreducible phenomenological singularity of the book-object at the centre of our experience of a text. This is existential reading: you are reading what you are reading and not anything else.

In the Clark Library at the University of California, Los Angeles, there are two copies of *An Answer to the Arguments in the Lord Bishop of Oxford's Speech, on the impeachment of Dr. Henry Sacheverell.*[4] In it the author rebuts the Bishop of Oxford's speech and accuses the Bishop of Jacobitism. The greater number of listeners and readers, writes the author:

> [C]onscious of some small mixture of Temporal views in the purest of their own Activities, and measuring your Lordship by themselves, are apprehensive of some Prodigiously deep design, and dread this Speech of yours as the leading Card to some glorious Aftergame, for retrieving that abandon'd exploded Thing, the *Good Old Cause*.[5]

This text documents one part of the ongoing and explosive political flashpoint that was known as the Sacheverell affair. On 5 November 1709, Reverend Henry Sacheverell had preached in St Paul's Cathedral in London that:

> The grand Security of our Government, and the very Pillar upon which it Stands, is founded upon the steady Belief of the Subject's Obligation to an Absolute, and Unconditional Obedience to the Supream Power, in All Things Lawful, and the utter Illegality of Resistance upon any Pretence whatsoever. But this Fundamental Doctrin, notwithstanding its Divine Sanction in the Express Command of God in Scripture, and without which, it is impossible any Government of any Kind, or Denomination in the World, should subsist with Safety, and which has been so long the Honourable, and Distinguishing Characteristic

[4] A. B., *An Answer to the Arguments in the Lord Bishop of Oxford's Speech, on the impeachment of Dr. Henry Sacheverell* (London: Anon, 1709).

[5] A. B. *An Answer to the Arguments*, p. 4. The 'Good Old Cause' referred to here is Jacobitism, the political movement agitating for the restoration of the House of Stuart to the throne of England and then Britain after the revolution of 1688 until, roughly, the Battle of Culloden in 1746.

> of Our Church, is now, it seems, quite Exploded and Redicul'd out of Countenance, as an Unfashionable, Superannuated, nay (which is more wonderful) as a Dangerous Tenet, utterly Inconsistent with the Right Liberty and Property of the PEOPLE; who as our New Preachers, and New Politicians teach us (I suppose by a New, and Unheard of Gospel, as well as Laws) have in Contradiction to Both, the Power Invested in Them, the Fountain and Original of it, to Cancel their Allegiance at pleasure, and call their Sovereign to account for High-Treason against his Supream Subjects, forsooth! nay to De-throne, and Murder Him for a Criminal, as they did the Royal Martyr by a Judiciary Sentence.[6]

The case is worth revisiting because the trial revolved around a written record of an evanescent oral performance attesting to a distortion of civil and ecclesiastical law. The fidelity of the written record as a trace of the performance is unknowable. The text with which I began, *An Answer to the Arguments in the Lord Bishop of Oxford's Speech*, is a response to a speech given at an evaluation of that trace itself. I draw out these layers of unreliable mediation to show the embeddedness and inextricability of distortion in the roots of this affair.

Sacheverell argues with heavy irony that 'Unconditional obedience' to the supreme monarch has been discarded as a tenet and supplanted by 'Supream Subjects' who are obedient, one imagines, only to themselves. These subjects, he suggests, have arrogated to themselves the power to dethrone a monarch at will. Given the events of the time, Sacheverell's sermon was interpreted as arguing that Parliament had had no authority to invite William of Orange to take the throne in 1688. Further, Sacheverell contended that, according to the doctrine of passive obedience to the monarch, it was in fact treasonous for Parliament to have done so and that William's accession to the throne was a civil and a religious deformity.

Sacheverell's sermon was subject to a wide variety of interpretations, but he was lionised by Tories and Jacobites alike, who saw in the sermon a noble defence of the exiled Stuart dynasty's right to rule. This sermon was printed under the title *The Perils of False Brethren, in Church, and State*, and the printer, Henry Clements, quickly ran off around 100,000 copies – a vast number. Sacheverell was tried and impeached in the House of Lords early in 1710 and, leniently, was only banned from preaching for three years.

The Bishop of Oxford referred to in this text's title, William Talbot, was one in fact of four bishops who spoke *against* Sacheverell in the

[6] Henry Sacheverell, *The Perils of False Brethren both in Church and State* (London: H. Clements, 1709), pp. 19–20.

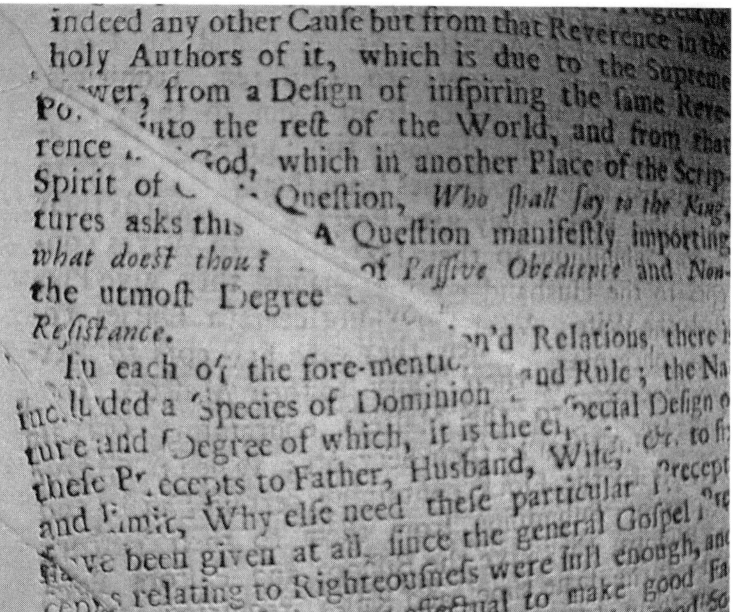

indeed any other Cauſe but from that Reverence in the
holy Authors of it, which is due to the Supreme
Po wer, from a Deſign of inſpiring the ſame Reve-
nto the reſt of the World, and from that
rence God, which in another Place of the Scrip-
Spirit of Queſtion, *Who ſhall ſay to the King,*
tures asks this A Queſtion manifeſtly importing
what doeſt thou? of *Paſſive Obedience* and *Non-*
the utmoſt Degree
Reſiſtance.
n'd Relations, there i
In each of the fore-mentio and Rule; the Na
included a Species of Dominion pecial Deſign o
ture and Degree of which, it is the ci &c. to fi
theſe Precepts to Father, Husband, Wife, Precept
and Limit, Why elſe need theſe particular
have been given at all, ſince the general Goſpel
relating to Righteouſneſs were full enough, and
effectual to make good Fa

Plate 1: UCLA Clark Library, Clark DA 496 1710 P28.

House of Lords, and one of two (along with arch-Whig Gilbert Wharton) to explicitly condemn the doctrine of passive obedience. It bespeaks the complexity of, and the intrigue surrounding, the Sacheverell affair that, despite this, Talbot himself is here under accusation of Jacobitism: even having condemned Sacheverell for his beliefs, Talbot fell under suspicion of adherence to the same creed. The integrity of states of authority and allegiance, as well as the very possibility of fixity, were under threat. Pamphlets like this one represented an effort to remove that threat.

This document, then, rebuts a speech in the House of Lords that condemned a printed version of a sermon given four months earlier. UCLA's Clark Library holds two copies. One copy of the text appears clean. Another, however (shelfmarked Clark DA 496 1710 P28), contains a page printed like that shown in Plate 1.

The sheet on which this text was printed before it was folded into octavo format, stitched, bound and cut, was not laid perfectly flat when it was printed. The result is that a series of white gashes appear through the text when the page is tugged on to unfold its creases. The distorted text pictured might be transcribed as follows:

> No Man, I suppose, will say that the Gospel's wanting particular Precepts, requiring certain Duties on the Sovereign's part, can proceed from Omission or Neglect, or indeed any other Cause but from that Reverence in the holy Authors of it, which is due to the Supreme Power, from a Design of inspiring the same Reverence of God, which in another Place of the Scriptures asks this Question, Who shall say to the King, what doest thou? A Question manifestly importing the utmost Degree of Passive Obedience and Non-Resistance.
>
> In each of the fore-mention'd Relations, there is included a Species of Dominion and Rule; the Nature and Degree of which, it is the especial Design of these Precepts to Father, Husband, Wife, &c. to fix.[7]

The white gash pictured in Plate 1, running diagonally across the page, literalises the partisanship characterising the debate of which this document is a part. The gash hits several key terms: 'Power', 'God', 'Degree of *Passive Obedience*', and 'Dominion and Rule'. Other folds riddle 'Resistance', 'Precepts' and 'limit'. The gash performs the sundering between 'Dominion' and 'Rule' that Sacherevell argued had occurred; it shows that the very terms 'Power' and 'God' were contested, unfixed, unstable territory. The flex of the paper possible by creasing or uncreasing the sheet instantiates the ontological instability that Sacheverell found so horrifying. The torsion exerted by the bound-in fold in the sheet of paper causes the volume to fall open to this page when the book is opened. The torsion on the binding wrought by the unfolded crease changes the appearance of the lineation of the text, so that it appears to be 'misaligned' so that '*what doest thou*' appears to run into 'of Passive Obedience'. This moment of physical distortion works on the book-object to accentuate the manifold fissures its inscribed text documents.

This much of a reading of the distortion in this book-object is acceptable. However, any speculation about the relationship of this book-object to other, more commonly occurring objects bearing the same text would reify the idea of a clean, undistorted, 'master' text. Any analysis of the possible valences of the accidental qualities of material object – as against how we might imagine most versions of that object to be – runs the risk of reinstituting an obsolete distinction between 'substance' and 'accidents'.[8] Look again at the image shown in Plate 1. The tightness of the

[7] This transcription performs its own distortions by, for example, modernising the long 's' into its contemporary form.

[8] Editorial theory that puts stock in an *ur*-text and that hold that distorted objects are, by corollary, deviations from that proper state has a clear correspondence in Thomas Aquinas's claims about the priority of substance over accidents.

binding and the fold in the sheet make traditional standards of photography impossible. These images document the book-object's physicality, and my own as I held it. The light rakes across the page at an angle and the folds in the paper cast faint shadows. The bend in the paper causes the text on the page to curve in and out of frame. The discernibility of these phenomena are considered below-standard in the practice of documenting book-objects. The International Federation of Library Associations and Institutions, in its *Guidelines for Planning the Digitization of Rare Book and Manuscript Collections,* writes that 'high-resolution digital cameras are recommended for medieval manuscripts and other materials for which researchers will want to study minute details'.[9] It makes recommendations on 'Resolution, colour depth, and lighting' and 'the absence of halos and other optical flaws'. Guidelines such as these seek to dematerialise the fact of the book-object's documentation as much as possible, to make the fact of mediation as close to invisible as possible.[10] My images can on these grounds be considered distortions of the physical object they represent: if so, however, they are merely representations that foreground a distortion that is inevitable.

The standard for representing printed rare books in English has long been set by Early English Books Online (EEBO) and Eighteenth-Century Collections Online (ECCO). Plate 2 shows the image provided by ECCO for the distorted page pictured in Plate 1.

It is difficult to remember that the text pictured in Plate 2 comes from a book-object, because the role of this image is to dematerialise the text. This image is a portable document format (PDF) version of a joint photographic experts group (JPEG) capture of a 1980s microfiche image of a book-object held at the British Library.[11] The portion of text presented in

See Henrik Lagerlund, 'Material Substance', in J. Marenbon, ed., *The Oxford Handbook of Medieval Philosophy* (Oxford: Oxford University Press, 2012), pp. 468–85.

9 International Federation of Library Associations and Institutions, *Guidelines for Planning the Digitization of Rare Book and Manuscript Collections*, available at: http://www.ifla.org/files/assets/rare-books-and-manuscripts/rbms-guidelines/guidelines-for-planning-digitization.pdf (accessed 5 February 2017).

10 These guidelines aim to prove the truth of Roland Barthes's dictum that 'a photograph is always invisible; it is not it that we see', in *Camera Lucida: Reflections on Photography*, trans. Richard Howard (New York: Hill and Wang, 1981), p. 4.

11 An excellent account of the history of the layers of mediation involved in creating these images can be found at Folgerpedia's 'History of Early English Books Online', available at: http://folgerpedia.folger.edu/History_of_Early_English_Books_Online (accessed 22 February 2017). This traces the core of EEBO back

(12)

But altho' the ſame Apoſtles give to Subjects many and moſt forcible Precepts requiring their Obedience to the Sovereign, repeat theſe Precepts oftner, and inculcate them ſtronger than they do any of thoſe Precepts in the Four forementioned Caſes; yet they no where give Precepts to Sovereigns requiring Duties from them towards their Subjects, but leave them to be directed by the general Precepts relating to Juſtice and Righteouſneſs at large. For what imaginable Reaſon cou'd theſe Apoſtles have acted thus? but that they might cut off all occaſion and pretence, for thinking there were, or ever ought to be any Exceptions to the Precepts which they had given to the Subject; or for fancying that the Duties between Sovereign and Subject were reciprocal, and that thoſe of the Subjects might ſlacken, ceaſe, or be ſuſpended, upon a failure on the Sovereign's Part. No Man, I ſuppoſe, will ſay, That the Goſpel's wanting particular Precepts, requiring certain Duties on the Sovereign's part, can proceed from Omiſſion or Neglect, or indeed any other Cauſe but from that Reverence in the holy Authors of it, which is due to the Supreme Power, from a Deſign of inſpiring the ſame Reverence into the reſt of the World, and from that Spirit of God, which in another Place of the Scriptures asks this Queſtion, *Who ſhall ſay to the King, what doeſt thou?* A Queſtion manifeſtly importing the utmoſt Degree of *Paſſive Obedience* and *Non-Reſiſtance.*

In each of the fore-mention'd Relations, there is included a Species of Dominion and Rule; the Nature and Degree of which, it is the eſpecial Deſign of theſe Precepts to Father, Husband, Wife, *&c.* to fix and limit, Why elſe need theſe particular Precepts have been given at all, ſince the general Goſpel Precepts relating to Righteouſneſs were full enough, and the Practice of them as effectual to make good Fathers, Maſters, Husbands, *&c.* as to make good Sovereigns?

In

Plate 2: A. B. *An Answer to the Arguments*, p. 12, accessed via Eighteenth-Century Collections Online, copy located in British Library.

a distorted form in Clark DA 496 1710 P28 appears differently here. The substrate, method of inscription and set text are the same, but the text presented by this book-object is manifestly different. Dematerialising the book-object into pure text implies several other sleights of hand: while the particular object presented here is effaced by the flat perspective, absence of discernible light gradients, and absence of warping effects of the binding on the shape of the page, it is also prioritised as *the* book-object referent for this text. Book-objects that differ in their representation of this text become deviants. And yet to confer priority on this view of a book-object is manifestly an arbitrary decision. Rarely, if ever, does any reader encounter a book-object at a perfect ninety-degree angle, with directionless light and with a completely flat substrate. In the totality of possibilities for encountering an object, this (black and white) view is simply one of an infinite set.

When images of book-objects in repositories like ECCO, EEBO or Google Books are distorted, an apparent paradox occurs as the authoritative and dematerialising source is suddenly revealed to have a singular and therefore partial material basis. Krissy Wilson has documented these in her Tumblr, The Art of Google Books, which shows disembodied hands, stray digitisation tools, perspectival warping, torn pages, and more.[12]

The page shown in Plate 3, page 246 of *Where Shall We Go? A Guide to the Healthiest and Most Beautiful Watering Places in the British Isles* (1866) shows a similar principle at work as in the image I have supplied of the Clark Library volume (Plate 1).[13] The mechanics by which this tear occurred are different from those that produced textual voids in the Clark volume, and are almost certainly the product of a reader's work, rather than a printer's. But this page of this volume has become the canonical site of its digitally-mediated existence, and the digital mediation of this

to Pollard and Redgrave's *Short-Title Catalogue* (1926). Chadwyck-Healey's own marketing for EEBO approvingly cites the collection's foundation on 'Great Literary Works' by 'revered authors', available at http://eebo.chadwyck.com/marketing/about.htm (accessed 22 February 2017). Medial histories are also histories of aesthetic value.

[12] Krissy Wilson, *The Art of Google Books*, available at: http://theartofgooglebooks.tumblr.com (accessed 22 February 2017). Kenneth Goldsmith discusses the phenomenon of actively seeking out these distorted scans in his article, 'The Artful Accidents of Google Books', *The New Yorker*, 4 December 2013.

[13] Cited by Wilson, *The Art of Google Books*, available at: http://theartofgooglebooks.tumblr.com/post/141485510700/torn-page-from-p-246-of-where-shall-we-go-a (accessed 22 February 2017).

246* THE WATERING-PLACES OF SCOTLAND.

of the advantages which flow from the railway system. The houses and shops are being altered and improved according to modern taste, and the town proper, which was comparatively limited, now boasts of handsome suburbs, consisting of elegant modern villas, many of them built with much taste, and occupying situations of singular beauty.

The High Street of Peebles is the main street, and from it diverge numerous closes or alleys running down the bank of the Tweed. One of the principal buildings is a large castellated edifice in the High Street, an old residence of the Queensberry family, and which has been renovated with great taste, and converted into a public institution by Mr. William Chambers, the well-known publisher. (Admission by ticket, price 3d.) The town is cleanly in appearance, and shews evident symptoms of becoming, at no distant period, a favourite resort during summer. Its greatest attraction is the Tweed, which is here a beautiful river, with fine grassy banks, along which there are many agreeable rambles. Between the town and the river there is a common of considerable extent, called "The Green," where games of various kinds are played, and which is a most suitable place for the amusements of the juvenile population or visitors.

CLIMATE.—Dry, bracing, and very healthy.

THE MINERAL WATERS OF INNERLEITHEN may not inappropriately be included here as a Spa of Peebles. Innerleithen is itself a village of considerable size, with numerous woollen mills, recently erected for the sake of the water-power derived from the rivers Leithen and Tweed. Like Peebles, it enjoys the advantage of the river Tweed, and numerous tributaries. The mineral well is situated on a rather elevated position, on the side of the hill called Lee Penn, about a mile from the inn (Riddle's) where the omnibus stops. The springs resemble in their properties those of the Bridge of Allan, being of a saline nature.

RECREATIONS.—The principal of these is trout-fishing in the Tweed, and its numerous tributaries, which flow from the extensive and beautiful range of hills in the neighbourhood. These have been minutely and well described in a work by Mr. Blaikie, entitled "The Tweed and its Tributaries," which will be found a useful work by those residing here. The places of interest in the neighbourhood to which walks and excursions may be made are numerous, and afford great scope for healthful recreation. The principal of these are the ruins of Neidpath Castle, a mile westwards, the old tower, the river Tweed, and its wooded banks, forming a scene of much beauty. To Yarrow and St. Mary's Loch is another favourite excursion, and Innerleithen, with its mineral well, is a third.

CHURCHES.—There is a good parish church and Free Church, and one belonging to the United Secession body.

Plate 3: *Where Shall We Go: A Guide to the Healthiest and Most Beautiful Watering Places in the British Isles*, 4th edn.

book-object gives this tear an ontological priority that scholars must confront if they choose to cite this mediation.[14]

Distortions such as these strike us with particular force because they are brought to our attention by new medial forms whose modes are primarily

[14] Randall McLeod is perhaps the foremost scholar of the manifestations of these so-called 'glitches' or distortions in print. Throughout his career he has used them to unravel with remarkable exactitude the precise material configurations and circumstances that they imply or necessitate. See, for example, Orlando F. Booke, 'IMAGIC / A Long Discourse', *Studies in the Literary Imagination*, 32.1 (1999), 190–215.

visual, and whose intention is to enable human readers to consume the text carried by the book-object. Other distortions are more naturalised. Optical character recognition (OCR) is a branch of software that seeks to process images of printed text and render an accurate transcription. Two tools I used, ABBYY and Google Books, performed well against an industry standard of 85 per cent accuracy, but still left considerable lacunae for a reader to fill in with contextual knowledge or guesswork. I supplied the digitised image of the twelfth page of A. B.'s pamphlet to ABBYY and Google and ran OCR on the images. I reproduce their results below with their breaches recorded in bold:

> ABBYY:
> indeed any other Cau**l**e but from that Reverence in the holy Authors of it, which is due to the Supreme Power, from a De**f**ign of in**f**piring the **l**ame Reverence into the re**f**t of the World, and from that Spirit of God, which in another Place of the Scriptures asks this Que**l**tion, Who **fl**a**i**l **f**ay to the King, •what doe**l?** thou? A Que**l**tion manife**l**tly importing the ut**rn**oft Degree of **1'**a**jf**iv**c** O**kc**d**km**e and No**&~** ■R**cft**s**l**ance..■■ In each of the for**c**-rnention'd Relations, there is included **ii** Species of Dominion and Rule **$** the Nature and Degree of which, it is the **d**peci**n**l De**f**ign of the**f**e Precepts to Father, Husband, Wife, **o**) **t.** to fix

> Google:
> indeed any other Cause but from that Rev**c**rence in the holy Authors of it, which is due to the Supreme Power, from a Design of inspiring the same Reverence into the re**c**t of the World, and from that Spirit of God, which in another Place of the Scriptures asks this Question, Who shall say to the King, **Ip**hat doest thou **F** A Question manifestly importing the utmost Degree of **1'**ssive Obedience and Non [- **+ 6**]] **kefi**ance. , , In each of the for**c**-mention'd Relations, there is included a Speci**c**s of **pun**i**t**ion and Rule; the Na[-]ture and **l**eg**cc[e]** of which, it is the [2]**cli**p**c**cial Design of these Precepts to Father, Husband, Wife, [1]**ci**c, to fix

ABBYY has 42 breaches in 511 non-space characters and is 91.79 per cent accurate. Google has 27 breaches in 523 non-space characters and is 94.84 per cent accurate. ABBYY struggles with the long 's'; Google recognises the long 's' and substitutes the modern form in its place, but has difficulty with this book-object's particular form of the letter 'e'. No other freely available OCR tools – such as that embedded in Adobe Acrobat – were able to process this image of a book-object at all. While both of these results represent a success in the OCR industry, they still rely heavily on the reader's ability to reconstruct, for example, 'Dominion' from 'punition', or 'Obedience' from 'Okcdkme'. Distortions such as these would be routinely caught and corrected by hand in the process of preparing this text for digital publication in a more dematerialised form.[15] The 'errors' that OCR software produces spring precisely from the material embodiment of the text that the OCR'd transcription will seek to efface.

Still other distortions of this text are possible and conventional. One preparation for text mining might represent the material OCR'd above as follows:

> indeed other cause from reverence holy authors due supreme power from design inspiring same reverence god another place scriptures asks question who shall say king what doest thou question manifestly importing utmost degree passive obedience non resistance each fore mentiond relations included species dominion rule nature degree especial design precepts father husband wife &c fix

To arrive at this set of tokens, a customised stop-list would be applied to a hand-corrected OCR of a PDF document showing a JPG of a scan of a book-object.[16] That stop-list would strip out words that the text-mining user would not wish to include in his or her analysis of significant semantic units of the text. This hypothetical user has stripped out all punctuation and put articles and some pronouns on the stop-list, but left 'from' and 'thou' off the stop-list. Each of these decisions corresponds to the objectives, perhaps disciplinarily defined, of the analyst, in processing this text, whether on its own or as part of a larger corpus. A topic model might be constructed from a corpus that included this snippet, and that model might further distort this text by returning words from it as part of a topic word list. That list would be a heavily distorted selection of tokens taken from the book-object.[17]

[15] Even in a 'fully digital' text, materiality perseveres as magnetic charges on a disk representing binary states.

[16] A stop-list, or skip-list, is a list of words that the processing script is instructed to ignore. This is a ubiquitous tool in text analysis to avoid common words of nugatory probative value – like 'I', 'the' or 'and' – from dominating numerical analyses.

[17] The complexity of the ways in which methods generally bracketed under the rubric of the digital humanities mediate text offers one reason more why the digital humanities has proven to be such a fruitful vein for disciplinary hand-wringers to mine. Digital humanities practices, like the humanities practices that came before them, rely on complex and sophisticated modes of remediating and distorting

An academically favoured distortion of the text under discussion here would be a scholarly edition. Such an edition might intersperse this passage with notes supplying context; clarifying terms such as passive obedience; offering variant readings; or summarising critical debates on particular cruces. That the editor's work distorts the author's text is an insight familiar to scholars of Pope's *Dunciad Variorum* (1729), which took aim at scholarly editing as it was practised by Richard Bentley in what has now come to be considered the standard method.[18] Pope claimed that Bentley's practices wrought a distortion on the text, and represented this by having spurious textual notes overwhelm all but two lines of the poem on the second page. The scholarly edition distorts by adding to a text, but, as a distortion, addition is not different in kind from subtraction, obscuring or transformation.

Distortions such as these – in OCR, in text preparation, in standards for photography – are not necessarily any different from the distortion at the centre of this discussion, a marked series of gashes traversing a page, adding interstices and ruffling the expected flatness of physical and discursive surfaces. And yet one set of distortions is regarded as acceptable, even desirable for certain purposes, and the other as aberrant.

Recuperating distorted texts is more than a matter of suppressing an Adornian shudder at a degraded artwork, or of redirecting that shudder into a reflection on the possibilities that the distortion offers for deciphering the circumstances of a book-object's production, transmission or

texts. The fresh visibility of these methods, however, combined with their widespread unfamiliarity, makes them a convenient stalking horse for other institutional and disciplinary *ressentiments*. Without a strong heuristic of distortion, that stalking horse will never be removed, and rather only fade into obsolescence once a new and more appealing object of transference hoves into view.

18 This 'standard method' is that discussed by Orgel in 'What is an Editor?'. The essential text on Pope's manipulation of the printed page to generate meaning remains James McLaverty's *Pope, Print and Meaning* (Oxford: Oxford University Press, 2001), esp. pp. 82–106 on the *Dunciad Variorum*. Pope's own editorial practices exerted far greater distortions, ironically enough, than did Bentley's. Pope rewrote the swathes of Shakespeare's verse that he considered to be incorrectly or laxly verified, and thought nothing of – absent historical evidence for such conjectures – presupposing compositorial transpositions that he would happily rectify. In Pope's hands, Macbeth opined that 'all our yesterdays have lighted fools / The way to dusty death': *The Tragedy of Macbeth, The Author William Shakespeare, According to Mr. Pope's Second Edition* (Glasgow: R. and A. Foulis, 1758), V.5, 80. Valerie Rumbold's unsurpassed edition of Pope's *Dunciad in Four Books* (London: Routledge, 2009) subjects Pope's texts to an appropriately Bentleyan treatment.

consumption. Nor am I positing distorted text as an image (rather than a text); a new and fetishisable aesthetic object to be contemplated rather than interpreted. By reifying distorted text into image I would both be affirming the primacy of a supposed *ur*-text and hiving off the distorted text into the state of a wholly new work. Moreover, distorted text is, in many cases, manifestly legible. What we call distortion in book-objects is simply a marker that reading that book-object's text is an experience that is irreproducible in other, supposedly congruent, objects.[19]

I wish to bear down on the nature of the similarity between two objects that closely resemble one another. The fact that a text has been reproduced is unaltered by the mode of that reproduction. Any sufficiently serious consideration of materiality, for example, reveals a distinction between digital and analogue reproduction to be chimerical. The interchangeability of different modes of reproduction entails that all the distortions wrought by reproduction be considered equally. Heidegger writes: 'Technology is therefore no mere means. Technology is a way of revealing. If we give heed to this, then another whole realm for the essence of technology will open itself up to us. It is the realm of revealing, i.e., of truth.' The sense of these lines includes a demand that the distortions produced as a part of reproduction be allowed a full seat at the hermeneutic table.[20] The order of priority between a master text and a distortion is satirised in Heidegger's aside that: 'The will to mastery becomes all the more urgent the more technology threatens to slip from human control.'[21] Those physical sites spoken of as distortions are fissures through which slip ideological category errors, moments that show the failure of technological challenging forth ever to fully enframe and hold in reserve whatever materials are at hand. Heidegger

[19] The difficulty of telling one object from another is eloquently spoken to by Nietzsche: 'The continual transitions do not permit us to speak of the "individual", etc.; the "number" of beings is itself in flux […] The principle of identity has as its background the "appearance" that things are the same. A world of becoming could not, in the strict sense, be "grasped", be "known"; only inasmuch as the "grasping" and "knowing" intellect finds an already created, crude world, cobbled together out of deceptions but having become solid, inasmuch as this kind of illusion has preserved life – only to that extent is there such a thing as "knowledge": i.e., a measuring of earlier and more recent errors against one another.' Friedrich Nietzsche, *Nietzsche: Writings from the Late Notebooks*, ed. Rüdiger Bittner (Cambridge: Cambridge University Press, 2003), Notebook 36, June–July 1885, para. 23, pp. 25–6. In this reading, all book-objects are errors that readers measure against one another.

[20] Martin Heidegger, 'The Question Concerning Technology', in David Farrell Krell, ed., *Basic Writings* (New York: Harper & Row, 1977), p. 5.

[21] Heidegger, 'The Question Concerning Technology', p. 2.

suggests that efforts to achieve an Adornian or even Kantian absorption in the artwork are futile because it is impossible to be certain that the materiality of that artwork is ever fully disciplined, fully enframed. The capacity of materials to escape their being held in reserve means that any material transmission of a text, whether in the form of a book-object or as a radio signal, is prone to the supersession of textual authority by material accident.

Adrian Johns has documented the way in which this very question was present at the inauguration of the status of the printed book-object as an authoritative and reliable vector for information.[22] To speak of the book as possessing an innate authority, writes Johns, 'would mean attributing to printed books themselves attributes of credibility and persuasion that actually took much work to maintain'.[23] Johns continues:

> The sources of print culture are therefore to be sought in civility as much as in technology, and in historical labors as much as in immediate cause and effect. The 'printing revolution', if there was one, consisted of changes in the conventions of handling and investing credit in textual materials, as much as in transformations in their manufacture. The point deserves to be stressed explicitly. I do not question that print enabled the stabilization of texts, to some extent […] I do, however, question the character of the link between the two. Printed texts were not intrinsically trustworthy. When they were in fact trusted, it was only as a result of hard work. Fixity was in the eye of the beholder, and its recognition could be maintained without continuing effort. At no point could it be counted on to reside irremissibly in the object.[24]

Material irruptions into the presentation of the text, like the folded and gashed page in the Clark library (Plate 1), are one way in which printed book-objects lack intrinsic trustworthiness. Epistemological authority relies in part in material stability, that is, authority over the material. Contemporary readers are sophisticated in negotiating the various and fluctuating epistemological and material authorities of printed objects they encounter in their day-to-day lives (printed grey literature, flyers, political and religious pamphlets, advertising inserts and billboards; online listicles, GIFs, data visualisations, pop-ups; television's 'lower-third', inset

[22] Adrian Johns, *The Nature of the Book: Print and Knowledge in the Making* (Chicago: University of Chicago Press, 1998).

[23] Johns, *The Nature of the Book*, p. 18. Johns correlates Elizabeth Eisenstein's 'fixity' of print with Bruno Latour's 'immutability' and historicises their development as a deliberate process of imbuing a medium with transcendent qualities.

[24] Johns, *The Nature of the Book*, pp. 35–6.

advertisements, i-dents, trailers, and so on), but archival and disciplinary literary practices both carry sedimented within themselves this historical-contingent belief in the durable and possibly irremissible authority – the aura, in Benjamin's terms – of the printed object.[25] Lisa Gitelman traces the afterlife of the struggle that Johns documents in her exploration of the forms of contemporary documentation and the tangled and shifting states of authority held by different medial forms over the twentieth and twenty-first centuries.[26] 'Documents', she writes, 'are integral to the ways people think as to the social order they inhabit [and] can never be disentangled from power – or, more properly, control.'[27] As the capacity to print and to copy has become more diffused through a more fully literate society, sites and forms of authority have shifted. Locating and understanding these new sites and forms is of paramount importance, Gitelman notes, because contemporary bureaucracies at all levels 'don't so much employ documents as they are partly constructed by and out of them'.[28] My slippage to document from text and book-object reflects the fact that the document represents the fused, total effect of the two.[29] If, as John Guillory and others have noted, the document exists *that it might be produced*, then the document encompasses the enframed material and textual whole, ready to be obediently challenged forth to substantiate whatever frame of authority in which it has been located.[30]

Arriving at authority brings us back to A. B.'s 1710 answer to the Bishop of Oxford's speech in the House of Lords, itself a response to the concerns that Henry Sacheverell expressed in his sermon about the instability of authority in the British state. Sacheverell's sermon was

[25] Walter Benjamin, 'The Work of Art in the Age of its Technological Reproducibility', in Michael W. Jennings, Brigid Doherty and Thomas Y. Levin, eds, *The Work of Art in the Age of its Technological Reproducibility and Other Writings on Media*, trans. Edmund Jephcott et al. (Cambridge, MA: Belknap Press, 2008), pp. 23–4.

[26] Lisa Gitelman, *Paper Knowledge: Towards a Media History of Documents* (Durham: Duke University Press, 2014).

[27] Gitelman, *Paper Knowledge*, p. 5.

[28] Gitelman, *Paper Knowledge*, p. 5.

[29] On the slippage between document and text, see Thomas G. Tanselle's seminal 'The Editing of Historical Documents', *Studies in Bibliography*, 31 (1978), 1–56; and Jerome J. McGann's commentary in 'The Socialization of Texts', *The Textual Condition* (Princeton: Princeton University Press, 1991), pp. 68–87.

[30] John Guillory, 'The Memo and Modernity', *Critical Inquiry*, 31.1 (2004), 108–32, esp. 114–22. Gitelman refers to this enframed situation as 'the know-show function' (*Paper Knowledge*, pp. 1–8).

documented by witnesses, but most substantively and consequentially by his subsequent printing of it. A. B.'s accusation of the Bishop of Oxford of crypto-Jacobitism, despite the Bishop's having given a speech that was pitched *against* political heterodoxy and *for* the stability of the Act of the Settlement of 1701, shows the intense anxiety riddling Britain about the location and the maintenance of authority.

Ironically enough, the fissures in Clark DA 496 1710 P28 ask us to weigh our 'Unconditional Obedience to the Supream Power' against the possibility that we might as citizens be instead 'Supream Subjects'.[31] The debates following Sacheverell's sermon and its appearance in print relied heavily on the supposedly immutable authority of print for an undergirding in ontological certainty.

The subjects Sacheverell speaks of, who have arrogated to themselves the authority to interpret phenomena, are familiar to us in the form of embodied readers empowered by Roland Barthes, Stanley Fish, Wolfgang Iser, Rita Felski and others. And one can, without much difficulty, imagine Sacheverell's reaction to reader response theory. I, however, am advocating for something more radical and disparate: a fully materially embedded rewriting of reader response theory that goes beyond Fish's suggestion that, for example, cruces are 'not *meant* to be solved, but to be experienced (they signify)'.[32] Fish does not go far enough, because of course cruces are not only interpretative but material; therefore they do not only signify, but *are.* Flagging a distortion as a deviation, or resolving the crux it provides, are acts of bad faith. The rewards of resisting these urges towards false resolution are richer than the standard perorations for ludic reading and interpretative plenitude would have you believe. Instead, that resistance opens a space for actually experiencing a book-object. That experience in turns reveals an object's full history. But most of all, the experience of the book-object reveals its presence. The object's history and presence are contingent on (among other things) trees, woodcutters, print-shop labourers, vendors, readers, collectors, libraries, universities, and the substrates and infrastructures of electricity, the internet and computing. Experiencing a book-object's presence makes it possible for the reader to experience his or her ramified contingencies as well as his or her own countervailing presence. Distortions are irruptions of the physical means by which texts and materials are challenged forth, moments at which our own embodiments are most problematically revealed to us.

31 Sacheverell, *The Perils of False Brethren*, pp. 19–20.

32 Stanley Fish, 'Interpreting the "Variorum"', *Critical Inquiry*, 2.3 (1976), 465–85 (p. 465).

Vilém Flusser writes that:

> [The] half-forgotten gesture of scratching […] is the essence ('eidos') of writing. It has nothing to do with constructing. It is, on the contrary, a taking away, a de-structing […] To write is to in-scribe, to penetrate a surface, and a written text is an inscription […] I believe that we have to start from this fact if we want to understand the gesture of writing: it is a penetrating gesture that informs a surface.[33]

The object's surface is formed, informed, destructed and penetrated in the process of creating a book-object, and I have suggested here some of the other transformations that render that object's text transferrable. Textual media will always be in some sense material. And those materials will continue to offer up countless distortions for readers to meditate upon. Those distortions should not be seized upon as rare deviations from the medium's proper form. Rather, they are opportunities to be conscious of, and to resist, our own ongoing enframing as mediated phenomena.

33 Vilém Flusser, 'The Gesture of Writing', in Nancy Roth, 'A Note on "The Gesture of Writing" by Vilém Flusser and The Gesture of Writing', *New Writing: The International Journal for the Practice and Theory of Creative Writing*, 9.1 (2012), 24–41.

Index